Practical . . . biblical . . . helpful. A tool that the church will not want to do without.
Ken Hemphill, President, Southwestern Baptist Seminary

The Peacemaker is the most thorough and comprehensive guide to resolving conflicts I have ever read. It is insightful, convicting, and biblical.
Josh McDowell

It is rare to find a Christian lawyer who will depend so wholly on the Scriptures.
Jay E. Adams, Pastor and Author

In an age when conflict is more often the norm in the world and the church, a practical guide to being a peacemaker is sorely needed. Ken Sande provides that guide. It is timely. It is biblical. It is user friendly. I have read it more than once. I have used it often. It belongs in everyone's library because it works.
Sam Casey, Executive Director, Christian Legal Society

[Sande] laces the book with examples of his experience in conciliation work. He makes a strong case for the "must" of reconciliation, and he demonstrates the "how-to's" with which to arrive at peace. In fact, *The Peacemaker* illustrates overwhelmingly that the Christian community has ignored or misused the many resources it has for settling disputes.
Rolf Bouma, *The Banner*

This well-written and thoughtful volume is must reading for all who care about peace in their families, their communities, and the world.
J. Martin Burke, Dean of the School of Law, University of Montana

The Peacemaker

The Peacemaker

*A Biblical Guide
to Resolving Personal Conflict*

Second Edition

Ken Sande

Baker Books

A Division of Baker Book House Co
Grand Rapids, Michigan 49516

Published by Baker Books
a division of Baker Book House Company
P.O. Box 6287, Grand Rapids, MI 49516-6287

Eighth printing, July 2000

Printed in the United States of America

Library of Congress Cataloging-in-Publication Data

Sande, Ken.
    The peacemaker : a biblical guide to resolving personal conflict / Ken Sande.—2nd ed.
       p.   cm.
    Includes bibliographical references and index.
    ISBN 0-8010-5741-8 (pbk.)
    1. Reconciliation—Religious aspects—Christianity. 2. Interpersonal relations—Religious aspects—Christianity. 3. Conflict management—Religious aspects—Christianity. 4. Peace—Religious aspects—Christianity. I. Title.
BV4509.5.S26   1997
253.5′2—dc20   96-40967

For information about academic books, resources for Christian leaders, and all new releases available from Baker Book House, visit our web site:
http://www.bakerbooks.com

To Corlette,
whose love and encouragement
kept me writing

and to Kris,
whose insights and common sense
added so greatly to this book

Contents

Preface   9

Part One   Glorify God
1   Conflict Provides Opportunities   16
2   Live at Peace   36
3   Trust in the Lord and Do Good   51

Part Two   Get the Log out of Your Eye
4   Is This Really Worth Fighting Over?   70
5   Examine Yourself   91
6   Free Yourself from Sin   107

Part Three   Go and Show Your Brother His Fault
7   Restore the Sinner Gently   132
8   Speak the Truth in Love   146
9   Take One or Two Others Along   168

Part Four   Go and Be Reconciled
10   Forgive as God Forgave You   186
11   Look Also to the Interests of Others   204
12   Overcome Evil with Good   226

Conclusion: The Peacemaker's Pledge   235
Appendix A: A Peacemaker's Checklist   238
Appendix B: Alternative Ways to Resolve Disputes   245
Appendix C: Principles of Restitution   252

Contents

Appendix D: When Is It Right to Go to Court? 255
Appendix E: Christian Conciliation Ministries 262

Notes 264
Bibliography 270
Index of Topics 272
Index of Persons 274
Index of Scripture References 275

Preface

My interest in peacemaking has grown considerably since I became a lawyer. When I first began to practice law, I was excited about the prospect of helping people solve problems and settle disagreements. Before long, however, I learned that our courts are not equipped to deal with the personal side of conflict. The adversarial process is designed to resolve legal issues, not to reconcile people or help them change the attitudes and habits that lead to conflict. In fact, lawsuits usually drive people further apart and often ingrain the beliefs and behavior that lead to controversy.

Wanting to avoid these problems and to help people find more complete solutions to their conflicts, I began to work with Peacemaker® Ministries in 1982. This ministry helps people resolve their disputes out of court in a cooperative rather than an adversarial manner (see Appendix E). The conciliation process is designed not only to solve legal issues but also to promote genuine peace by restoring broken relationships and helping people change in constructive ways.

As a conciliator, I soon discovered that the personal aspects of conflict often are more complicated than the legal considerations. Interpreting a contract can be challenging, but it is nothing compared to dealing with the attitudes and emotions that lead to and grow out of conflict. Finding little help in contemporary textbooks, I was forced to dig deeper into the one book that consistently provided me with reliable guidance: the Bible. As I applied the peacemaking principles presented in God's Word, I discovered that they are remarkably effective in today's complicated society. As a conciliator, I have used these principles to resolve a wide variety of conflicts, including contract and employment disputes, divorces, personal-injury actions, family feuds, church divisions, malpractice cases, landlord/tenant disagreements, neighborhood quarrels, construction disputes, and real estate controversies.

At the same time, I learned that these principles are equally effective in my personal life. The same concepts that enabled me to conciliate complicated lawsuits have helped me to resolve disagreements with my wife, friends, neighbors, and business contacts. I have found this to be the case even when I am dealing with people who do not profess to be Christians.

As I shared my experiences with John Hughes, a close friend and a member of my board of directors, he encouraged me to write a book that would describe these principles and explain how to use them in the typical conflicts of everyday life. At first I questioned whether I had anything new to say in this area. As I saw these principles work in case after case, however, I finally agreed that it would be worthwhile to describe them in a book. Nevertheless, I have not created anything new with this book. As C. S. Lewis wrote, "*Creation* as applied to human authorship seems to me to be an entirely misleading term. We re-arrange elements He has provided."[1] That is what I have done in this book. I have identified, arranged, explained, and illustrated the essential elements of peacemaking revealed in God's Word. In the process, I have developed a systematic theology for conflict resolution that can easily be applied in everyday life. This approach to resolving conflict may be summarized in four basic principles:

Glorify God (1 Cor. 10:31). Biblical peacemaking is motivated and directed by a desire to please and honor God. His interests, reputation, and commands should take precedence over all other considerations. This focus not only shows our love and respect for God but also protects us from the impulsive, self-centered decisions that make conflicts even worse.

Get the log out of your eye (Matt. 7:5). Peacemaking requires facing up to our own attitudes, faults, and responsibilities before pointing out what others have done wrong. Overlooking the minor offenses of others and honestly admitting our own faults often will encourage similar responses from our opponents and open the way for candid dialogue, reconciliation, and constructive negotiation.

Go and show your brother his fault (Matt. 18:15). At times peacemaking also requires constructive confrontation. When others fail to accept responsibility for their actions, we may need to confront them in a gracious yet firm manner. If they refuse to respond appropriately, we may need to involve respected friends, church leaders, or other neutral individuals who can help restore peace.

Go and be reconciled (Matt. 5:24). Finally, peacemaking involves a commitment to restoring damaged relationships and developing agreements that are just and satisfactory to everyone involved. Forgiveness and cooperative negotiation clear away the debris left by conflict and make possible reconciliation and genuine peace.

This book shows how these principles may be applied in the home, workplace, church, and neighborhood. Among other things it explains:

How to use conflict as an opportunity to please and honor God.

The differences between negotiation, mediation, arbitration, litigation, and Christian conciliation.

Why Christians should resolve disputes in church and not in court.

Why you can trust God to help you even in the most difficult conflicts.

When it is appropriate simply to overlook an offense.

When and how to assert your rights.

How to confess wrongs honestly and effectively.

When it is necessary to pay restitution.

How to change attitudes and habits that lead to conflict.

When it is appropriate to confront others regarding sinful behavior.

11

How to confront others in an effective manner.

When and how to ask other people or the church to intervene in a conflict.

When and how to forgive others and to achieve genuine reconciliation.

How to negotiate just and reasonable agreements.

How to deal with people who refuse to be reasonable.

As you learn to deal with these issues in a biblical way, you can develop an entirely new approach to resolving conflict. Instead of reacting to disputes in a confused, defensive, or angry manner, you can learn to *manage conflict* confidently and constructively. This book describes the principles required for effective conflict management and provides numerous illustrations of how they have been used to resolve actual disputes and lawsuits. (The stories told in this book are based on real situations, but the names of the people and some distinguishing facts have been changed to protect the privacy of those involved.)

The more you study and apply God's peacemaking principles, the more you will see how practical and powerful they are. When used properly these principles can rob conflict of its destructive tendencies and turn it into an opportunity to find lasting solutions to serious problems, to experience significant personal growth, to deepen relationships, and, best of all, to know and enjoy God in a new and vibrant way. I hope that this book will encourage this process in your life and allow you to experience the joy and satisfaction that come from being a peacemaker.

Ken Sande

PART 1

Glorify God

So whether you eat or drink or whatever you do, do it all for the glory of God.

1 Corinthians 10:31

When someone opposes or mistreats me, my instinctive reaction is to devote all my energies to defending myself and defeating my opponent. This self-absorbed attitude usually leads to further problems. When I follow my feelings, I am likely to make impulsive decisions that often offend my opponent and make matters worse.

I have found that the best way to counteract this tendency is to get my eyes off myself and to focus on God. As Colossians 3:1–2 instructs, "Since, then, you have been raised with Christ, set your hearts on things above, where Christ is seated at the right hand of God. Set your minds on things above, not on earthly things." This focus is especially helpful when dealing with conflict. When I give God's interests and commands top priority, I invariably see things more clearly and respond to problems more wisely. Two of my earliest clients learned the same thing after they had been involved in months of expensive litigation.

Deficiencies in the construction of Steve's new home had resulted in a lawsuit, a countersuit, months of legal discovery, and thousands of dollars in attorneys' fees. During a deposition, one of the attorneys finally realized what a contradiction he was watching: two prominent businessmen, both Christians, were growing increasingly bitter and hostile as each continued to justify his own actions and focus on the other's faults. The attorney's concern led him to suggest that the men submit their dispute to Christian conciliation.

Although there was some initial reluctance on the part of the other attorney, Steve and Bill (the builder) eventually agreed to meet with a panel of Christian conciliators, which included a builder, a businessman, and an attorney. At first, progress was slow; each man refused to admit much personal fault and blamed most of the problem on the other person. The conciliators inspected the new home and observed that some of Steve's complaints were legitimate. Even so, both men remained defensive and disagreed about how to assess the damage and make repairs.

In spite of the disappointing progress, the conciliators kept working. They asked each man to spend time studying specific Bible passages and praying about his responsibility for the problem. As God worked in their hearts over the next few days, Bill began to see that his behavior was not pleasing or honoring to God. He also realized that he was providing his attorney and his family with a terrible example of how a Christian should deal with conflict. This new insight led to an attitude change and a remarkable breakthrough at the next meeting.

Moments after the meeting began, Bill asked to make a statement. He admitted that there were defects in the home, and he confessed that he had aggravated the problem by reacting poorly to Steve's complaints. Bill then explained how he would like to repair the house and showed Steve a checklist he had developed to prevent similar problems in future projects.

Bill's statement had a profound effect on Steve. His expression softened and he said, "This is really more my fault than yours. I'm too much of a perfectionist, and I've done a terrible job of communicating with you. My wife can tell you how difficult I can be! I think I need your forgiveness more than you need mine." After months of hostile litigation and weeks of frustrating mediation, everyone was amazed at the breakthrough. Bill and Steve forgave past offenses and began to work out a plan to rcpair the home and offset the expenses. One of the conciliators even offered to donate some materials that would help with the repairs.

It did not end there, however. Bill also went to Steve's wife to apologize for the inconvenience and stress he had caused her. They, too, were reconciled. Later, when unforeseen delays occurred in the repairs and the conciliators were planning to advise Bill to work faster, Steve surprised everyone by coming to Bill's defense. Instead of criticizing the delays as he had earlier, Steve explained why they were reasonable and asked the conciliators not to bother Bill.

Bill's change in attitude also had a powerful effect on his attorney. The day after the dispute was settled, I returned some papers to the attorney's office. Seeing me in the waiting room, he asked me to step into his office. When he told me to close the door, I thought he was going to complain about the outcome of the case. Instead he said, "What happened over there yesterday? I've watched those two fight for over a year, and I know how bitter they were. But when Bill came in to talk with me this morning, his attitude was completely changed. He said God had helped him to see his fault in the situation, and he explained the repairs he is going to make. When I pointed out what Steve had done wrong, Bill came to his defense! I've never seen anything like this."

When I affirmed Bill's assertion that it was God who had brought about these changes, the attorney said, "Well, I guess it had to be God; I know that neither of these men was about to give an inch on this matter."

By showing a concern for God's commands and reputation, Bill and Steve had resolved their dispute and restored important relationships. Better yet, they had brought praise and honor to God and shown at least one other person how good and powerful he is.

1

Conflict Provides Opportunities

"Well done, good and faithful servant!"

Matthew 25:21

In 1986 I was hiking with three friends in the Beartooth Mountains in southern Montana. It was early in the summer, and the streams were still swollen from melting snow. Ten miles into the mountains, we came to a stream where the bridge had been washed away. The water was deep and icy cold. There was one place where we might have been able to cross by leaping from rock to rock, but it would have meant risking a fall into the rapids.

As we stood there trying to decide what to do, three different perspectives surfaced. One person saw the stream as a dangerous obstacle. Afraid that one of us might fall in and be swept away, he wanted to turn back and look for another trail. Another friend saw the stream as a means to show how tough he was. He wanted to wade straight across, even if that meant we would be wet and cold for a few hours. But two of us saw the stream as an interesting challenge. We studied the rocks leading to the other side and determined where we would need additional footing. Finding a fallen tree in the woods, we laid it across the largest gap between the rocks.

At this point, our two friends began to cooperate with us. Working together, we managed to get one person over to the other bank. Then two of us stood on rocks in the middle of the stream and the packs were passed to the other side. One by one, we jumped from rock to rock, receiving support from the person ahead. Before long, we were all on the far bank and we were perfectly dry and exhilarated by our accomplishment.

I have found that people look at conflict in much the same way that my friends and I viewed that stream. To some, conflict is a hazard that threatens to sweep them off their feet and leave them bruised and hurting. To others, it is an obstacle that they should conquer quickly and firmly. But a few people have learned that conflict is an opportunity to solve common problems in a way that honors God and offers benefits to those involved. As you will see, the latter view can transform the way you respond to conflict.

The Slippery Slope of Conflict

There are three basic ways that people respond to conflict. These responses may be arranged on a curve that resembles a hill. On

the left slope of the hill we find the *escape responses* to conflict. On the right side we find the *attack responses.* And in the center we find the *conciliation responses* to conflict.

Imagine that this hill is covered with ice. If you go too far to the left or the right, you can lose your footing and slide down the slope. Similarly, when you experience conflict, it is easy to become defensive or antagonistic. Both responses make matters worse and can lead to more extreme reactions.

Fortunately, there are two things you can do to stay on top of this slippery slope: You can learn to resist the natural inclination to escape or attack when faced with conflict, and you can develop the ability to use the conciliation response that is best suited to resolving a particular conflict. Let's look at all the responses in more detail.

Escape Responses

The three responses found on the left side of the slippery slope are called the *escape responses.* People tend to use these responses when they are more interested in avoiding a conflict than in resolving it. This attitude is common within the church because many Christians believe that all conflict is wrong or dangerous. Thinking that Christians should always agree, or fearing that conflict will inevitably damage relationships, these people will usually do one of three things to escape from conflict.

Denial. One way to escape from a conflict is to pretend that it does not exist. Another way is to refuse to do what should be done to resolve a conflict properly. These responses bring only temporary relief and usually make matters worse (see 1 Sam. 2:22–25).

Flight. Another way to escape from a conflict is to run away. This may mean ending a friendship, quitting a job, filing for divorce, or changing churches. Flight may be a legitimate response in extreme circumstances when it is impossible to resolve the conflict in a constructive manner (see 1 Sam. 19:9–10). In most cases, however, running away only postpones a proper solution to a problem (see Gen. 16:6–8).

Suicide. When people lose all hope of resolving a conflict, they may seek to escape the situation (or make a desperate cry for help) by attempting to take their own lives (see 1 Sam. 31:4). Suicide is never the right way to deal with conflict. Tragically, however, suicide has become the second leading cause of death among adolescents in the United States, partly because our children have never learned how to deal with conflict constructively.

Attack Responses

The three responses found on the right side of the slippery slope are called the *attack responses.* These responses are used by people who are more interested in winning a conflict than in preserving a relationship. This attitude is seen in people who view conflict as a contest or an opportunity to assert their rights, to control others, and to take advantage of their situation. Attack responses are used not only by people who are strong and confident but also by those who feel weak, fearful, insecure, or vulnerable. Whatever the motive, these responses are directed at bringing as much pressure to bear on opponents as is necessary to defeat the claim and eliminate the opposition.

Litigation. Some conflicts may legitimately be taken before a civil judge for a decision (see Acts 24:1–26:32; Rom. 13:1–5). Lawsuits usually damage relationships, however, and they often fail to achieve complete justice. Moreover, Christians are commanded to settle their differences within the church rather than the civil courts (1 Cor. 6:1–8). Therefore, it is important to make every effort to settle a dispute out of court whenever possible (Matt. 5:25–26).

Assault. Some people try to overcome an opponent by using various forms of force or intimidation such as verbal attacks (including gossip and slander), physical violence, or efforts to damage a person financially or professionally (see Acts 6:8–15). Such conduct always makes conflicts worse.

Murder. In extreme cases, people may be so desperate to win a dispute that they will try to kill those who oppose them (see Acts 7:54–58). While most Christians would not kill someone, we should never forget that we stand guilty of murder in God's eyes when we harbor anger or contempt in our hearts toward others (see Matt. 5:21–22).

There are two ways that people move into the attack zone. Some resort to an attack response the minute they encounter a conflict. Others move into this zone after they have tried unsuccessfully to escape from a conflict. When they can no longer ignore, cover up, or run away from the problem, they go to the other extreme and attack those who oppose them.

Conciliation Responses

The six responses found on the top portion of the slippery slope are called the *conciliation responses*. These responses are specifically commended by God and directed toward finding just and mutually agreeable solutions to conflict. The first three conciliation responses may be referred to as "personal peacemaking" because they may be carried out personally and privately, just between you and the other party.

Overlook an offense. Many disputes are so insignificant that they should be resolved by quietly and deliberately overlooking an offense and forgiving the person who has wronged you. "A man's wisdom gives him patience; it is to his glory to overlook an offense" (Prov. 19:11; see 12:16; 17:14; Col. 3:13; 1 Peter 4:8).

Discussion. If a personal offense is too serious to overlook, it should be resolved through confession or loving confrontation. "[If] your brother has something against you . . . go and be reconciled" (Matt. 5:23–24; see Prov. 28:13). "If your brother sins against you, go and show him his fault, just between the two of you" (Matt. 18:15; see Gal. 6:1–3).

Negotiation. Substantive issues related to money, property, or other rights should be resolved through a bargaining process in which the parties seek to reach a settlement that satisfies the legitimate needs of each side. "Each of you should look not only to your own interests, but also to the interests of others" (Phil. 2:4).

When a dispute cannot be resolved through one of the personal peacemaking responses, you should use one of the three "assisted responses." These require the involvement of other people from your church or community.

Mediation. If two Christians cannot reach an agreement in private, they should ask one or more others to meet with them to help them communicate more effectively and explore possible solutions. "If he will not listen [to you], take one or two others along" (Matt. 18:16). These mediators may ask questions and give advice, but they cannot force you to accept a particular solution.

Arbitration. When you and an opponent cannot come to a voluntary agreement on a substantive issue, you should appoint one or more arbitrators to listen to your arguments and render a binding decision to settle the matter. In 1 Corinthians 6:1–8, Paul indicates that this is how Christians ought to resolve even their legal conflicts with one another. "If you have disputes about such matters, appoint as judges even men of little account in the church" (1 Cor. 6:4).

Church discipline. If a person who professes to be a Christian refuses to be reconciled and do what is right, his or her church leaders should be asked to formally intervene to promote repentance, justice, and forgiveness. "If he refuses to listen [to others], tell it to the church" (Matt. 18:17).

Interesting Trends on the Slope

The slippery slope reveals several interesting trends regarding the various responses to conflict. As we move from the left side of the slope to the right (clockwise), our responses tend to go from being private to being public. When we fail to resolve a matter through a private response, more people must get involved as we look to mediation, arbitration, church discipline, or even litigation to settle a dispute.

Moving from left to right on the curve also involves a move from consensual to coercive solutions. In all the responses on the left side of the curve from suicide to mediation, the parties decide on their own solution. In arbitration and the attack responses, a result is imposed by others. This is usually less palatable to everyone involved.

In addition, the extreme responses to conflict result in greater losses. Every response to conflict costs you something; you must give up one thing to gain another. Personal peacemaking responses generally produce the most "profitable" exchange; the benefits of your solution are usually worth the time and energy you invest to reach an agreement, especially from a spiritual standpoint. The further you move away from this zone in either direction, the greater your losses will be, whether in time, money, effort, relationships, or a clear conscience.

There are also three noteworthy parallels between the two sides of the slippery slope. Both extremes of the spectrum result in death, either through suicide or murder, which are growing problems in our culture. Similarly, assault and flight often come together in classic "fight/flight" behavior, both sides of which avoid dealing with the underlying causes of the conflict. Finally, litigation is often nothing more than "professionally assisted denial." When you enter the legal adversarial system, your attorney is expected to make you look faultless and to paint your opponent as the one who is entirely responsible for the problem—which is seldom the case.

There are also some interesting contrasts between the various responses to conflict. First, there is a difference in focus. When I resort to an escape response, I am generally focusing on "me." I am looking for what is easy, convenient, or nonthreatening for myself. When I use an attack response, I am generally focusing on "you," blaming you and expecting you to give in and solve the problem. When I use a conciliation response, my focus is on "us." I am conscious of everyone's interests in the dispute, especially God's, and I am working toward mutual responsibility in solving a problem.

The issue of goals reveals a second difference between various responses. People who use escape responses are usually intent on "peacefaking," or making things look good even when they are not. (This is especially common in the church, where people are often more concerned about the appearance rather than the reality of peace.) Attack responses are used by people who are prone to "peacebreaking." They are more than willing to sacrifice peace and unity to get what they want. Those who use the conciliation responses to conflict are committed to "peacemaking" and will work as hard and as long as necessary to achieve true justice and genuine harmony with others.

Finally, there is a difference in results. When a person earnestly pursues the conciliation responses to conflict, there is a greater likelihood that he or she will eventually see reconciliation. In contrast, both the escape and attack responses to conflict almost inevitably result in KYRG: Kiss your relationship good-bye.

The different responses to conflict and their associated dynamics were dramatically revealed in the first family conflict I conciliated. I was asked to help seven adult brothers and sisters settle a guardianship dispute over whether they should keep their elderly mother in her home or place her in a retirement center. Five of the siblings were doing all they could to escape from the situation, either by pretending that a conflict did not exist or by refusing to meet with the others to talk about it. The other two attacked each other intensely and frequently, slandering one another to family and friends and fighting in court to obtain control through legal guardianship.

The first step in resolving the dispute was to help the parties change the way they had been responding to the situation. The five siblings who had been trying to escape from the problem quickly saw the benefits of mediation and agreed to meet together. The other two sisters grudgingly consented to mediation, but they continued to attack each other during our meetings, accusing each other of improper motives and demanding opposing solutions. Our investment of time and energy was producing no results, and relationships were suffering further damage.

I finally asked to talk with the two sisters in private to help them discuss the personal offenses that were obviously fueling their quarrel. Putting the guardianship issue aside for a moment, I helped them to examine their attitudes and behavior toward each other. As we studied a few relevant Bible passages, the Lord began to work in their hearts. After about thirty minutes, the real cause of the conflict finally came to the surface. Almost twenty years earlier, one of the women had said something that deeply hurt the other one. The offended sister had tried to pretend that she was not hurt, but she could not help brooding over the insult, and their relationship was steadily poisoned. Consequently, they opposed each other in everything, even if it involved their mother's care.

As we continued to talk about their relationship, they began to deal honestly with their feelings and actions. They saw how they had been dishonoring God and hurting other people. As God opened their hearts, they confessed their sins and forgave each other. With tears in their eyes, they embraced each other for the first time in twenty years. They soon joined their brothers and sister and explained what had happened. Within five minutes, all seven children agreed that their mother would be happier in her own home, and in another fifteen minutes they negotiated a schedule for her care. As you can imagine, when they told her the news that evening, the reconciliation of her children brought her even more joy than the decision about her living arrangement.

A Biblical View of Conflict

Many of the problems associated with the escape and attack responses to conflict can be prevented if you learn to look at and respond to conflict in a biblical way. In his Word, God has explained why conflicts occur and how we should deal with them. The more we understand and obey what he teaches, the more effective we will be in resolving disagreements with other people. The following are a few of the basic principles behind a biblical view of conflict.

Let's begin our discussion by defining conflict as "a difference in opinion or purpose that frustrates someone's goals or desires." This definition is broad enough to include innocuous variations in taste, such as one spouse wanting to vacation in the mountains while the other prefers the ocean, as well as hostile arguments, such as fights, quarrels, lawsuits, or church divisions.

The Bible does not teach that all conflict is bad; instead, it teaches that *some* differences are natural and beneficial. Since

God has created us as unique individuals, human beings will often have different opinions, convictions, desires, perspectives, and priorities. Many of these differences are not inherently right or wrong; they are simply the result of God-given diversity and personal preferences. When handled properly, disagreements in these areas can stimulate productive dialogue, encourage creativity, promote helpful change, and generally make life more interesting. Therefore, although we should seek *unity* in our relationships, we should not demand *uniformity* (see Eph. 4:1–13). Instead of avoiding all conflicts or demanding that others always agree with us, we should rejoice in the diversity of God's creation and learn to accept and work with people who simply see things differently than we do (see Rom. 15:7; cf. 14:1–13).

Not all conflict is neutral or beneficial, however. The Bible teaches that many disagreements are the direct result of sinful motives and behavior. As James 4:1–2 tells us, "What causes fights and quarrels among you? Don't they come from your desires that battle within you? You want something but don't get it. You kill and covet, but you cannot have what you want. You quarrel and fight. . . ." When a conflict is the result of sinful desires or actions that are too serious to be overlooked, we need to deal with them in a straightforward manner. This is why Jesus said, "If your brother sins against you, go and show him his fault, just between the two of you" (Matt. 18:15a). Loving confrontation is often the key to repentance, which can remove the root causes of conflict and open the way for genuine peace.

Most importantly, the Bible teaches that we should see conflict neither as an inconvenience nor as an occasion for selfish gain, but rather as an opportunity to demonstrate the presence and power of God. This is what Paul told the Christians in Corinth when religious, legal, and dietary disputes threatened to divide their church:

> So whether you eat or drink or whatever you do, do it all for the glory of God. Do not cause anyone to stumble, whether Jews, Greeks, or the church of God—even as I try to please everybody in every way. For I am not seeking my own good but the good of

many, so that they may be saved. Follow my example, as I follow the example of Christ (1 Cor. 10:31–11:1).

This passage presents a radical view of conflict; it encourages us to look at conflict as an opportunity to glorify God, to serve others, and to grow to be like Christ. This perspective may seem naive and foolish at first glance, especially to anyone who is presently embroiled in a dispute. As you will see, however, this view can inspire remarkably practical responses to conflict. These responses are described in detail later in this book, but it will be helpful to have an overview now.

Glorify God

Conflict always provides an opportunity to glorify God, that is, to show him honor and bring him praise. In particular, conflict gives you a chance to show God that you love, respect, and trust him. At the same time, it allows you to show others that God is loving, wise, powerful, and faithful. You can do this in several ways.

First, *you can trust God.* Instead of giving in to the pressures produced by conflict and taking matters into your own hands, you can decide to rely on God's grace and depend on the principles taught in his Word (Prov. 3:5–7). In chapter 3 we will examine the basis for this trust and see how it has been demonstrated by Christians for centuries.

Second, *you can obey God.* One of the most powerful ways to glorify God is to do what he commands (Matt. 5:16; John 17:4). As Jesus said, "This is to my Father's glory, that you bear much fruit, showing yourselves to be my disciples" (John 15:8). This principle is revealed even in the Lord's Prayer, where Jesus indicated that God's name is "hallowed"—that is, greatly respected—when his will is "done on earth as it is in heaven" (Matt. 6:9–10; cf. Ps. 23:3; Phil. 1:9–10). Obeying God's commands shows that you love and trust him. Jesus highlighted the relationship between love and obedience in a dramatic way. In the Jewish culture, one way to emphasize a point was to say it two or three times. Thus, to repeat something five times gave it great weight. This is exactly

26

what Jesus did when he said: "If you love me, you will obey what I command. . . . Whoever has my commands and obeys them, he is the one who loves me. . . . If anyone loves me, he will obey my teaching. . . . He who does not love me will not obey my teaching. . . . the world must learn that I love the Father and that I do exactly what my Father has commanded me" (John 14:15–31; cf. 1 John 5:3 and 2 John 5–6).

Third, *you can imitate God.* Instead of following the ways of the world when dealing with conflict, you should follow Paul's command to "Be imitators of God, therefore, as dearly loved children" (Eph. 5:1; see 1 John 2:6). As we will see throughout this book, when you are involved in conflict there will be many opportunities to follow the example of Christ as you love your enemies, pray for those who mistreat you, and do good to those who oppose you (see Ps. 103:9–10; Luke 6:27–28, 35–36; 23:34).

Every time you encounter a conflict, you have an opportunity to show what you really think of God. If you trust, obey, and imitate him, you will show that you love him "with all your heart and with all your soul and with all your mind" (Matt. 22:37). This honors God and shows others how worthy he is of your devotion. This principle was powerfully illustrated in the apostle Peter's life. Just before Jesus ascended into heaven, he warned Peter that he would be executed for his faith. In John 21:19 we are told that, "Jesus said this to indicate the kind of death by which Peter would glorify God." How would Peter glorify God by dying? He would show that God is so excellent and trustworthy and his ways are so perfect that it is better to die than to turn away from him or disobey his commands (cf. Dan. 3:1–30; 6:1–28; Acts 5:17–42; 6:8–7:60). Peter was willing to pay the highest price possible, his very life, to show how much he loved and trusted God.

Glorifying God will benefit *you* as well, especially when you are involved in a conflict. Many disputes begin or grow worse because one or both sides give in to their emotions and say or do things that they later regret. When you focus on trusting, obeying, and imitating God, you will be less inclined to stumble in these ways. As Psalm 37:31 says, "The Law of his God is in his heart; his feet do not slip."

The other benefit of a God-centered approach to conflict resolution is that it makes you less dependent on results. Even if others refuse to respond positively to your efforts to make peace, you can find comfort and encouragement in the knowledge that God is pleased with your obedience. That knowledge can help you to persevere in difficult situations.

It is important to realize that if you do not "glorify God" when you are involved in a conflict, you will inevitably glorify someone or something else. By your actions you will show that either you have a big God or that you have a big self and big problems. To put it another way, if you do not focus on God, you will inevitably focus on yourself and your will, or on other people and the threat of their will.

One of the best ways to keep your focus on the Lord is to continually ask yourself this question: *How can I please and honor God in this situation?* This thought governed Jesus' life and ministry: "I seek not to please myself, but him who sent me" (John 5:30). "The one who sent me is with me; he has not left me alone, for I always do what pleases him" (John 8:29). King David was motivated with the same desire when he wrote: "May the words of my mouth and the meditation of my heart be pleasing in your sight, O LORD, my Rock and my Redeemer" (Ps. 19:14).

When pleasing God is more important than pleasing yourself, it becomes increasingly natural to trust, obey, and imitate him. This attitude and behavior brings glory to God and sets the stage for a constructive approach to conflict.

Serve Others

As Paul reminded the Corinthians, conflict also provides an opportunity to serve others. This sounds absurd from a worldly perspective, because the world says, "Look out for number one." But Jesus says, "Love your enemies, do good to those who hate you, bless those who curse you, pray for those who mistreat you" (Luke 6:27–28). We are *not* released from the command to love our neighbor as ourselves even when that neighbor is hating, cursing, and mistreating us. Instead of reacting harshly or seeking revenge, God calls us to be merciful to those who offend us, just as he is merciful to us (Luke 6:36). You can do this in several ways.

In some situations, God may use you to help an opponent find better solutions to his problems than he would have developed alone. If you follow the principles of negotiation described in chapter 11, you can often develop creative ways to satisfy both your needs and the needs of your opponent. Instead of allowing a conflict to pit you and your opponent against each other, sometimes you can turn it around so that the two of you are working together against a common problem.

In other cases, the Lord may give you an opportunity to carry your opponent's burdens by providing for his or her spiritual, emotional, or material needs (Gal. 6:2, 9–10). It may be that your conflict has little to do with actual differences between the two of you and much to do with unresolved problems in your opponent's life. When others lash out at you, it is sometimes symptomatic of other frustrations. (This behavior is particularly common in families and close friendships.) Instead of reacting defensively, try to discern ways that you can help others deal with those problems. This does not mean you should take on their responsibilities. Rather, you should help them lift those burdens that are beyond their abilities. At the very least, your efforts will show that you are a child of God (Luke 6:29–36), which brings him glory. As you will see in the final chapter of this book, there may also be times when your kindness will eventually soften an opponent's heart and open the way for reconciliation (see Rom. 12:20).

The Lord may also use you to help others learn where they have been wrong and need to change (Gal. 6:1–2). As we will see later, this will sometimes require private confrontation. If that does not work, God may lead you to involve other people who can help bring about needed changes.

Best of all, conflict may provide an opportunity to encourage others to put their trust in Jesus Christ. When you are involved in a conflict, your opponent and various bystanders will be observing you closely. If you behave in a worldly way, you will give nonbelievers yet another excuse for mocking Christians and rejecting Christ. On the other hand, if you behave in a wise and loving manner, those who are watching you may become open to hearing the gospel (1 Peter 3:15–16).

Another way to serve others is to teach and encourage by your example. In many situations, other Christians will be watching how you handle a difficult conflict. If you succumb to sinful emotions and lash out at your enemies, those who are watching will feel justified in doing the same. But if you respond with love and self-control, others will be encouraged to be faithful to God as well (1 Cor. 4:12–13, 16; 1 Tim. 4:12; Titus 2:7). This is particularly important if you are a parent or grandparent. Your children constantly observe how you handle conflict. If you are defensive, critical, unreasonable, and impulsive, they are likely to handle their problems the same way. But if you handle disputes in a godly manner, your children will be encouraged to do the same. What they learn about peacemaking from you may have a profound impact on how they handle conflict at school, in the workplace, and in their own marriages.[1]

Grow to Be like Christ

Most conflicts also provide an opportunity to become more Christlike. As Paul urged in his letter to the Corinthians, "Follow my example, as I follow the example of Christ" (1 Cor. 11:1). Paul elaborated on this opportunity when he wrote to the Christians in Rome: "And we know that in all things God works for the good of those who love him, who have been called according to his purpose. For those God foreknew he also predestined *to be conformed to the likeness of his Son*, that he might be the firstborn among many brothers" (Rom. 8:28–29, emphasis added; cf. 2 Cor. 3:18).

Contrary to what you may have heard, God's highest purpose for you is not to make you comfortable, wealthy, and happy. If you have put your faith in him, he has something far more wonderful in mind for you—he plans to conform you to the likeness of his Son! He began to change you the day you yielded yourself to him, and he will continue this process throughout your life. Conflict is one of the many tools that God can use to help you develop a more Christlike character. To begin with, he may use conflict to remind you of your weaknesses and to encourage you to depend more on him (2 Cor. 12:7–10). The more you depend on his grace, wisdom, and power, the more you will be imitating the Lord Jesus (Luke 22:41–44).

God may also use conflict to uncover sinful attitudes and habits in your life. Conflict is especially effective in breaking down appearances and revealing stubborn pride, a bitter and unforgiving heart, or a critical tongue. When you are squeezed through controversy and these sinful characteristics are brought to the surface, you will have an opportunity to admit their existence and ask for God's help in overcoming them.

There is more to being like Jesus than simply recognizing weaknesses and confessing sin. To grow, you must also practice new attitudes and habits. Just as athletes develop their muscles and skills through strenuous training, you will see greatest growth when you repeatedly think and behave properly in response to challenging circumstances. For example, when people provoke and frustrate you, practice love and forgiveness. When they fail to act promptly, develop patience. When you are tempted to give up on someone, exercise faithfulness. Conflict provides a rich mixture of such trials, each of which can strengthen and refine your character. As Chuck Swindoll points out: "If you listen to the voices around you, you'll search for a substitute—an escape route. You'll miss the fact that each one of those problems is a God-appointed instructor ready to stretch you and challenge you and deepen your walk with him. Growth and wisdom await you at the solution of each one, the pain and mess notwithstanding."[2]

God uses the problems found in conflict to stretch and challenge you in carefully tailored ways. This process is sometimes referred to as the "ABC of spiritual growth"—Adversity Builds Character. As you worry less about *going* through conflict and focus more on *growing* through conflict, you will enhance that process and experience the incomparable blessing of being conformed to the likeness of Jesus Christ.

Stewarding Conflict

A biblical view of conflict forms the foundation for the most effective style of conflict management, which I refer to as *"stewarding."* This style gives the phrase *conflict management* a unique emphasis. When Jesus talked about managing something, he was usually referring to a servant who had been entrusted by his master with certain resources and responsibilities (e.g., Luke 12:42). The Bible calls such a person a steward. A steward is not supposed to manage things for his pleasure, convenience, or benefit. Instead, he is expected to follow his master's instructions and look out for his master's interests, even if they conflict with his personal desires or convenience (John 12:24–26).

The concept of stewardship is especially relevant to peacemaking. Whenever you are involved in a conflict, God has given you a management opportunity. He has entrusted you with natural abilities and spiritual resources, and his Word clearly explains how he wants you to manage the situation. The more faithfully you follow his instructions, the more likely you are to see a proper solution and genuine reconciliation. Moreover, faithful stewarding will leave you with a clear conscience before God, regardless of what the other people do. The Bible provides a detailed description of the character traits needed to manage conflict productively. Many of these qualities will be discussed later in this book, but a few of them deserve immediate attention. If you want to be an effective steward, you need to be:

Informed. As a steward, you need to understand your Master's will (see Luke 12:47). This should not be difficult, because God has already written out his instructions for you. Through the Bible he provides clear and reliable guidance on how he wants you to deal with every aspect of life. The Bible is not merely a collection of religious rituals and commendable ideals. In addition to showing us how to know God personally, it provides detailed and practical instructions on how to deal with the problems that arise in daily living (2 Tim. 3:16–17). Understanding God's Word is an essential ingredient of wisdom, which is the ability to apply God's truth to life's complexities. Having wisdom does not mean that you understand all of God's ways; it means that you respond to life God's way (Deut. 29:29). The better you know the Bible, the wiser you will be, and the more effectively you will deal with conflict.[3]

Dependent. You are not alone when you are stewarding conflict: "For the eyes of the LORD range throughout the earth to strengthen those whose hearts are fully committed to him" (2 Chron. 16:9a; cf. 1 Cor. 10:13). God provides this strength to all Christians through the Holy Spirit, who plays an essential role in peace-making. In addition to helping you understand God's will (1 Cor. 2:9–15), the Spirit will provide you with the spiritual gifts, grace, and strength you need to respond to conflict in a way that will bring honor to Christ and build up his church (Gal. 5:22–23; Eph. 3:16–21; 1 Peter 4:10–11; 2 Tim. 1:7). This help is available to you on request, which is why prayer is emphasized throughout this book.[4]

Realistic. At times, conflict can push you beyond your limits. You may have a difficult time understanding how to respond to a particular situation, or you may become so weary that you lose your determination to do what you know is right. When this happens, it is wise to turn to the church and seek out spiritually mature Christians who will encourage you, give you biblically sound advice, and support your efforts to be faithful to God (Prov. 12:15; 15:22; 1 Thess. 5:10–11; Heb. 10:24–25). You won't be helped by people who are likely to tell you only what they think you want to hear (2 Tim. 4:3). Therefore, be sure you turn to people who will love you enough to be honest with you. By being realistic about your abilities and needs and humbly calling on fellow Christians at the proper time, you can resolve many conflicts that would otherwise defeat you.

Faithful. Perhaps the most important characteristic of a steward is faithfulness: "Now it is required that those who have been given a trust must prove faithful" (1 Cor. 4:2). Faithfulness is not a matter of results; it is a matter of obedience. Because God knows that you cannot control other people, he will not hold you responsible for the ultimate outcome of a conflict (Rom. 12:18). What he will look at is whether or not you have obeyed his commands and wisely used the resources he has given you. If you have done your best to resolve a conflict in a loving and biblical manner, no matter how the situation turns out, you will have earned that marvelous commendation: "'Well done, good and faithful servant!'" (Matt. 25:21a).

Summary and Application

Conflict provides opportunities to glorify God, to serve others, and to grow to be like Christ. These opportunities, which are sometimes described as being faithful to God, merciful to others, and acting justly ourselves, are mentioned throughout Scripture. In Micah 6:8 we are told, "He has showed you, O man, what is good. And what does the LORD require of you? To act justly and to love mercy and to walk humbly with your God." Jesus teaches us to pay attention to "the more important matters of the law—justice, mercy and faithfulness" (Matt. 23:23). As you pursue these opportunities with God's help, you can use conflict as a stepping-stone to a closer relationship with God and a more fulfilling and fruitful Christian life.

If you are presently involved in a conflict, these questions will help you to apply the principles presented in this chapter to your situation:

1. Briefly summarize your dispute as you perceive it, placing events in chronological order as much as possible. In particular, describe what you have done to resolve the dispute.
2. What have you done that has probably made this dispute worse?
3. What have your primary goals been as you've tried to resolve this dispute?
4. Which response to conflict have you been using to resolve this dispute? How has your response encouraged or inhibited progress toward a meaningful solution?
5. How can you glorify God—that is, please and honor him—through this conflict?
6. How can you serve others through this conflict?
7. How can you grow to be more like Christ through this conflict?

8. What have you been relying on for guidance in this situation: your feelings and personal opinions about what is right, or the careful study and application of what is taught in the Bible? What will you rely on in the future?
9. What are you struggling with most at this time (e.g., your opponent's attacks, controlling your tongue, fear of what is going to happen, a lack of support from others)?
10. How could you use the resources God has provided (the Bible, the Holy Spirit, or other Christians) to deal with these struggles?
11. If God were to evaluate this conflict after it is over, how would you like him to complete these sentences:
    "I am pleased that you did not . . ."
    "I am pleased that you . . ."
12. Go on record with the Lord by writing a prayer based on the principles taught in this chapter.

2

Live at Peace

If it is possible, as far as it depends on you, live at peace with everyone.

Romans 12:18

As noted in the previous chapter, peacemaking may be viewed as a matter of stewardship. Whenever you are involved in a conflict, God has given you an opportunity to manage yourself in a way that will glorify him, benefit others, and allow you to grow in character. Fulfilling these responsibilities comes more easily if you understand why peace is so important to our heavenly Father.

The Three Dimensions of Peace

The Bible teaches that God is deeply interested in peace. From Genesis to Revelation, the prophets and apostles constantly urge God's children to seek peace. Consider these recurrent themes:

1. Peace is part of God's character, for he is frequently referred to as "the God of peace" (see Rom. 15:33; 2 Cor. 13:11; Phil. 4:9; Heb. 13:20; cf. Judg. 6:24).
2. Peace is one of the great blessings that God gives to those who follow him (see Lev. 26:6; Num. 6:24–26; Judg. 5:31; Ps. 29:11; 119:165; Prov. 16:7; Micah 4:1–4; Gal. 6:16).
3. God repeatedly commands his people to seek and pursue peace (see Ps. 34:14; Jer. 29:7; Rom. 14:19; 1 Cor. 7:15; 2 Cor. 13:11; Col. 3:15; 1 Thess. 5:13; Heb. 12:14); he promises to bless those who do so (see Ps. 37:37; Prov. 12:20; Matt. 5:9; James 3:18).
4. God describes his covenant in terms of peace (Num. 25:12; Isa. 54:10; Ezek. 34:25; 37:26; Mal. 2:5).
5. God taught his people to use the word *peace* (Hebrew, *"shalom,"* and Greek *"eirene"*) as a standard form of greeting (Judg. 6:23; 1 Sam. 16:5; Luke 24:36) and also of wishing one another well when parting (1 Sam. 1:17; 2 Kings 5:19; Luke 7:50; 8:48). Nearly all of the New Testament Epistles either begin or end with a prayer for peace (Rom. 1:7; 15:13; Gal. 1:3; 2 Thess. 3:16).

Nothing reveals God's concern for peace more vividly than his decision to send his beloved Son to "guide our feet into the path of peace" (Luke 1:79; cf. Isa. 2:4). From beginning to end, Jesus' mission was one of peacemaking. Long before he was born, he was given the title "Prince of Peace" (Isa. 9:6). Throughout his ministry he was constantly preaching and giving peace (John 14:27; Eph. 2:17). As the supreme Peacemaker, Jesus sacrificed his life so we could experience peace both now and forever.

There are three dimensions to the peace that God offers to us through Christ: peace with God, peace with one another, and peace within ourselves. Many people care little about their relationships with God and other people; all they want is peace within themselves. As you will see, it is impossible to know genuine internal peace unless you also pursue peace with God and others.

Peace with God

Peace with God does not come automatically, since all of us have sinned and alienated ourselves from him (Isa. 59:1–2). Instead of living the perfect lives needed to enjoy fellowship with him (Matt. 5:48), each of us has a record stained with sin (Rom. 3:23). As a result, we deserve to be eternally separated from God (Rom. 6:23a). That is the *bad* news.

The *good* news is that "God so loved the world that he gave his one and only Son, that whoever believes in him shall not perish but have eternal life" (John 3:16). By sacrificing himself on the cross, Jesus has made it possible for us to have peace with God. The apostle Paul wrote:

> For God was pleased to have all his fullness dwell in him [Christ], and through him to reconcile to himself all things . . . by making peace through his blood, shed on the cross (Col. 1:19–20).
>
> Therefore, since we have been justified through faith, we have peace with God through our Lord Jesus Christ, through whom we have gained access by faith into this grace in which we now stand (Rom. 5:1–2).

Believing in Jesus means more than being baptized, going to church, or trying to be a good person. None of these activities can erase the sins you have already committed and will continue to commit throughout your life. Believing in Jesus means, first of all, admitting that you are a sinner and acknowledging that there is no way you can earn God's approval by your works (Rom. 3:20; Eph. 2:8–9). Second, it means believing that Jesus paid the *full* penalty for your sins when he died on the cross (Isa. 53:1–12; 1 Peter 2:24–25). In other words, believing in Jesus means trusting that he exchanged records with you at Calvary—that is, he took your sinful record on himself and paid for it in full, giving you his perfect record, which opens the way for peace with God. As you learn more about God and draw closer to him, this peace can fill every part of your life.

Peace with Others

In addition to giving you peace with God, Jesus' sacrifice on the cross opened the way for you to enjoy peace with other people (Eph. 2:11–18). This peace, which is often referred to as "unity" (Ps. 133:1), is not simply the absence of conflict and strife. Unity is the presence of genuine harmony, understanding, and goodwill. God commands us to do all we can to "live at peace with everyone," whether or not they are Christians (Rom. 12:18). This kind of peace is the result of obedience to the second great commandment, "Love your neighbor as yourself" (Matt. 22:39). As you will see, such unity is an essential part of an effective Christian witness.

Peace within Yourself

Through Christ, you can also experience genuine peace within yourself. Internal peace is a sense of wholeness, contentment, tranquility, order, rest, and security. Although nearly everyone longs for this kind of peace, it eludes most people. Genuine internal peace cannot be obtained directly; it is a gift that God gives only to those who believe in his Son and obey his commands (1 John 3:21–24). In other words, *internal peace is a by-product of righteousness.* This truth is revealed throughout Scripture:

> You will keep in perfect peace him whose mind is steadfast, because he trusts in you (Isa. 26:3).
> The fruit of righteousness will be peace; the effect of righteousness will be quietness and confidence forever (Isa. 32:17; cf. Ps. 85:10; 119:165).
> If only you had paid attention to my commands, your peace would have been like a river, your righteousness like the waves of the sea (Isa. 48:18).

These passages show why it is impossible to experience internal peace if you fail to pursue peace with God and peace with others. Internal peace comes from obeying what God commands. "And this is his command: to believe in the name of his Son, Jesus Christ,

39

and to love one another as he commanded us" (1 John 3:23). The three dimensions of peace are inseparably joined by God's design. As one author expressed it, "Peace with God, peace with each other and peace with ourselves come in the same package."[1] Therefore, if you want to experience internal peace, you must seek harmonious relationships with God and those around you.

Jesus' Reputation Depends on Unity

Unity is more than a key to internal peace. It is also an essential element of your Christian witness. When peace and unity characterize your relationships with other people, you show that God is present in your life. The converse is also true; when your life is filled with unresolved conflict, you will have little success in sharing the Good News about Jesus Christ. This principle is taught repeatedly throughout the New Testament.

One of the most emphatic statements on peace and unity in the Bible is found in Jesus' prayer shortly before he was arrested and taken away to be crucified. After praying for himself and for unity among his disciples (John 17:1–19), Jesus prayed for all who would someday believe in him. These words apply directly to every Christian today:

> "My prayer is not for [my disciples] alone. I pray also for those who will believe in me through their message, that all of them *may be one*, Father, just as you are in me and I am in you. May they also be in us so that the world may believe that you have sent me. I have given them the glory that you gave me, that they *may be one as we are one*: I in them and you in me. *May they be brought to complete unity to let the world know that you sent me and have loved them even as you have loved me*" (John 17:20–23, emphasis added).

Jesus prayed these words during the final hours of his life. As death drew near, the Lord focused on a single concept he knew to be of paramount importance for all those who would believe in him. He did not pray that his followers would always be happy, that they would never suffer, or that their rights would always be defended. *Jesus prayed that his followers would get along with one another.* This was so important to him that he tied his reputation and the credibility of his message to how well his followers would display unity and oneness. Read his prayer once more and think about how important unity is to him. Is it equally important to you?

Similar words are recorded in John 13:34–35, where Jesus tells his disciples that their public witness would be closely related to the way they treated one another: "A new command I give you: Love one another. As I have loved you, so you must love one another. By this all men will know that you are my disciples, if you love one another."

The love Jesus commands us to show to one another has very little to do with warm feelings; in fact, he commands us to show love even when it is the last thing in the world we feel like doing (Luke 6:27–28). The love that Jesus wants us to show for one another leaves no room for unresolved conflict:

> Love is patient, love is kind. It does not envy, it does not boast, it is not proud. It is not rude, it is not self-seeking, it is not easily angered, it keeps no record of wrongs. Love does not delight in evil but rejoices with the truth. It always protects, always trusts, always hopes, always perseveres (1 Cor. 13:4–7).

The theme of peace and unity also occupied an important part of Jesus' Sermon on the Mount. He said, "Blessed are the peacemakers, for they will be called sons of God" (Matt. 5:9). Peacemakers provide a powerful testimony to those who observe their efforts. The world is so contaminated by conflict that even the ungodly will eventually recognize that God himself is working in and through those who make peace (1 Peter 2:12).

Later in his sermon, Jesus again urged his followers to seek peace and unity. Knowing that God will sternly judge anyone who condemns or harbors anger toward his brother (Matt. 5:21–22), Jesus gave this command: "Therefore, if you are offering your gift at the altar and there remember that your brother has something against you, leave your gift there in front of the altar. First go and be reconciled to your brother; then come and offer your gift" (vv. 23–24).

Peace and unity are so important that Jesus commands us to seek reconciliation with a brother even ahead of worship! This command shows that we cannot love and worship God properly if we are at odds with another person and have not done everything in our power to be reconciled (1 John 4:19–21). It also reminds us that our Christian witness depends greatly on our commitment to deal faithfully with unresolved conflict.

The pastor of a church I attended during college clearly understood the importance of seeking peace with an estranged brother. He demonstrated this the Sunday I brought a friend named Cindy to church for the first time. I had met Cindy at school and learned that she was struggling in her spiritual life, largely because the church she attended provided little biblical teaching. Thinking that she might find meaningful instruction and encouragement from my church, I had invited her to worship with me one Sunday.

I was unprepared for what took place shortly after Cindy and I took our seats, because I had forgotten that during the previous week's Sunday school period my pastor and an elder had gotten into a public argument. Pastor Woods called for the attention of the congregation and asked the elder with whom he had quarreled to join him at the pulpit. "As most of you know," Pastor Woods said, "Kent and I had an argument during Sunday school last week. Our emotions got out of hand, and we said some things that should have been discussed in private."

As I thought of the first impression Cindy must be getting, my stomach sank. "Of all the days to bring someone to church," I thought, "why did I pick this one?" I was sure this incident would discourage Cindy from coming to my church again.

Pastor Woods put his arm around Kent's shoulders and went on. "We want you to know that we met that same afternoon to resolve our differences. By God's grace, we came to understand each other better, and we were fully reconciled. But we need to tell you how sorry we are for disrupting the unity of this fellowship, and we ask for your forgiveness for the poor testimony we gave last week."

Many eyes were filled with tears as Pastor Woods and Kent prayed together. Unfortunately, I was so worried about what Cindy might be thinking that I completely missed the significance of what had happened. Making a nervous comment to Cindy, I opened the hymnal to our first song and hoped she would forget about the whole incident. The rest of the service was a blur, and before long I was driving her home. I made light conversation for a few minutes, but eventually Cindy referred to what had happened: "I still can't believe what your pastor did this morning. I've never met a minister in my church who had the courage and humility to do what he did. I'd like to come to your church again."

During subsequent visits, Cindy's respect for my pastor and for Kent continued to grow, and before long she made our church her spiritual home. She saw real evidence of God's presence and power in those two men. Their humility highlighted God's strength and helped Cindy to take Christ more seriously. As a result, she committed herself to Christ and began to grow in her faith. As I watch that growth continue to this day, I still thank God for those two men and their willingness to obey the Lord's call to peace and unity.

The Enemy of Peace

Since peace and unity are essential to an effective Christian witness, you can be sure that there is one who will do all he can to promote conflict and division within the fellowship of believers. Satan, whose name means "adversary," likes nothing better than to see us at odds with one another. "Your enemy the devil prowls around like a roaring lion looking for someone to devour" (1 Peter 5:8b).

Satan promotes conflict in many ways. Among other things, he fills our hearts with greed and dishonesty (Acts 5:3), deceives us as to what will make us happy (2 Tim. 2:25–26), and takes advantage of unresolved anger (Eph. 4:26–27). Worst of all, he uses false teachers to propagate values and philosophies that encourage selfishness and stimulate controversy (1 Tim. 4:1–3). Here are some of the expressions that often reflect the devil's influence:

"Look out for number one."
"God helps those who help themselves."

43

"Surely God doesn't expect me to stay in an unhappy situation."
"I'll forgive you, but I won't forget."
"Don't get mad, get even."
"I deserve better than this."

Satan prefers that we do not recognize his role in our conflicts. As long as we see other people as our only adversaries and focus our attacks on them, we will give no thought to defending ourselves against our most dangerous enemy. Both James and Peter were aware of this danger, and they warn us to resist Satan's schemes (James 4:7; 1 Peter 5:9). Paul gives a similar warning, reminding us that "our struggle is not against flesh and blood, but against the rulers, against the authorities, against the powers of this dark world and against the spiritual forces of evil in the heavenly realms" (Eph. 6:12). He then describes the weapons needed to withstand Satan's power: truth, righteousness, the gospel, faith, Scripture, and prayer. (I will refer to these weapons frequently throughout this book.)

Of course, it would be a serious mistake to blame all conflict on Satan. We need to take responsibility for our sins and encourage others to do the same. We must also face up to the practical problems that conflict raises and develop realistic solutions. At the same time, we should be aware of Satan's goals and guard against his influences. By doing so, we can avoid being led astray in our efforts to restore and maintain peace.[2]

Strive like a Gladiator

The apostles understood the importance of peacemaking, and they realized that Satan will do all he can to promote conflict. The depth of their concern is revealed by the fact that every Epistle in the New Testament contains a command to live at peace with one another. For example:

May the God who gives endurance and encouragement give you a spirit of unity among yourselves as you follow Christ Jesus, so that with one heart and mouth you may glorify the God and Father of our Lord Jesus Christ. Accept one another, then, just as Christ accepted you, in order to bring praise to God (Rom. 15:5–7).

I appeal to you, brothers, in the name of our Lord Jesus Christ, that all of you agree with one another so that there may be no divisions among you and that you may be perfectly united in mind and thought (1 Cor. 1:10).

The acts of the sinful nature are obvious: . . . hatred, discord, jealousy, fits of rage, selfish ambition, dissensions, factions and envy. . . . But the fruit of the Spirit is love, joy, peace (Gal. 5:19–22).

Bear with each other and forgive whatever grievance you may have against one another. . . . Let the peace of Christ rule in your hearts, since as members of one body you were called to peace (Col. 3:13, 15).

Live in peace with each other. . . . Make sure that nobody pays back wrong for wrong. . . . (1 Thess. 5:13b–15).[3]

Half of Paul's letter to the Ephesians is devoted to peacemaking. The first three chapters of this letter provide a glorious description of God's plan of salvation. In the fourth chapter, Paul begins to explain how we should respond to what Christ has done for us. Note carefully what Paul places at the top of his list of practical applications: "As a prisoner for the Lord, then, I urge you to live a life worthy of the calling you have received. Be completely humble and gentle; be patient, bearing with one another in love. Make every effort to keep the unity of the Spirit through the bond of peace" (Eph. 4:1–3). The Greek word that is translated "make every effort" in this passage means to strive eagerly, earnestly, and diligently. It is a word that a gladiator trainer in Rome might have used when he sent one of his men to fight to the death in the coliseum: "Make every effort to stay alive today!" So, too, must a Christian agonize for peace and unity. Obviously, token efforts and halfhearted attempts at reconciliation fall far short of what Paul had in mind.

Paul also shows that unity does not mean uniformity (Eph. 4:7–13), for God has richly blessed his children with every kind of gift, talent, and calling (1 Cor. 12:12–31). Mature Christians rejoice in the diversity that God has given to his people, and they realize that believers can legitimately hold differences of opinion on "disputable matters" (Rom. 14:1). When differences rob us of harmony and peace, however, there is work to do.

Later in Ephesians, Paul uses even stronger language to emphasize the importance of harmonious relationships. He warns us that we "grieve the Holy Spirit" when we indulge in "unwholesome talk . . . bitterness, rage and anger, brawling and slander" (Eph. 4:29–31). Knowing that such conduct grieves God and quenches the work of the Holy Spirit in our lives, Paul earnestly urges us to "be kind and compassionate to one another, forgiving each other, just as in Christ God forgave you" (v. 32).

Lawsuits among Believers

God's concern for peace and unity is further emphasized by the instructions he has given on how to resolve lawsuits. When Paul learned that Christians in Corinth were suing one another in secular courts, he was dismayed. Because he knew that lawsuits between Christians were inconsistent with Jesus' teachings and would do serious damage to the witness of the church, he sharply rebuked the Corinthians:

> If any of you has a dispute against another, dare he take it before the ungodly for judgment instead of before the saints? Do you not know that the saints will judge the world? And if you are to judge the world, are you not competent to judge trivial cases? Do you not know that we will judge angels? How much more the things of this life! Therefore, if you have disputes about such matters, appoint as judges even men of little account in the church! I say this to shame you. Is it possible that there is nobody among you wise enough to judge a dispute between believers? But instead, one brother goes to law against another—and this in front of unbelievers!
>
> The very fact that you have lawsuits among you means you have been completely defeated already. Why not rather be wronged? Why not rather be cheated? Instead, you yourselves cheat and do wrong, and you do this to your brothers (1 Cor. 6:1–8).

When Christians cannot resolve their differences privately, God commands that we turn to the church rather than to the civil courts. Unfortunately, many Christians are unaware of this command or believe that it no longer applies today. Worse yet, many churches ignore this passage and do nothing to help Christians settle their disputes in a biblical manner. This failure was specifically noted by Chief Justice Warren Burger in 1982.

> One reason our courts have become overburdened is that Americans are increasingly turning to the courts for relief from a range of personal distresses and anxieties. Remedies for personal wrongs that once were considered the responsibility of institutions other than the courts are now boldly asserted as legal "entitlements." The courts have been expected to fill the void created by the decline of church, family and neighborhood unity.[4]

The church's neglect in fulfilling its traditional peacemaking responsibilities has deprived Christians of valuable assistance, contributed to the congestion of our court system, and, worst of all, damaged the witness of Christ. Fortunately, there are still some Christians who take Paul's rebuke seriously. For example, Associate Supreme Court Justice Antonin Scalia made this observation:

> I think this passage [1 Cor. 6:1–8] has something to say about the proper Christian attitude toward civil litigation. Paul is making two points: first, he says that the mediation of a mutual friend, such as the parish priest, should be sought before parties run off to the law courts. . . . I think we are too ready today to seek vindication or vengeance through adversary proceedings rather than peace through mediation. . . . Good Christians, just as they are slow to anger, should be slow to sue.[5]

Thank God that a Justice of the United States Supreme Court has such a high view of Scripture! Justice Scalia reminds us that Paul's instructions to the Corinthians are as relevant today as they were two thousand years ago. Furthermore, these instructions are extremely practical and beneficial.

When Paul commanded Christians to resolve their disputes in the church, he had a specific process in mind. Jesus had already established a format that Christians are to follow when they are dealing with sin and conflict (see Matt. 18:15–20). This process, which will be discussed more thoroughly in chapters 7 through 9, involves private discussions, a type of mediation, and authority to make a binding decision. The approach is so wise and effective that even the secular legal system is imitating it.[6]

There are many benefits to resolving conflicts in the church rather than the courts. Litigation usually increases tensions and often destroys relationships. In contrast, the church can actively encourage forgiveness and promote reconciliation, thus preserving valuable relationships. Furthermore, a court process usually fails to deal with the underlying causes of conflict. In fact, the adversarial process, which encourages people to focus on what they have done right and what others have done wrong, often leaves the parties with a distorted view of reality and may actually ingrain the flawed attitudes that caused the conflict in the first place.

In contrast, the church can help people to identify root problems. Once the personal issues are resolved, the legal issues can often be settled with little additional effort. At the same time, the church can help people change harmful habits so they will experience less conflict and enjoy healthier relationships in the future.

The church can also develop more complete and effective remedies than a court. A judge is usually limited to awarding money damages, transferring property, or enforcing a contract. When a dispute is resolved within the church, the parties are encouraged to work together to develop creative solutions that resolve both substantive and relational issues. For example, when one church helped several brothers resolve a dispute regarding their farming operations, it suggested that the men and their families get together for dinner once a month and talk about anything but farming. That advice proved to be sound. As the bonds between various family members were strengthened through more regular personal contact, there were fewer disagreements regarding the operation of the family farm.

The primary benefits of resolving disputes through the church are that this process prevents a public quarrel that would dishonor Christ, and encourages biblical solutions and genuine reconciliation. These results bring praise to God by revealing his peace, goodness, and power. At the same time, we improve our ability to tell others how they can be reconciled with God through Christ (see 2 Cor. 5:18–20). For these reasons alone, we should make every effort to resolve our differences outside of a courtroom.[7]

Summary and Application

The message given by Jesus and the apostles is resoundingly clear: whether our conflicts involve minor irritations or major legal issues, peace and unity are of paramount importance to God. Therefore, peacemaking is not an optional activity for a believer. If you have committed your life to Christ, he commands you to make peace and unity a high priority in your life. Token efforts will not satisfy this command; God wants you to strive earnestly, diligently, and continually to maintain harmonious relationships with those around you. Your obedience to this call will advance the gospel and allow you to enjoy the personal peace that God gives to those who faithfully serve him.

If you are presently involved in a conflict, these questions will help you to apply the principles presented in this chapter:

1. Have you made peace with God by accepting Jesus Christ as your Savior, Lord, and King? If not, you can do so right now by sincerely praying this prayer:

   Lord Jesus,
      I know that I am a sinner, and I realize that my good deeds could never make up for my wrongs. I need your forgiveness. I believe that you died for my sins, and I want to turn away from them. I trust you now to be my Savior, and I will follow you as my Lord and King, in the fellowship of your church.

If you have prayed this prayer, it is essential that you find fellowship with other Christians in a church where the Bible is faithfully taught and applied. This fellowship will help you to learn more about God and to be strengthened in your faith.

2. Are you at peace with other people? If not, from whom are you estranged? Why?

3. Are you experiencing the kind of internal peace that you desire? If not, why?

4. Has the peace and unity of the Christian community been disrupted by your dispute? How?

5. What effect might this conflict be having on the reputation of Christ?

6. Is there someone who might have something against you? What have you done to be reconciled? Do you believe that you are free to worship God, or do you need to make another effort to restore unity with that person?

7. Why and how might Satan be aggravating this dispute?

8. On a scale of 0 to 100 (with 100 being "maximum possible effort"), how would you rate the effort you have made thus far to restore peace and resolve this dispute? What kind of effort would please and honor God?

9. Read Ephesians 4:29–32. Are you thinking, speaking, or acting in a way that might grieve the Holy Spirit?

10. Are you involved in a lawsuit? If so, what have you done to follow 1 Corinthians 6:1–8?

11. Go on record with the Lord by writing a prayer based on the principles taught in this chapter.

3

Trust in the Lord and Do Good

The LORD's unfailing love
surrounds the man who trusts in him.

Psalm 32:10

The more you trust God, the easier it is to do his will. This is especially true when you are involved in conflict. If you believe that God is watching over you with perfect love and unlimited power, you will be able to serve him faithfully as a peacemaker, even in the most difficult circumstances. In this chapter, you will see why God is worthy of this kind of trust.

God Is Sovereign

The Bible provides many examples of people who trusted God even in the midst of terrible hardship and suffering. Our prime example is Jesus; when faced with the horror of the cross, Jesus responded to his human fears with these words: "My Father, if it is not possible for this cup to be taken away unless I drink it, may your will be done" (Matt. 26:42) and "Father, into your hands I commit my spirit" (Luke 23:46; cf. 1 Peter 2:23).

The apostle Paul responded to his imprisonment, suffering, and impending execution in a similar way: "That is why I am suffering as I am. Yet I am not ashamed, because I know whom I have believed, and am convinced that he is able to guard what I have entrusted to him for that day" (2 Tim. 1:12).

One reason that Jesus and Paul trusted God so completely was that they knew he was in complete control of everything that happened in their lives. This perfect control is often referred to as "the sovereignty of God." It would take an entire book to address the implications of God's sovereignty, and even then many questions and mysteries would remain unanswered. Still, a fundamental understanding of this important doctrine is invaluable to anyone who wants to serve as a peacemaker.

To be sovereign means to be supreme, unlimited, and totally independent of any other influence. God alone has such power (Isa. 46:9–10). The Bible teaches that God's dominion is so great that he has ultimate control over all things. His sovereignty extends over both creation and preservation (Ps. 135:6–7; John 1:3; Col. 1:16–17; Rev. 4:11). He rules over all governments (Prov. 21:1; Dan. 2:20–21; 4:35). He alone controls individual lives and destinies (Jer. 18:6; John 6:39; Rom. 9:15–16; 15:32; Eph. 1:11–12; James 4:15). At the same time, he watches over events as small as a sparrow's fall from a tree (Matt. 10:29).

As these and dozens of other passages show, God has ultimate control over all that happens in this world. Yet he does not exercise this power from a distance or relate to us as a mass of anonymous people. Rather, he takes personal interest in individual people and knows the smallest details of our lives (Ps. 8:3–4; 139:1–18; Prov. 16:1, 9, 33; 19:21; Matt. 10:30–31). Such power and attention is beyond our comprehension. When King David tried to understand the wonders of God's intimate involvement in his life, he could only conclude, "Such knowledge is too wonderful for me, too lofty for me to attain" (Ps. 139:6).

God's sovereignty is so complete that he exercises ultimate control even over painful and unjust events (Exod. 4:10–12; Job

1:6–12; 42:11; Ps. 71:20–22; Isa. 45:5–7; Lam. 3:37–38; Amos 3:6; 1 Peter 3:17). This is difficult for us to understand and accept, because we tend to "judge" God's actions according to our notions of what is right. Whether consciously or subconsciously, we say to ourselves, "If I were God and could control everything in the world, I wouldn't allow anyone to suffer or be hurt." Such thoughts show how little we understand and respect God. Isaiah warned, "You turn things upside down, as if the potter were thought to be like the clay! Shall what is formed say to him who formed it, 'He did not make me'? Can the pot say of the potter, 'He knows nothing'?" (Isa. 29:16).

Certainly, God takes no pleasure in what is hurtful (Ezek. 33:11), and he is never the author of sin (James 1:13–14; 1 John 1:5). Yet, for his eternal purposes, he sometimes allows suffering and permits unjust acts by men and women he decides not to restrain, even though he has the power to do so. Nowhere is this more vividly revealed than when the apostle Peter described the trial and execution of the Lord Jesus: "This man was handed over to you *by God's set purpose and foreknowledge*; and you, with the help of wicked men, put him to death by nailing him to the cross" (Acts 2:23, emphasis added; cf. Luke 22:42; Acts 4:27–28). Jesus did not die because God had lost control or was looking in the other direction. God was fully in control at all times. He *chose* not to restrain the actions of evil men so that his plan of redemption would be fulfilled through the death and resurrection of Christ (Rom. 3:21–26). As John Piper puts it:

> People lift their hand to rebel against the Most High only to find that their rebellion is unwitting service in the wonderful designs of God. Even sin cannot frustrate the purposes of the Almighty. He himself does not commit sin, but he has decreed that there be acts which are sin—for the acts of Pilate and Herod were predestined by God's plan.[1]

Even when sinful and painful things are happening, God is somehow exercising ultimate control and working things out for his good purposes. Moreover, at the right time God administers justice and rights all wrongs. As Proverbs 16:4–5 promises, "The

LORD works out everything for his own ends—even the wicked for a day of disaster. The LORD detests all the proud of heart. Be sure of this: They will not go unpunished" (cf. Ps. 33:10–11; Rom. 12:19).

The fact that God has ultimate control of all things does not release us from responsibility for our actions. He has allowed us to exercise immediate control of ourselves, and he will hold us fully accountable for the decisions we make in life (Matt. 12:36; Rom. 14:12). Therefore, we should never think of God's sovereignty as an excuse for our sin. Instead, knowledge of the sovereignty of God should motivate us to be even more responsible. As the passages cited above indicate, nothing in our lives happens by chance. We will never suffer trials or be involved in disputes unless God allows it. In other words, every conflict that comes into our lives has somehow been ordained by God. Knowing that he has personally tailored the events of our lives should dramatically affect how we respond to them.

God Is Good

If all we knew was that God is in control, we could have reason to fear. Indeed, if he used his power arbitrarily, sometimes for good and sometimes for evil, we would be in great danger. But this is not the case. God is good—his power is always wielded with perfect love—"One thing God has spoken, two things have I heard: that you, O God, are strong, and that you, O Lord, are loving" (Ps. 62:11–12).

The foundation for our trust in God is constructed of both power and love. He is not only in control over us; he is *for* us! In love, he gives us life, provides for our needs, and never takes his eyes off us. As Christians, we can say with J. I. Packer:

> He knows me as a friend, one who loves me; and there is no moment when his eye is off me, or his attention distracted from me, and no moment, therefore, when his care falters. This is momentous knowledge. There is unspeakable comfort . . . in know-

ing that God is constantly taking knowledge of me in love, and watching over me for my good.[2]

The fact that God is good does not mean that he will protect us from all suffering. Rather, it means that he will be with us in our suffering and accomplish good through it (Isa. 43:2–3). We have already seen several ways that God can use trials and difficulties for good. He often uses them to bring glory to himself by displaying his goodness, power, and faithfulness (e.g., John 9:1–5; 11:1–4; 1 Peter 1:6–7). J. I. Packer writes, "We see that he leaves us in a world of sin to be tried, tested, belaboured by troubles that threaten to crush us—in order that we may glorify him by our patience under suffering, and in order that he may display the riches of his grace and call forth new praises from us as he constantly upholds and delivers us."[3]

God also uses our trials to teach us how to minister to others when they are suffering (2 Cor. 1:3–5). Through our trials, we can set an example that will encourage others to trust in God and remain faithful to his commands (2 Cor. 1:6–11). In doing so, we are passing on the example given to us by Christ:

> If you suffer for doing good and you endure it, this is commendable before God. To this you were called, because Christ suffered for you, leaving you an example, that you should follow in his steps. . . . When they hurled their insults at him, he did not retaliate; when he suffered, he made no threats. Instead, he entrusted himself to him who judges justly. . . . So then, those who suffer according to God's will should commit themselves to their faithful Creator and continue to do good (1 Peter 2:20, 23; 4:19).[4]

By allowing us to suffer insults, conflict, and other hardships, God teaches us to rely more on him (2 Cor. 1:9; 12:7–10). He also allows us to suffer the unpleasant consequences of our sins so that we will see our need for repentance (Ps. 119:67–71). In addition, God uses difficulties to conform us to the likeness of Christ (Rom. 8:28–29). The trials he gives us require that we practice the character qualities that will make us like our Lord. The apostles recognized and accepted this dynamic. Paul wrote that "we also rejoice in our sufferings, because we know that suffering produces perseverance; perseverance, character; and character, hope" (Rom. 5:3–4). And James elaborated: "Consider it pure joy, my brothers, whenever you face trials of many kinds, because you know that the testing of your faith develops perseverance. Perseverance must finish its work so that you may be mature and complete, not lacking anything" (James 1:2–4).

One reason that these men could face problems with such confidence was that they knew God would never give them more than they could handle. They trusted that every time he gave them a challenge, he would also give them the guidance, strength, and abilities needed to deal with it (cf. Exod. 4:11–12). As Paul promised the Corinthians: "No temptation [or trial] has seized you except what is common to man. And God is faithful; he will not let you be tempted beyond what you can bear. But when you are tempted, he will also provide a way out so that you can stand up under it" (1 Cor. 10:13). As this passage promises, God will always make available the strength and help we need to deal with the difficulties of life. It is up to us to take hold of that assistance. He also promises to provide "a way out" of our problems, and he will do this in one of two ways. Sometimes he removes the problems after they have accomplished their purpose in our lives (2 Cor. 1:3–11). At other times, he leaves the problems but gives us his strength so that we can have victory over them on a day-to-day basis (2 Cor. 12:7–10).

Although we can be sure that God is always working for our good and the good of others, even through trials and suffering, we will not always know exactly what that good is. In many cases his ultimate purposes will not be evident for a long time. In other situations his ways and objectives are simply too profound for us to comprehend, at least until we see God face to face (see Rom. 11:33–36). This should not diminish our confidence in him or our willingness to obey him, however. As Deuteronomy 29:29 tells us, "The secret things belong to the LORD our God, but the things revealed belong to us and to our children forever, that we may follow all the words of this law."[5]

This passage provides the key to dealing faithfully with painful and unjust situations. God may not tell us everything we *want* to know about life, but he has told us all we *need* to know. Therefore, instead of wasting time and energy trying to figure out things that are beyond our comprehension, we need to turn our attention to the information and instructions that God has revealed to us through Scripture. The Bible tells us that God is both sovereign and good, so we can be sure that whatever he has brought into our lives can be used to glorify him, to benefit others, and to help us to grow. The Bible also provides clear and practical instructions on how to respond effectively to the challenges God allows in our lives. As we trust God with the "secret things" and focus our attention on obeying his revealed will, we will experience greater peace within ourselves (Ps. 131; Isa. 26:3) and be able to serve him more effectively as peacemakers (Prov. 3:5–7).[6]

The Path Has Been Marked

Trusting God does not mean that we will never have questions, doubts, or fears. We cannot simply turn off the natural thoughts and feelings that arise when we face difficult circumstances. Trusting God means that *in spite of our questions, doubts, and fears* we draw on his grace and continue to believe that God is loving, that he is in control, and that he is always working for good. Such trust helps us to continue doing what is good and right, even in difficult circumstances.

The Bible is filled with examples of people who experienced all kinds of misgivings and yet continued to trust in God. For example, when Job suffered incredible hardship, he voiced many doubts and apprehensions. Even so, he eventually came to this conclusion: "I know that you can do all things; no plan of yours can be thwarted. You asked, 'Who is this that obscures my counsel without knowledge?' Surely I spoke of things I did not understand, things too wonderful for me to know" (Job 42:2–3; see 40:1–41:34).

One of my favorite Bible characters, Joseph, had a similar experience, which is described in Genesis 37 through 50. Because he was favored by his father, his brothers envied him and sold him into slavery in Egypt. Although Joseph probably struggled with times of doubt and frustration, he did not take things into his own hands. Instead, he continued to serve God faithfully (e.g., Gen. 39:9). In spite of Joseph's honesty and diligence, however, false charges were brought against him, and his master threw him into prison. Even there, Joseph continued to trust in God and faithfully served those who imprisoned him (Gen. 39:11–23).

The Lord showed kindness to Joseph, giving him great wisdom and empowering him to interpret dreams. This led Pharaoh to make Joseph prime minister of Egypt. In that position, Joseph was able to save the entire nation of Egypt, as well as his family, from starvation when famine devastated the Middle East. His brothers eventually came to him in fear, seeking forgiveness for the great wrong they had done to him. Joseph's reply revealed remarkable humility and a profound trust in the sovereignty of God: "'Don't be afraid. Am I in the place of God? You intended to harm me, but God intended it for good to accomplish what is now being done, the saving of many lives. So then, don't be afraid. I will provide for you and your children.' And he reassured them and spoke kindly to them" (Gen. 50:19–21).

King David likewise observed that God allowed evil men to flourish for a time. Although he could not understand why, David was convinced that God was in control and that all his ways are good. This confidence inspired David to obey God even in the midst of severe persecution. David's feelings and insights are recorded in Psalm 37, which provides great encouragement to those who are being opposed or mistreated by others. The following thoughts are the first six verses of that psalm:

> Do not fret because of evil men
>   or be envious of those who do wrong;
> for like the grass they soon wither,
>   like green plants they will soon die away.
> Trust in the Lord and do good;
>   dwell in the land and enjoy safe pasture.
> Delight yourself in the Lord
>   and he will give you the desires of your heart.
> Commit your way to the Lord;
>   trust him and he will do this:

> He will make your righteousness shine like the dawn,
> the justice of your cause like the noonday sun.

Like Joseph, the apostle Peter was often mistreated and wrongly imprisoned. At times he, too, struggled with questions and fears. Even so, he continued to trust God and made every effort to obey his revealed will. This is particularly apparent in the prayer spoken after Peter and John had been arrested and threatened by the Jewish authorities: "Sovereign Lord, you made the heaven and the earth and the sea, and everything in them. . . . Indeed Herod and Pontius Pilate met together with the Gentiles . . . [and] did what your power and will had decided beforehand should happen. Now, Lord, consider their threats and enable your servants to speak your word with great boldness" (Acts 4:24, 27–29). When the authorities' threats later turned into floggings, Peter and the other apostles continued to trust in God, "rejoicing because they had been counted worthy of suffering disgrace for the Name" (Acts 5:41).

The apostle Paul had the same habit of trusting God regardless of his circumstances. In Philippi, he and Silas were falsely accused, severely flogged, and thrown into prison. Incredibly, instead of wallowing in doubt or despair, they spent the night "praying and singing hymns to God" (Acts 16:25). God responded by bringing about an earthquake, the conversion of the jailer and his family, and an apology from the city officials.

Trusting God proved to be the pattern in Paul's life. Even when the Lord did not immediately relieve his sufferings, Paul continued to view everything that happened to him as God's sovereign will (2 Cor. 4:7–18). This doesn't mean that Paul never had doubts or that he never asked God to relieve his suffering (2 Cor. 12:7–8). But when the Lord's response did not match Paul's request, he was willing to believe that God had something better in mind (vv. 9–10).

This was especially evident during Paul's many imprisonments, which he always considered to be part of God's plan for advancing his kingdom (Eph. 4:1; Phil. 1:12–14; Col. 4:3). The longer Paul walked with God, the more he trusted God. Therefore, Paul did not spend all of his time thinking about when he would be released from prison. Instead of asking his supporters to pray for his prison door to be opened, Paul urged them to pray that "God may open a *door for our message*" (Col. 4:3–4, emphasis added; cf. Eph. 6:19–20). Knowing that he was safely in God's hands no matter what his circumstances, Paul was always free. This knowledge saved him from crippling worry and allowed him to respond effectively to the opportunities God had set before him.

God has continued to provide us with examples of the kind of trust that honors him. One of the most profound examples in recent years was given by Jim and Elisabeth Elliot. In 1956, Jim and four other missionaries were murdered when they tried to carry the gospel to the Aucas, an isolated tribe in South America. Elisabeth was deeply grieved by the loss of her husband, and she had to wrestle through many unanswered questions. As this excerpt from her subsequent book reveals, however, she continued to trust in the sovereignty of God: "To the world at large this was a sad waste of five young lives. But God has his plan and purpose in all things. . . . The prayers of the widows themselves are for the Aucas. We look forward to the day when these savages will join us in Christian praise. Plans were promptly formulated for continuing the work of the martyrs."[7]

The widows carried on the work their husbands had begun; three years after the killings, God answered their prayers and began to open Auca hearts to the gospel. Even some of the men who had killed the five missionaries eventually came to Christ. Although Elisabeth praised God for the conversions he brought about, she acknowledged that they were not the sole measure of God's purpose in her husband's death. In 1981, she added an epilogue to her book, which included these words:

> The Auca story . . . has pointed to one thing: God *is* God. If he is God, he is worthy of my worship, and my service. I will find rest nowhere but in his will, and that will is infinitely, immeasurably, unspeakably beyond my largest notions of what he is up to. God is the God of human history, and he is at work continuously, mysteriously, accomplishing his eternal purposes in us, through us, for us, and in spite of us. . . . Cause and effect are in God's hands. Is it not the part of faith simply to let them rest there? God is God. I

dethrone him in my heart if I demand that he act in ways that satisfy my idea of justice. . . . The one who laid the earth's foundations and settled its dimensions knows where the lines are drawn. He gives all the light we need for trust and obedience.[8]

Similar trust has been displayed in the life of Joni Eareckson Tada. In 1967, Joni was paralyzed from the shoulders down as the result of a diving accident. She too struggled for a time with many questions and doubts. By God's grace, however, she did not succumb to resentment or hopelessness. Instead, as the Lord steadily increased her faith and knowledge, she learned to see her situation as an opportunity to exalt Christ and minister to disabled people. She now leads an organization that ministers to hundreds of thousands of people throughout the world. When writing about God's sovereignty, she says:

> Nothing is a surprise to God; nothing is a setback to his plans; nothing can thwart his purposes; and nothing is beyond his control. His sovereignty is absolute. Everything that happens is uniquely ordained of God.
>
> Sovereignty is a weighty thing to ascribe to the nature and character of God. Yet if he were not sovereign, he would not be God. The Bible is clear that God is in control of everything that happens.
>
> As Moses learned, when God gives a disability, he also gives us the means to deal with it (Exod. 4:11–12). God does not delight in our afflictions, but when they are in his will for us, he delights in working everything out for our good and for his glory (Rom. 8:28)—whether he removes the affliction or not!
>
> If examining the sovereignty of God teaches us anything, it teaches us that real satisfaction comes not in understanding God's motives, but in understanding his character, in trusting in his promises, and in leaning on him and resting in him as the Sovereign who knows what he is doing and does all things well.[9]

Each of the people mentioned in this section experienced extremely difficult problems and wrestled with the same kinds of questions and concerns we have today. What was it that allowed them to keep going in spite of these challenges? Among other things, they had the humility to recognize the limits of their own understanding and the wisdom to bow before God's eternal purposes. Through prayer, study, and experience, they learned to trust completely in the sovereignty of God. Even in the midst of incredible hardship or injustice, they believed that God was in control and that he loved them with an everlasting love. That trust released them from the burden of unanswered questions, helping them overcome the fears and doubts that naturally challenged them. That trust opened their hearts to receive God's grace and gave them freedom to continue doing good as they responded to the challenges God brought into their lives.

Trust Is a Decision

Your view of God will have a profound effect on how much you trust him. If you do not believe that he is both sovereign and good, trust will be an elusive thing, for a god who is loving but not in control is simply "a heavenly Santa Claus . . . who means well, but cannot always insulate his children from trouble and grief."[10] Such a god offers little security or hope in the face of affliction and fails to inspire either trust or obedience.

On the other hand, if you believe that God is sovereign and good, you will be able to trust and obey him, even in the midst of difficult circumstances. A woman I counseled several years ago learned this principle when she was about to leave her husband. Her experience was so encouraging that I later asked her to write an anonymous letter for the benefit of others who were facing similar problems. Here is what she wrote:

Dear Friend,

If you are now in Ken's office, maybe you are feeling as I did. You're saying you want to improve your marriage, but what you really want deep inside is to get out. You can't take the way you are living any more, and you wish your husband would just disappear, leaving behind lots of cash.

The day I first called the CCS, I was ready to take 30 painkillers if I'd had them. I was full of anger, resentment, and hatred for what my life had become. I had reached the point where I couldn't even talk to my husband. I'm not talking about serious conversations—I couldn't even answer a simple question with a yes or no. When he entered a room, I left. When he touched me, I cringed. I felt trapped, and I would drive by apartment complexes with the idea of finding a place where the kids and I could run away and live.

This had gone on for so long that I didn't see how it could ever change. Talking to Ken was going to be my last effort to change things, but I really felt that the marriage was hopeless, and I told my husband that I wanted out.

After talking with Ken, I prayed and prayed about the biblical principles he had explained to me. I was deeply concerned about my future. I began to see that God is sovereign, and I realized my marriage was not an "accident." I also saw that I had no right to leave my husband. On a retreat God showed me through Scripture (Deut. 30:11–20; please read it) that really committing myself to my marriage was God's way. He had set before me a choice—his way or my way. If I chose my own way, I was on my own.

I decided to trust God and go his way. I agreed to go with my husband to a Christian counselor whom Ken had recommended. It was very hard at times. Sometimes I couldn't even talk, but we went for a few months and things started to get better.

We were "getting along," yet I was deeply bothered by the fact that I felt no love for my husband. I no longer felt anger or hatred toward him, but there was no warmth either. Although our relationship had improved, I knew marriage had to be much more than just "getting along."

I didn't believe God had brought us through so much to leave us in a relationship that was so empty. I wanted to continue to trust the Lord and to depend on him for hope. When I looked up "hope" in my Bible concordance, I found this verse: "And hope does not disappoint us, because God has poured out his love into our hearts by the Holy Spirit, whom he has given us" (Rom. 5:5). To me this verse meant that by hoping in God for my future I would not be disappointed. He would give me love for my husband. I could depend on him. I was following his way and therefore I could trust in him to meet my needs.

And do you know what? Something absolutely amazing happened. I'm in love with my husband. I enjoy being with him. I appreciate his sense of humor. I depend on him as a friend. He's my favorite lunch date, and I find myself wanting to give him a hug and a kiss while he's watching television.

The Lord has so turned around my feelings. I thank him almost every day that he didn't let me go my own way. I would have thrown away so much and never realized how God can work when I let him. The change in our family is truly a miracle!

A year after she wrote this letter, I called her to ask how things were going in her marriage. She said her relationship with her husband "still went up and down at times," and they continued to work with a counselor to deal with the root causes of their marital problems. She told me that she and her husband were both growing in their faith. Even when she was very frustrated with her husband, she seldom struggled with the hopelessness that had plagued her two years earlier. She also said she was confident that God knew what he was doing in her life, and she trusted that things would continue to improve as he kept working in both of them.

Then she said something that touched me deeply. She and her husband had just invested in an apartment, and she had been painting it that day. Remembering the times she had driven around looking for a place to run away to, she began to think about what it would be like to live there alone. She said she had shuddered at the thought of how empty and lonely she would be without her husband. "I am so glad," she said, "that I trusted God and didn't go my own way."[11]

Summary and Application

When you are involved in a conflict, you, too, must decide whether or not you will trust God. Trusting God does not mean believing that he will do all that you want, but rather that he will do everything that he knows is good. If you do not trust God, you will inevitably place your trust in yourself or someone else, which ultimately leads to grief. On the other hand, if you believe that God is sovereign and that he will never let anything into your life unless it can be used for good, you will see conflicts not as *accidents* but as *assignments*. This kind of trust glorifies God and inspires the faithfulness needed for effective peacemaking.

If you are presently involved in a conflict, these questions will help you to apply the principles presented in this chapter:

1. Have you been looking at this dispute as something that happened by chance, as something done to you by someone else, or as something that God allowed in your life for a specific purpose?
2. What questions, doubts, or fears do you have because of this dispute?
3. Read Psalms 37 and 73. What do these psalms warn you not to do? What do they instruct you to do? What comforting promises do they provide?
4. How would your feelings, attitude, and behavior change if you started seeing this dispute as an assignment from a perfectly loving and all-powerful God?
5. What good might God bring about if you respond to this conflict in a biblical manner?
6. Go on record with the Lord by writing a prayer based on the principles taught in this chapter.

Part 2

Get the Log out of Your Eye

"You hypocrite, first take the plank out of your own eye, and then you will see clearly to remove the speck from your brother's eye."

Matthew 7:5

As we saw in part one, peacemaking always begins by focusing on God and his concerns. Next you should focus on yourself—not to justify yourself and develop a scheme to get your way, but to examine your attitude and evaluate your faults and responsibilities in the situation. This personal inspection will help you see things more clearly, overlook minor offenses, and take responsibility for your contributions to the dispute. Many times, this will evoke a positive response in your opponent and accelerate a solution to the conflict. Two friends of mine learned this lesson as they stood on the brink of a lawsuit.

Betty and Elaine had been close friends since high school. They had worked at a variety of jobs for a few years after graduation, and eventually Betty was able to start her own clothing store. Elaine was looking for something new to do, and before long Betty hired her as manager.

At first things went well. Both women were hard workers, and the company grew. Later, when Betty decided that she needed to spend more time with her family, she gradually reduced the number of hours she spent at work. Elaine continued at the same pace, however, even when Betty urged her to slow down. Although she worked many hours overtime, Elaine was content with a flat salary each month, especially when Betty gave her a car allowance and other benefits that had not been in their original employment contract.

As time passed the company prospered, but problems developed between Betty and her manager. Elaine was assertive and didn't hesitate to express her ideas about the business in a forceful way. Betty was rather easygoing and avoided confrontations with Elaine as much as possible, even when their opinions differed on important issues. Without meaningful communication, their frustration grew until it erupted in a heated argument at the end of a long, hot day. Tempers flared, and soon Betty said, "That's it! I'm tired of you always telling me how to run my company. You're fired!"

Over the next few weeks Elaine's resentment at being fired deepened, and soon she was talking to an attorney about suing Betty to force her to pay $8,000 for Elaine's overtime during the previous three years. Fortunately, a mutual friend learned of their falling out and was able to persuade them to submit their dispute to Christian conciliation. A panel consisting of an attorney, a respected friend, and myself met with them several times over the next few weeks.

During the early meetings both women were extremely defensive. Each justified her conduct and placed all the blame for the conflict on the other. After several fruitless meetings we were losing hope of settling the dispute. We agreed to meet one last time, however, and we asked both women to study certain Bible passages before we came together again.

God used those passages to change Betty's heart. The next time we met, she took an entirely new approach to the situation. Instead of defending herself and focusing on her own interests, she began to admit the things she had done that had contributed to the dispute. She confessed that she had developed a critical attitude toward Elaine over the past year, which added to the tension in their relationship. In addition, she acknowledged that she had done a poor job of communicating with Elaine and had given her many inconsistent instructions. She also admitted that she had let greed control some of her business decisions, and that she had been wrong to let her temper get out of control. Finally Betty looked at Elaine and said, "You know, I've not only ruined a good friendship through this, but I've also lost a great manager. I can't find anyone who works as hard or manages the store as well as you did."

Elaine's eyes filled with tears when she heard this. "You don't know what that means to me," she said. "I've never been fired before, and this really destroyed my confidence." She paused and then went on. "These events have forced me to see some changes I need to make in my life, too. What you just said helps me believe that I can do it."

Since Elaine had already accepted a new job, reinstatement was not an issue. Elaine agreed that Betty did not owe her any money, but Betty still decided to give her a generous gift to help her get back on her feet financially. Elaine accepted the gift with gratitude. By changing their attitudes and taking responsibility for their own faults, Betty and Elaine averted a lawsuit and preserved a valuable friendship.

4

Is This Really Worth Fighting Over?

A man's wisdom gives him patience;
it is to his glory to overlook an offense.

Proverbs 19:11

Jesus had much to say about resolving conflict. One of his most famous commands is recorded in Matthew 7:3–5:

"Why do you look at the speck of sawdust in your brother's eye and pay no attention to the plank in your own eye? How can you say to your brother, 'Let me take the speck out of your eye,' when all the time there is a plank in your own eye? You hypocrite, first take the plank out of your own eye, and then you will see clearly to remove the speck from your brother's eye."

This passage is sometimes interpreted as forbidding us to confront others about their faults. If you read it carefully, however, you will see that it does not forbid confrontation. Rather, it forbids premature and improper confrontation. Before you talk to others about their faults, you need to face up to yours. Once you have dealt with *your* contribution to a conflict, you may approach others about theirs.

You may have to deal with two kinds of faults when you are involved in a conflict. First, you may be overly sensitive to the wrongs of others, which makes their sins seem more serious than they really are. Second, you may have contributed to the conflict through your sinful behavior. We will deal with the first problem in this chapter, and the second in the following two chapters. Then, in Part Three, we will look at ways you can help others come to grips with their wrongs.

Define the Issues

Conflicts generally involve two kinds of issues: material and personal. Material issues involve substantive matters that must be resolved to settle a disagreement. These issues may be expressed in questions like these: Where will we spend our vacation? Should we build a new church? Did Alice breach the contract? How much money does Ted owe Sue? How can we get this property sold? Was it right for Bill to fire Don? (In chapter 11 I will explain how to resolve such issues through cooperative negotiation.)

Personal issues are those things going on inside of or between persons. These matters involve our attitudes, feelings, and motives, as well as our words, behavior, and conduct toward one another. When a relationship has been damaged by sinful words or actions, genuine peace and unity will not be restored until these personal issues are resolved through repentance, confession, and forgiveness.

Some disputes involve only personal issues and others only material issues. In most conflicts, however, both kinds are present, in which case the personal issues often have a strong influence on how we will deal with the material ones. This influence is described in Luke 12:13–15. "Someone in the crowd said to him, 'Teacher, tell my brother to divide the inheritance with me.' Jesus replied. . . . 'Watch out! Be on your guard against all kinds of greed; a man's life does not consist in the abundance of his possessions.'" The material issue in this situation was, "How should the family inheritance be divided?" The primary personal issue was the brothers' greed, which kept them from resolving the material issue in a cooperative and generous way.

As this brief story illustrates, it is generally wise to address the related personal issues before attempting to resolve a conflict. Once people have repented of sinful attitudes, motives, and behavior, they are in a far better position to deal reasonably with the specific disagreement that divides them. However, since personal reconciliation may be blocked until there is substantial progress on the material issues, both factors must sometimes be dealt with simultaneously.

One of the first things to do when you are involved in a conflict is to define the personal and material issues and discern how they relate to one another. Once you have a clear understanding of these dynamics, you can begin to decide which steps you must take to resolve the problem. It is usually wise to begin this process by asking yourself, "Is this really worth fighting over?" When significant personal or material issues are involved, the answer to this question will be yes, and you will need to follow the steps described in subsequent chapters. In many cases, however, if you look at the situation from a biblical perspective, the answer will be no, which means you should settle the matter as quickly and quietly as possible. Below are some of the principles that will help you answer this question properly.

Overlook Minor Offenses

In many situations, the best way to resolve a conflict is simply to overlook the offenses of others. This approach is highly commended throughout Scripture:

> A man's wisdom gives him patience; it is to his glory to overlook an offense (Prov. 19:11; cf. 12:16; 15:18; 20:3).
> Starting a quarrel is like breaching a dam; so drop the matter before a dispute breaks out (Prov. 17:14; cf. 26:17).
> Above all, love each other deeply, because love covers over a multitude of sins (1 Peter 4:8; cf. Prov. 10:12; 17:9).

Be completely humble and gentle; be patient, bearing with one another in love (Eph. 4:2).

Bear with each other and forgive whatever grievances you may have against one another. Forgive as the Lord forgave you (Col. 3:13; cf. Eph. 4:32).

When we overlook the wrongs that others commit against us, we are imitating God's extraordinary forgiveness toward us: "The LORD is compassionate and gracious, slow to anger, abounding in love. He will not always accuse, nor will he harbor his anger forever; he does not treat us as our sins deserve or repay us according to our iniquities" (Ps. 103:8–10).

Since God does not deal harshly with us every time we sin, we should be willing to treat others in a similar fashion. While this does not mean that we must overlook all sins, it does require that we make every effort to overlook inconsequential wrongdoing. This should take place under two conditions. First, the offense should not have created a wall between you and the other person or caused you to feel differently toward him or her for more than a short period of time. Second, the offense should not be doing serious harm to God's reputation, to others, or to the offender. (We will discuss these criteria more fully in chapter 7.)

If you decide to overlook an offense, you should not simply file it away in your memory for later use against the other person. Instead, you need to forgive the offense in a biblical way: making a commitment not to dwell on it or to use it against the other person in the future. (Chapter 10 will provide more details on forgiveness.) If you cannot overlook the offense this way, or if overlooking it would not be biblically appropriate, talk to the other person about it in a loving and constructive manner.

Check Your Attitude—and Change It

When someone has wronged you and you are still feeling frustrated or hurt, it is difficult to overlook the offense. It is even more difficult if you are overly sensitive to the wrongs of others and tend to dwell excessively on what they have done. One way to guard against this problem is to check your attitude in the light of God's Word.

Paul's letter to the Philippians contains an excellent formula for examining one's attitudes during a conflict. Apparently Paul had heard that two friends in Philippi were having an argument. It must have been a significant one, because word of it had crossed the sea and reached Paul in prison. Therefore, as part of his open letter to the church at Philippi, Paul took the time to urge these two women to seek peace:

> I plead with Euodia and I plead with Syntyche to agree with each other in the Lord. Yes, and I ask you, loyal yokefellow, help these women who have contended at my side in the cause of the gospel, along with Clement and the rest of my fellow workers, whose names are in the book of life.
>
> Rejoice in the Lord always. I will say it again: Rejoice! Let your gentleness be evident to all. The Lord is near. Do not be anxious about anything, but in everything, by prayer and petition, with thanksgiving, present your requests to God. And the peace of God, which transcends all understanding, will guard your hearts and your minds in Christ Jesus.
>
> Finally, brothers, whatever is true, whatever is noble, whatever is right, whatever is pure, whatever is lovely, whatever is admirable—if anything is excellent or praiseworthy—think about such things. Whatever you have learned or received or heard from me, or seen in me—put it into practice. And the God of peace will be with you (Phil. 4:2–9).

All of the major peacemaking principles we have looked at so far are reflected in this letter. Paul implicitly reminds the women that their conflict provides an opportunity to glorify God, to serve others, and to grow to be like Christ. He also emphasizes the importance of peace and unity in God's kingdom, and he says that Euodia and Syntyche should receive help from the church if they cannot resolve their dispute privately. Most importantly, he reminds them that God is intimately involved in their situation and able to help them resolve it.

Paul does not explain every action that Euodia and Syntyche need to take to settle their differences. Apparently they had already received sufficient instruction in that area. Instead, he focuses on the steps they must take to develop a proper attitude toward their situation and toward each other. Paul has broken his instructions into five basic principles, which you, too, can use whenever you are involved in a conflict.

1. Rejoice in the Lord always. As usual, Paul urges us to be God-centered in our approach to conflict. Moreover, he wants us to be *joyfully* God-centered. Realizing we may skip over this point, Paul repeats it: "Rejoice in the Lord always. I will say it again: Rejoice!" What on earth is there to rejoice about when you are involved in a dispute? To begin with, you can rejoice over the most wonderful fact in your life: If you have put your trust in Jesus Christ, you are "in the Lord," and your name is written "in the book of life." If your opponent is a Christian, that person, too, has salvation. Nothing, not even the difficulties of a conflict, should ever overshadow the joy of having received forgiveness through Christ. The more you rejoice in that forgiveness, the easier it can be for you to forgive others.

You can also rejoice that God has given you the Bible, the Holy Spirit, and the church to guide, strengthen, and support you. (If you are not rejoicing over these resources, you may be neglecting them.) If your opponent is a believer, these resources are available to him or her as well. As God works in you through these channels, you can receive reliable direction, grow in character, develop creative solutions, and see a return of genuine peace.

Finally, you can rejoice that your situation is not an accident. Knowing that God is sovereign and good, you can have confidence that he is working through this conflict for your ultimate good. With this confidence as your foundation, you can avoid pointless anxiety and focus your attention on the opportunities that your disagreement provides. Salvation, the motivation and power to change, sound guidance through God's Word and Spirit, the resources of the body of Christ, opportunities that come through a sovereign God—all these blessings are available when you are "in the Lord." That is much to rejoice about!

2. Let your gentleness be evident to all. The second step in developing a proper attitude toward conflict is to "let your gentleness be evident to all" (cf. Gal. 6:1–2). The Greek word translated as "gentleness" in this passage is rich in meaning: "[*Epiaches*] means forbearing, large-hearted, gentle, courteous, considerate, generous, lenient, moderate. In summary, it is describing a quality which is the opposite of irritability, rudeness, and abrasiveness; it is describing a quality that would make a person nice instead of nasty. It is saying that if you are a Christian, you can be a nice person."[1] Being gentle in the midst of conflict produces several benefits, especially when it is "evident to all." It reflects Christ's presence and power in your life, which pleases and honors him. It also guards you from speaking and acting harshly, which would only make matters worse. Finally, your gentleness may encourage similar behavior in your opponent.

Gentleness is especially appropriate if the person who wronged you is experiencing unusual stress. In such cases, the wrong done to you is often only a symptom of a deeper problem. By responding in a gentle and compassionate manner, you can often be of great service to the other person. I recently observed a couple practice this principle in their marriage. The husband had been under a lot of stress recently, and he was more irritable than usual. As a result, he was unfairly critical of his wife and said some harsh things to her in my presence. She had every right to confront him for his sin, but God gave her grace to be gentle. Instead of rebuking him, she overlooked her husband's offense, responded with kind words, and acknowledged the difficulties he was facing. After asking questions to learn more about his situation and feelings, she offered to help him in some concrete ways. He was touched by her gentleness and apologized for the way he had treated her. Thanks to this wife's gentle response, a situation that could have turned into a major quarrel was transformed into a time of real ministry and growth.

3. Replace anxiety with prayer. The third step in developing a godly attitude toward conflict is to get rid of anxious thoughts. Paul is not just talking about trivial concerns. *Merimnao,* the Greek word translated as "anxious," means laden with cares and trouble, pressured, squeezed, burdened, under stress. These feelings tend to multiply when we are in the middle of a dispute, especially if it involves a person who is very important to us or if valuable interests are at stake.

Since Paul knew that anxious thoughts have a way of creeping back into our minds, no matter how hard we try to ignore them, he instructs us to replace worrying with "prayer and petition, with thanksgiving." When you are in a dispute, it will be natural to dwell on your difficult circumstances or on the wrong things that the other person has done or may do to you. The best way to overcome this negative thinking is to thank God for the many things he has already done for you in this situation (and in others) and to request his assistance in dealing with your current challenges (cf. Matt. 6:25–34).

When you remind yourself of God's faithfulness in the past and ally yourself with him today, you will discover that your anxiety is being steadily replaced by confidence and trust (cf. Isa. 26:3). In fact, recalling God's faithfulness and thanking him for his deliverance in the past was one of the primary ways the Israelites overcame their fears when they were faced by overwhelming circumstances (e.g., Pss. 18, 46, 68, 77, 78, 105, 106, 107, 136; Neh. 9:5–37).

When you place your focus on God through prayer, you can begin to experience something that does not seem logical: The hostility, anxiety, and inner conflict with which you have been dealing will begin to give way to a peace so unexpected that Paul says it will "transcend all understanding." Although this peace may be only internal at first ("guarding your heart and mind"), it will often grow into an external peace—or reconciliation—that will likewise surpass the comprehension of those who have been observing your conflict. When God works in his people, things begin to happen that don't make sense to the world. This brings him glory.

4. See things as they really are. As you replace anxiety with prayer, you will be ready to follow Paul's fourth instruction, which is to develop a more accurate view of your opponent. If you respond to conflict like most people, you will tend to focus on the negative characteristics of the person who is disagreeing with you, exaggerating faults and overlooking virtues. The more distorted your perspective becomes, the more likely you are to imagine the worst about your opponent, which may lead you to misjudge completely his or her values, motives, and actions. A negative perspective usually also leads to bitterness, to dwelling on your hurt and thinking how undeserving of it you are.

The best way to overcome this prejudicial tendency is to think deliberately about aspects of your opponent that are true, noble, right, pure, lovely, admirable—in short, "excellent, or praiseworthy." Paul is not saying that we should think *only* about the good things in others, for he clearly understands the necessity of confronting sin and encouraging repentance (Gal. 6:1–2; Col. 3:16). Rather, Paul is teaching us to counterbalance our natural tendency to focus only on what is bad in those who oppose us.

This change does not come about naturally for most of us. It requires a deliberate decision, followed by perseverance. If you shift your focus to positive things, you can experience the principle described in Proverbs 11:27: "He who seeks good finds good will, but evil comes to him who searches for it." If you look for something bad in another person, you will usually be able to find it. On the other hand, if you look for what is good, you are likely to find that, too—and then more and more that is good.

As you regain a more balanced view of the other person, you will often find it easier to overlook minor offenses. I have experienced this process many times in my marriage. I remember one day when Corlette said something that really disappointed me. I don't remember what she said, but I do remember going out into the back yard a few minutes later to rake leaves. For about fifteen minutes I treated myself to a real "pity party," and I was increasingly convinced that I should go back inside and let her know how hurt I was. But then, by God's grace, Philippians 4:8 came to mind.

"Ha!" I thought at first. "What's noble, right, or lovely about the way she's treating me?" But the Holy Spirit wouldn't give up. Within a few moments, I grudgingly conceded that Corlette is a good cook. (This counterbalancing process often begins with the basics.) Then I admitted that she keeps a beautiful home and practices wonderful hospitality. And, yes, she has been very kind and thoughtful toward my family. And she is certainly pure and faithful—I remembered how much she had supported me through some difficult times in my work. Every chance she gets, she attends the seminars I teach and sits smiling and supportive through hours of the same material (always saying she has learned something new). Corlette is a marvelous counselor and has helped hundreds of children. And didn't she even take up backpacking because she knew I loved it? I realized that the list could go on and on.

Within minutes my attitude was turned upside down and I saw the offensive comment for what it was—a momentary and insignificant flaw in an otherwise wonderful person. I did go back inside, but not to confront Corlette about what she had said. Instead, I just wanted to give her a hug and tell her how glad I was to be married to her.

Even if a change in focus does not allow you to overlook every offense, it can often help you in two other ways. First, by recalling what is good in another person, you often will realize how much you will lose if your differences are not resolved. Many marriages, friendships, and business relationships are damaged or destroyed when people focus exclusively on a point of disagreement and forget about all that they have enjoyed in and with one another. Remembering the good may provide the motivation it takes to work through the painful differences that temporarily separate people.

Second, the process of thinking right can be contagious. The more negatively you view opponents, the more inclined they will be to view you in the same way. Conversely, as you focus on what is good about another person and openly acknowledge those qualities, he or she may begin to do the same in return. As you gain a more accurate assessment of each other and as goodwill grows between you, you will both have a greater freedom to deal honestly and realistically with your differences. This will increase your ability to set aside imagined problems and offenses and give proper attention to areas of genuine disagreement. When both of you bring your attention and energy to bear on fewer, more clearly defined issues, you will be more likely to find workable solutions. As mentioned earlier, making progress on the personal concerns that divide you will generally make the material issues more manageable.

5. Practice what you've learned. Paul's final instruction to Euodia and Syntyche (and to us) is both straightforward and encouraging: "Whatever you have learned or received or heard from me, or seen in me—put it into practice. And the God of peace will be with you." Paul knew what he was talking about when it came to conflict. He had to deal with intense conflict and opposition during his stay with the Christians in Philippi (see Acts 16:16–40), so they had seen him in action. He had taught and demonstrated how to deal with disputes, but he understood our human tendency to be hearers rather than doers of the Word. Therefore, he exhorted Euodia, Syntyche, and the rest of the Philippian church to put their knowledge into practice. Otherwise, all their learning was in vain.

Paul's instruction will apply equally well in *your* life. When you find yourself estranged from another person, especially when that person professes to be a follower of Jesus, it is not good enough simply to study the Bible—knowledge isn't really knowledge (in a biblical sense) unless you put it into practice. When you use God's principles to check your attitude and make some changes, you will discover how much easier it becomes to overlook minor offenses. Even when further dialogue or action is necessary, it can be surprisingly productive when you practice the peacemaking principles contained in God's Word. Regardless of what else happens, as long as you are faithful to your Master, you can know the truth of Paul's promise: "The God of peace will be with you."

Count the Cost

Another reason to overlook some offenses and examine your attitude toward the offender is to spare yourself from unnecessary grief and distraction. Conflict is often far more costly than you may realize. In addition to draining your personal finances, prolonged litigation can consume a great amount of time and energy, leaving you emotionally and spiritually exhausted. Worst of all, as long as a disagreement is unresolved, there is the potential for further damage to a relationship. This is one of the reasons for Jesus' command to settle disputes, even lawsuits, as quickly as possible: "Settle matters quickly with your adversary who is taking you to court. Do it while you are still with him on the way, or he may hand you over to the judge, and the judge may hand you over to the officer, and you may be thrown into prison. I tell you the truth, you will not get out until you have paid the last penny" (Matt. 5:25–26).

Unresolved conflict can lead to several types of "prisons" and exact a variety of prices. In some cases you may lose money or property if you do not settle a dispute voluntarily. At other times you may lose your good reputation in your community as a result of continuous negative gossip or publicity. Worst of all, you may get caught in a prison of bitterness. As the verses preceding this passage indicate (vv. 21–24), ongoing hostility can destroy you from the inside and alienate you from God (cf. Ps. 73:21–22). Moreover, the anxiety and negative thinking generated by conflict can spill over and hurt people who are close to you, such as your family or co-workers.

It is all too easy to ignore these costs when we are actually embroiled in a dispute. This is why we need to make a conscious effort to evaluate the true costs of a conflict and to compare them to the benefits of a desired settlement. For example, I was once asked to help four partners divide the assets of a business. One of the men wanted much more than the other three were willing to give him. It was soon evident that the one partner was not going to participate in a negotiation process; if he could not have the share he demanded and believed was rightfully his, he was going to file a lawsuit. For several weeks the other partners had firmly refused to concede to his demands. When I met with those three and asked them why they wouldn't settle, they said, "It isn't just the money; it's the principle of the matter."

In response, I asked, "How much is this principle costing you? How much time has this dispute already taken away from your business, and how much time will a lawsuit consume? More importantly, what effect has this conflict had on you personally and on your families? Are you pleasant to be around at home, or are you more anxious and irritable than usual?"

There was a long pause, and then one of the partners pulled out his calculator. After a few key strokes, he said, "I'd say we have already lost over two thousand dollars in billable time. A lawsuit could easily cost us ten times that amount." Then one of the other partners admitted that he hadn't been sleeping well because of the tensions created by the conflict. He also conceded that his critical attitude had created problems with his wife and children. The third partner made a similar comment.

When these three men added up the real cost of their dispute and compared it to the cost of settling the matter, they saw that the wisest thing to do would be to settle the matter as quickly as possible. Although it was difficult for them to do at the time, one of them later told me that within two weeks of the settlement he was completely free of the matter. "When I look back," he said, "I have a hard time understanding why we didn't settle it much earlier. It sure wasn't worth all that fighting."

What About "Rights"?

Some people resist overlooking offenses and forgiving others by arguing, "I have my rights—and it wouldn't be *just* to let him off so easily." I am always grieved when I hear this type of comment from a Christian. Where would we be if God administered rigid justice? We would already be condemned to hell. Fortunately, God does not treat us as our sins deserve: To those who have trusted in Christ, he is compassionate and merciful—and he expects us to treat one another the same way. Jesus commanded, "Be merciful, just as your Father is merciful" (Luke 6:36; cf. Micah 6:8; Matt. 5:7; James 2:12–13).

The truth of the matter is that it may actually be *unjust* in God's eyes to exercise certain legal rights. Much of what is legal today is not "right" when viewed from a biblical perspective. As Supreme Court Justice Antonin Scalia has noted:

> What is lawful is not always right. Confusing the two concepts is particularly easy for the English-speaking because we use the word "right" to refer both to legality and to moral appropriateness. . . . We say "I have a *right* to plead the Fifth Amendment and refuse to answer questions about possible criminal activity"— even when the consequences of exercising that "right" may cause an innocent person to be convicted. Exercising such a "right" is certainly wrong.[2]

82

Many conflicts arise or grow worse because people use legal rights wrongly. For example, some people avoid moral obligations or liabilities by pleading the statute of frauds or the statute of limitations. Others reap windfalls from less powerful people by rigidly enforcing certain business advantages. In addition, much of what employees and employers can do by law today is flatly inconsistent with biblical teachings regarding the workplace.

When exercising a "right" allows you to avoid a moral responsibility or to take unfair advantage of others, you have not acted justly, regardless of what a court might say. Therefore, you should always strive to exercise only those rights that will pass both a legal and a heavenly review. The basic principle to follow at all times is to "do to others what you would have them do to you . . ." (Matt. 7:12).

Even if you would be legally and morally justified in exercising a particular right, it may be better not to. One aspect of "mercy" is to show sympathy, kindness, and compassion toward someone who is in need of help, *whether or not he deserves it* (see the parable of the good Samaritan, Luke 10:30–37). One way to do this is to refrain from exercising legitimate rights and thus release others from their obligations (see the parable of the unmerciful servant, Matt. 18:21–35). The Bible is filled with examples of this kind of mercy.

Abraham relinquished his rights and gave his nephew Lot first choice on where to settle in Canaan (Gen. 13:5–12). Joseph did not exercise his right to bring his brothers to justice for kidnapping and selling him into slavery (Gen. 50:19–21). King David chose not to punish Shimei for cursing him when he was fleeing from Absalom (2 Sam. 16:5–12; 19:19–23; cf. Exod. 22:28). Paul gave up his right to financial support from the church in Corinth (1 Cor. 9:3–15). In addition, he once relinquished his right to a just trial and consequently was flogged (Acts 16:22–24). Jesus did not exercise his right to be exempt from the temple tax (Matt. 17: 24–27), and he declined to call down legions of angels to rescue him from the Jews (Matt. 26:53–54). Most importantly, he willingly laid down his right to justice by allowing himself to be crucified as a substitute for sinful men (1 Peter 2:22–25).

On the other hand, the Bible teaches that it is sometimes appropriate to exercise our rights, to confront others, and to hold them fully accountable for their responsibilities and their wrongs. For example, after Paul was flogged in Philippi, he asserted his rights and insisted that the civil authorities apologize for their unjust conduct (Acts 16:35–39). On other occasions Paul quickly asserted his rights as a Roman citizen, to avoid a flogging and also to secure an appeal of his case (Acts 22:25–29; 25:11).

As these examples indicate, there are times when it is proper to assert rights, as well as times when we should willingly lay them aside. How can you know when to do which? Paul's first letter to the Corinthians provides a guiding principle. In it Paul discusses various rights the Corinthians were concerned about, including legal rights (6:1–8), marital rights (7:1–40), dietary rights (8:1–13; 10:23–33), and the rights of apostles (9:1–18). He concludes his discussion of "rights" with words that we looked at earlier:

> So whether you eat or drink or whatever you do, do it all for the glory of God. Do not cause anyone to stumble, whether Jews, Greeks, or the church of God—even as I try to please everybody in every way. For I am not seeking my own good but the good of many, so that they may be saved. Follow my example, as I follow the example of Christ (1 Cor. 10:31–11:1).

Here again the concept of stewardship serves as a guiding principle. Rights are simply privileges given to you by God, and he wants you to use them for his glory. A secondary concern should be how exercising your rights can be of benefit to others, especially by helping them to know Christ. As a steward it is likewise appropriate to consider your needs and personal responsibilities (Phil. 2:3–4). Thus, whenever there is a question about your rights, you should ask yourself questions like these:

"Will exercising my rights please and honor God?"
"Will exercising my rights advance God's kingdom—or will it advance only my interests at the expense of his kingdom?"

"Will exercising my rights benefit others?"

"Is exercising my rights essential for my own well-being?"

A brief review of the examples mentioned above shows how the stewardship principle was lived out by many people in the Bible. Paul gave up his right to financial support "rather than hinder the gospel of Christ" (1 Cor. 9:12). When he allowed himself to be flogged by the Philippian authorities and then insisted that they apologize to him, he alarmed them and vividly reminded them of their responsibility to administer justice properly (Acts 16:36–38). This probably caused them to act more carefully in the future, which would be to the benefit of the fledgling church in Philippi if others attempted to persecute its members (Acts 19:35–41; 22:22–29). Likewise, when Paul asserted his rights as a Roman citizen to avoid being flogged, to defend himself in court, and to appeal his case to Caesar, he was securing the opportunity to carry the gospel to the Gentiles and to testify about Christ in Rome (Acts 9:15–16; 22:25; 23:11; 25:11).

Similarly, Abraham's deference to Lot prevented conflict that would have dishonored God in the eyes of those around them (Gen. 13:5–10). Joseph's mercy reunited the house of Israel and allowed it to grow to great numbers (Gen. 50:19–21; Exod. 1:6–7). When David had mercy on Shimei, he provided a powerful example of forgiveness and reconciliation to war-torn Israel and discouraged his followers from taking revenge against others (2 Sam. 19:22–23). Jesus relinquished his right to be exempt from the temple tax so that he would not offend the Jews and generate unnecessary distractions to his ministry (Matt. 17:27). Even greater than all of these acts was Jesus' refusal to exercise his right to justice: laying down this right allowed him to carry out his salvation mission and save all of those who put their faith in him (1 Peter 2:22–25; cf. Isa. 53:1–7; Phil. 2:5–11).[3]

By exercising or laying down their rights with God's kingdom in mind, all of these people brought him glory, expanded the ultimate outreach of the gospel, and sought the good of others. This should be our goal as well. In many cases giving up rights will prevent unnecessary conflicts that would detract from our daily purpose to serve Christ and to spread the gospel. In other cases, however, the best way to achieve these results will be to assert our rights. For example, asserting rights is sometimes the best way to help others learn that they are accountable for their decisions and must "pay the penalty" (Prov. 19:19). Such accountability may help them realize that one day they will be answerable to God. You may also need to exercise certain rights to provide for your family or others who depend on you.

When you are weighing your personal interests and responsibilities, be careful not to twist the concept of stewarding to your advantage. I have seen many people who believe that stewardship means *preserving* everything they have. Thus, they refuse to lay down any rights or to sacrifice any property in the interest of peace. Jesus condemns this notion—he does not want us to hoard what he has given us but to invest our resources and thereby gain the maximum return for his kingdom (Matt. 25:24–27). This certainly means protecting our rights and assets from *wasteful* sacrifices, but it also means expending them on profitable ventures. Just as seed must be sacrificed to produce a crop, our personal rights and material assets must sometimes be surrendered to sow the gospel and produce a spiritual harvest (John 12:24–26).

The principle of relinquishing rights is illustrated in one of my first conciliation cases. Ted worked for a government agency. As a new Christian, he was enthusiastic about his salvation and had tried to talk to his co-workers about Christ, but no one had shown any interest. Ted and his supervisor, Joan, had never gotten along well, especially since Ted continually tried to tell her how she could run her department more effectively. His enthusiasm for Christ provoked her further. As her frustration toward Ted increased, Joan had given him particularly difficult work assignments, even though she knew he had a back problem. Eventually he injured his back and had to leave work for several months. Although he received some disability benefits, Ted lost several thousand dollars in wages and medical expenses. As a result, he filed a lawsuit against Joan and the agency.

By the time Ted came to see me, he had returned to work, and the lawsuit was moving slowly through the court system. During our first conversation, Ted and I identified several things he had done that had contributed to the conflict with Joan. Seeing his own fault more clearly, Ted began to consider settling the lawsuit by accepting the $5,000 the agency had offered him a few days earlier. Although his damages exceeded that amount, his attorney advised him to accept the settlement. On the other hand, several of Ted's friends were encouraging him to either demand more money or continue the litigation.

A few days later Ted called to tell me that he was going to drop his lawsuit without accepting the settlement offer. The more he had reflected on his own fault in the matter, the less comfortable he felt about accepting money from the agency. At the same time, he had concluded that laying down his right to restitution would be an effective way to demonstrate the mercy and forgiveness that he himself had received from God.

The next morning, Ted went to talk with Joan. He admitted that he had been disrespectful, arrogant, and rude, and he asked for her forgiveness. Joan seemed suspicious of his motives and did not say anything in response. Ted went on to explain that he had forgiven her for ordering him to move the heavy boxes and that he was dropping his lawsuit. Finally he said he hoped they could start over in their relationship and learn to work together in the future.

More suspicious than ever, Joan asked why he was doing this. He replied, "I became a Christian a year ago, and God is slowly helping me to face up to a lot of my faults, including those that contributed to the problems between you and me. God has also shown me that his love and forgiveness for me is absolutely free and that I can do nothing to earn or deserve it. Since he has done that for me, I decided I want to act the same way toward you."

Amazed by his answer, Joan mumbled something like, "Oh, I see. Well, let's let bygones be bygones. Thanks for coming in."

Although Joan's response wasn't quite what Ted had hoped for, word of their meeting got around. The next day a union representative who had heartily supported the lawsuit against Joan confronted Ted and asked whether he had really dropped his lawsuit. When Ted said yes, the man asked, "Is it true that you did it because you're a Christian?" Ted again said yes, and the man's scowl turned to a look of puzzlement. As the man walked away,

Ted heard him say to a bystander, "Well, that's the first time I've ever seen a Christian's faith cost him anything."

Like ripples in a pond, the effect of Ted's decision moved slowly throughout the department. A few days after Ted dropped his lawsuit, two co-workers asked to meet with him over lunch once a week to discuss the Bible. Later, other co-workers asked him questions about his faith. For the first time since Ted's conversion, he felt he was really helping people to learn about God's love.

Although Joan continued to treat Ted rudely at times, he learned to submit to her authority and to use her provocations as further opportunities to show God's work in his life. When she was replaced a few months later, there was no doubt in Ted's mind who had arranged for him to have a more pleasant and supportive boss.

Three years later, I asked Ted whether he regretted his decision to give up the settlement. "No," he replied, "that was the best five thousand dollars I ever spent. God used those events to bring several people to Christ. He also helped me to overcome some personal weaknesses. My family saw me put my faith into practice, and we all grew through that. If faced with the same situation today, the only thing I would do differently would be to try to restore peace more quickly."

Summary and Application

There are many conflicts that can be properly resolved only through confrontation, confession, forgiveness, and cooperative negotiation. But there are hundreds more that can be properly resolved simply by overlooking minor offenses or relinquishing rights for the sake of God's kingdom. Therefore, before focusing on your rights, take a careful look at your responsibilities, and before you go to remove the speck from your brother's eye, ask yourself, "Is this really worth fighting over?"

If you are presently involved in a conflict, these questions will help you to apply the principles presented in this chapter.

1. Define the material issues in this conflict.
2. Define the personal issues in this conflict.
3. Which personal issues are having the greatest influence on you? On your opponent?
4. What has the other person done that has offended you?
5. Check your attitude:
   (a) Why can you "rejoice in the Lord" in this situation?
   (b) Have you been irritable, rude, or abrasive in this situation? From this point on, where or how can you make a special effort to be "forbearing, large-hearted, gentle, courteous, considerate, generous, lenient, or moderate"? How could your gentleness be more "evident" to others?
   (c) What have you been worried or anxious about? How has God shown himself to be loving, powerful, and faithful to you in previous conflicts or difficulties? What would you like him to do for you or accomplish through this conflict?
   (d) What is good about the person with whom you are in conflict? What is right about his or her concerns? Do you have any good memories of your relationship? How has God helped you through that person?
   (e) What principles taught in Scripture are most difficult for you to put into practice in this situation? Will you apply those principles? How?
6. What effect is this dispute having or likely to have on:
   (a) Your family life?
   (b) Your occupation?
   (c) Your finances or property?
   (d) Your friendships?
   (e) Your relationship with God?
   (f) Your service to your church and community?
7. Consider your rights:
   (a) What legal rights could you exercise in this situation? Would it be morally right to do so?
   (b) What other rights could you exercise? How might *exercising* these rights glorify God, advance his kingdom, benefit others, and benefit you? How might *laying down*

these rights glorify God, advance his kingdom, benefit others, and benefit you?

8. Which of the offenses described in answer to question 4 can you simply overlook? How might doing so please and honor God?

9. Which of the material issues described in answer to question 1 can you simply give in on?

10. Go on record with the Lord by writing a prayer based on the principles taught in this chapter.

5

Examine Yourself

Let us examine our ways and test them,
and let us return to the LORD.

Lamentations 3:40

In the preceding chapter we saw that Jesus commands us to get the log out of our eye before we try to show others where they have been wrong. Self-examination is especially important when we are involved in a dispute. Until we have dealt with our faults, it will be difficult to help others see how they have contributed to a dispute. But once we have confessed our wrongs and repaired any damage we have done, others will often be encouraged to follow our example and listen to our words. Here are some of the steps we can take to begin this process.

Be Honest about Sin

After many years of marriage, I can think of only one time I may have been entirely innocent of wrongdoing when Corlette and I had an argument (and I am probably mistaken about that incident). Every other time we have experienced a conflict, I either caused it or made it worse through sinful words or actions. Of course, when I am embroiled in the heat of battle, the last thing I naturally think about is my sin. But after the smoke clears, I can always see something that I should have done differently. With God's help, I am trying to speed up this process so I can avoid sinful reactions more often, or at least face up to them more quickly.

Later in this chapter we will look at some of the sinful words, actions, attitudes, and desires that contribute to conflict. But first we need to understand what sin really is. Literally speaking, to sin means "to miss the mark." More specifically, sin may be described as failing to be and do what God commands and doing what God forbids (1 John 3:4). Sin is not an action against an impersonal set of rules. Rather, it is a rebellion against God's personal desires and requirements. This is true even when our thoughts, words, or actions are not consciously directed against God himself. Even seemingly small wrongs against other people are serious in God's eyes, because every wrong is a violation of his will (Gen. 39:9; Num. 5:6–7; Ps. 51:3–4; James 2:10–11).

In fact, we can sin against God by omission—by doing nothing. As James 4:17 tells us, "Anyone, then, who knows the good he ought to do and doesn't do it, sins." Therefore, if we are involved in a conflict and neglect opportunities to serve others (through gentle responses, loving confrontation, etc.), we are guilty of sin in God's eyes.

Because most of us do not like to admit that we have sinned, we tend to conceal, deny, or rationalize our wrongs. If we cannot completely cover up what we have done, we try to minimize our wrong-doing by saying that we simply made a "mistake" or an "error in judgment." Another way to avoid responsibility for our sins is to shift the blame to others or to say that they made us act the way we did. When our wrongs are too obvious to ignore, it is easy to practice what I call the 40/60 Rule. It goes something like this: "Well, I know I'm not perfect, and I admit I am partially to blame for this problem. I'd say that about 40% of the fault is mine. That means 60% of the fault is hers. Since she is 20% more to blame than I am, she should be the one to ask for forgiveness." I never actually say or think these exact words, but I sometimes catch myself using this general concept in subtle ways. By believing that my sins have been more than canceled by another's sins, I can divert attention from what I have done and avoid the call to repentance and confession. "If there is any confessing that needs to be done," I convince myself, "it needs to start with her."

Of course, we are only kidding ourselves when we try to cover up our sins. As 1 John 1:8 indicates, "If we claim to be without sin, we deceive ourselves and the truth is not in us" (cf. Ps. 36:2). Whenever we refuse to face up to our sins, we will eventually pay an unpleasant price. This is what King David discovered when he did not immediately repent of his sins. Psalm 32:3–5 describes the guilty conscience, emotional turmoil, and even the physical side effects that he experienced until he confessed his sins to God: "When I kept silent, my bones wasted away through my groaning all day long. For day and night your hand was heavy upon me; my strength was sapped as in the heat of summer. Then I acknowledged my sin to you and did not cover up my iniquity. I said, 'I will confess my sins to the LORD'—and you forgave the guilt of my sin."

Clearly, ignoring sin never pays. If it is difficult for you to identify and confess your wrongs, there are two things you can do. First, you can ask God to help you to see your sin clearly and repent of it, regardless of what others may do. As David prayed, "Search me, O God, and know my heart; test me and know my anxious thoughts. See if there is any offensive way in me, and lead me in the way everlasting" (Ps. 139:23–24). One of the ways that God will help you to see your sin is through the study of his Word. As you spend time in the Bible, learning what God has to say about the issues you face and the things you have done, you will often see where you have fallen short of his standards.

Second, it is often helpful to ask for the candid insights and advice of a spiritually mature friend (Prov. 12:15; 19:20). This proved to be of real benefit to me one day after a woman called to confront me about a statement I had made about a mutual acquaintance. Although I "won" the discussion we had on the telephone (at least I thought so), my conscience bothered me afterward. Therefore, I described the situation to a friend and asked for his advice. Fortunately, Terry loved me enough to tell me the truth. He asked a few questions to clarify the situation and to unearth some facts I had conveniently passed over. Then he gently but firmly said that he thought I was wrong.

That was not what I wanted to hear, but when Terry explained his reasoning, I knew he was right. Five minutes later, after God helped me to overcome my pride, I called the woman back and admitted I was wrong. She graciously thanked me for my confession and freely forgave me. As I hung up the phone, I realized once more how much freedom we can experience if only we will deal with sin in God's way: "He who conceals his sins does not prosper, but whoever confesses and renounces them finds mercy" (Prov. 28:13).

Control Your Tongue

Before we can confess and renounce our sins, we must identify them. It is often wise to begin this process by examining what we have been saying to and about our opponents. Scripture warns us, ". . . Consider what a great forest is set on fire by a small spark. The tongue also is a fire, a world of evil among the parts of the body. It corrupts the whole person. . . . It is a restless evil, full of deadly poison" (James 3:5–6, 8b).

Sinful speech takes many forms. In many cases we simply use *reckless words*. When faced with an offense or disagreement, we unthinkingly blurt words that will inflame rather than extinguish conflict. Many disagreements that might have been resolved quickly get worse before they get better, simply because we do not restrain our tongues or choose our words more carefully. The Bible repeatedly warns us against this habit. "Reckless words pierce like a sword, but the tongue of the wise brings healing" (Prov. 12:18). "He who guards his lips guards his life, but he who speaks rashly will come to ruin" (Prov. 13:3; cf. 17:28; 21:23; 29:20). Although we may seldom set out deliberately to hurt others with our words, sometimes we do not make much of an effort *not* to hurt others. We simply say whatever comes to mind without thinking about the consequences. In the process, we may hurt and offend others, which only aggravates conflict.

Grumbling and complaining also contribute greatly to discord, which is why we are warned to avoid such talk (Phil. 2:14; James 5:9). Negative and critical talk irritates, offends, and depresses other people, which often leads them to begin grumbling and complaining as well. The more we focus on things we do not have or like, the less we will notice and give thanks for the good things others do for us. When others feel we are critical of them or ungrateful for what they do, it is only a matter of time before conflict breaks out.

Falsehood is another kind of talk that incites and aggravates conflict. Falsehood involves more than outright lies; it includes any form of misrepresentation or deceit (Prov. 24:28; 2 Cor. 4:2). Thus many of us give false testimony more often than we realize. For example, we may resort to *exaggeration* as a means of strengthening a weak position. At other times we find it convenient to tell only *part of the truth* about a particular situation. Or, if all else fails, we occasionally *distort the truth* by emphasizing favorable facts while minimizing those that are against us. Any time we use words that give a false impression of reality, we are guilty of practicing deceit. In doing so, we are following a dangerous example, for Satan himself is known as "the father of lies" (John 8:44; cf. Gen. 3:13; Rev. 12:9).

Gossip is often both the spark and the fuel for conflict. "A perverse man stirs up dissension, and a gossip separates close friends" (Prov. 16:28). "Without wood a fire goes out; without gossip a quarrel dies down" (Prov. 26:20). To gossip means to reveal or discuss personal facts about another person for no legitimate purpose; it often betrays a confidence. Such conversation is sinful and a sign of spiritual immaturity (2 Cor. 12:20; cf. Prov. 11:13; 20:19; 1 Tim. 5:13).

Another problem area for many of us is *slander,* which involves speaking false and malicious words about another person. The Bible repeatedly warns against such talk (e.g., Lev. 19:16; Titus 2:3) and even commands us to "have nothing to do" with slanderers who refuse to repent (2 Tim. 3:3). One warning in particular will discourage us from slandering others. The Greek word *diabolos,* translated as "slanderer" or "accuser," is used thirty-four times in the Bible as a title for Satan, the devil (e.g., Zech. 3:1; Matt. 4:1). This dual usage warns us whom we are imitating and serving whenever we falsely accuse others.

People who generally refrain from reckless words, falsehood, gossip, and slander may still be guilty of *worthless talk,* which can also contribute to conflict, even if they intend no harm. God has set a very high standard to follow whenever we are talking to or about others: "Do not let any unwholesome talk come out of your mouths, but only what is helpful for building others up according to their needs, that it may benefit those who listen" (Eph. 4:29).

The word translated "unwholesome" *(sapros)* means "rotten or worthless." What exactly is worthless talk? Paul answers that question in this passage by using a contrast. The word translated "building up" *(oikodome)* can also be translated as "edifying," which in a physical sense means to construct or strengthen a building. The word is used throughout the New Testament to describe the process of building others up in their faith (e.g., Rom. 14:19; 15:2; 1 Cor. 8:1; 10:23; 14:26; Eph. 4:12, 16). The word translated "benefit" *(didomi)* means "to minister or to give freely" (2 Cor. 8:1; 1 John 3:1). Thus, Paul teaches that instead of indulging in worthless talk, we should say only those things that will promote spiritual growth and encourage the development of a godly character in other believers. To put it another way, he is telling us to avoid saying anything that may be destructive.

In effect, "worthless talk" could describe all six of the specific categories of sinful speech described above, as well as other obviously negative kinds of speech such as cursing others, bad language, and harsh or abusive speech (e.g., 1 Cor. 5:11; Eph. 4:31; Col. 3:8; 2 Tim. 3:2; 1 Peter 3:9).[1] Worthless talk also occurs in more subtle forms. For example, a great deal of tearing down can take place under the guise of offering others "constructive criticism." We have already seen that the Bible endorses loving confrontation, which sometimes requires saying things that people do not want to hear. But Ephesians 4:29 forbids us to confront others in a way that will discourage spiritual growth. Thus, if we believe confrontation is called for, we must guard against a critical spirit, selfish motives, or anything else that may tear down rather than build up the other person.[2]

Another way to tear down a person is to talk about the person behind his or her back ("backbite") and to judge without giving the person a chance to explain or defend actions. This often takes place while we are passing on rumors or hearsay, or when we are discussing others' opinions, actions, or problems. It may also occur when we are seeking advice regarding a friend or co-worker, or even sharing a prayer need. Whenever such conversation diminishes another person's reputation in the eyes of others and serves no legitimate and constructive purpose, it is "worthless talk." A more subtle way to tear down others is to speculate on their thoughts and motives, which is common during disputes. When someone is opposing or mistreating us, it is easy to assume that he or she has selfish, dishonest, or even malicious motives. But the Bible warns that only God can know a person's heart (e.g., 1 Sam. 16:7; Prov. 16:2; Jer. 17:10; 1 Cor. 4:5; 2 Cor. 10:7). When we judge and discuss others' motives without having hard facts to go on (such as their own admissions), we may be guilty of sinful presumption (cf. James 4:11–12).

Sinful speech contributes greatly to conflict. Furthermore, it destroys us from the inside out. Paul provides this warning: "Avoid godless chatter, because those who indulge in it will become more and more ungodly" (2 Tim. 2:16). If you indulge in reckless talk, falsehood, gossip, slander, or any other form of worthless talk, your character will be eroded and your relationship with God will suffer. Therefore, for the sake of peace and spiritual growth, it is important to control your tongue—renounce such talk and seek God's help in overcoming it.

Heed Your Responsibilities

Our country has become so preoccupied with rights that many people give little thought to their responsibilities. Such neglect is often a major cause of conflict. There are three responsibilities in particular that seem to be increasingly ignored in our society.

Keep Your Word

Although I have no personal memory of my mother's father, he has had a powerful impact on my life. When I was young and visited my mother's hometown, she would often introduce me to people who had known my grandfather. Again and again, they would shake my hand and say, "Your grandfather was a man of his word; once he said he'd do something, you could be sure that it would get done." What a precious legacy to leave to your descendants! But such faithfulness is not only rare today; it is often ridiculed. Many of our most popular television shows endorse every form of unreliability and mock people who believe it is important to keep one's word.

A great deal of conflict is the direct result of someone's failure to keep a commitment, whether it was expressed in a contract, a marriage vow, an oath to God, or by a simple yes or no (Matt. 5:33–37; cf. Num. 30:2; Deut. 23:23; Prov. 2:17). People usually justify their unfaithfulness by saying that they didn't know what they were agreeing to, that things didn't turn out as they expected, or that it would be too difficult to keep their promises. The Bible clearly teaches that such developments do not justify breaking one's word, whether or not it is in writing. God expects us to keep our word, even if we made an unwise and impulsive commitment and will have to suffer to be faithful (e.g., Josh. 9:1–19; Eccles. 5:1–7). God commends the person "who keeps his oath even when it hurts" (Ps. 15:4).

In light of this high standard of faithfulness, you should never make commitments lightly, because there are only a few ways you may legitimately get out of them. If you have foolishly committed yourself to something or if unforeseen circumstances arise, you may *appeal* to the other person for mercy and ask (not demand) to be released from your obligation (Prov. 6:1–5; cf. Matt. 18:22–33). In some cases, you may also be freed from your commitments if the other party fails in a substantial way to keep his or her word (e.g., Matt. 19:9; 1 Cor. 7:15). If you cannot be released in a biblical way, however, do not devise dishonest ways to avoid keeping your word (e.g., by resorting to technicalities of law; see Matt. 15:3–9). Instead, ask God to help you learn from your mistake and fulfill your obligations, and then work as long and as hard as necessary to live up to your promises.

Respect Authority

Another common source of conflict is the abuse of or rebellion against the authority God has established in the church, the government, the family, and the workplace. All legitimate authority has been established by God, primarily for the purpose of maintaining peace and order (Rom. 13:1–7). He has given those in authority strict commands not to take advantage of their positions, but rather to diligently serve and look out for the well-being of those whom they are called to lead (Mark 10:42–45; cf. Eph. 5:25–33; 6:4, 9; 1 Peter 3:7; 5:1–3). When people in authority violate the position God has given them, God himself will eventually hold them accountable for that sin (Deut. 24:15; Job 31:13–14; Jer. 22:13; Mal. 3:5; Col. 4:1; James 5:4).

At the same time, God commands us to submit to biblically established authority, both for his sake and for our own good (Eph. 5:21–24; 1 Thess. 5:12–13; 1 Tim. 6:1–2; Titus 2:9–10; Heb. 13:17). Because submission to authority is not a popular concept these days, a variety of excuses are offered to justify overthrowing God's authority structure. But those who rebel against biblically established authority are rebelling against God himself (Rom. 13:2). R. C. Sproul writes, "All authority is under Christ. When we disobey lesser authorities, we are guilty of disobeying Christ. You cannot serve the King and honor his authority by rebelling against his appointed governors. To say you honor the kingdom of Christ while you disobey his authority structure is to be guilty not only of hypocrisy but of cosmic treason."[3]

Respect for authority is so important that Jesus commands us to submit to those over us, even when they behave hypocritically or harshly (Matt. 23:1–3; 1 Peter 2:13–3:6). In other words, God calls us to respect the *positions* of those in authority even when their *personalities* leave much to be desired.

Authority does have its limits, however. Since God has not given anyone the authority to command you to sin, it is proper to disobey any instructions that contradict the clear teaching of Scripture (Acts 4:18–19; 5:29; cf. Dan. 3:9–18; 6:6–10). When a person in authority instructs you to do something that you believe is unwise, unfair, or sinful, it is appropriate to make an appeal and respectfully try to persuade that person to do what is right and wise (Esther 7:1–6; Prov. 25:15; Acts 4:5–17; 24:1–26:32). When doing so, it is helpful to try to discern the purpose or goal of the person in authority and seek to offer creative alternatives that will accomplish the same end (assuming it is a proper one), but in a proper and efficient manner (e.g., 1 Sam. 25:1–35; Dan. 1:6–16; 2:14–16; Eccles. 8:2–5).[4] If this does not lead the person in authority to change course, you should obey any instructions that do not violate Scripture and trust God to take care of the results (1 Peter 2:19–23).

Apply the Golden Rule

One of the most effective ways to determine your responsibilities and thereby discover whether or not you have sinned is to refer to the principle set forth in Matthew 7:12: "So in everything, do to others what you would have them do to you, for this sums up the Law and the Prophets." All you have to do is ask yourself questions like these:

> "Would I want someone else to treat me the way I am treating So-and-So?"
>
> "If our positions were reversed, how would I feel if So-and-So was saying and doing what I am saying and doing?"
>
> "If someone broke a contract for the same reasons I am using, would I feel that was right?"
>
> "If I owned this business, would I want my employees to behave the way I am behaving?"

Anytime you see that you would not want someone else to treat you the way you are presently treating others, you need to reconsider what you are doing. It may very well be that you are engaged in sinful conduct; until you repent of it, your problems will only get worse.

Acknowledge Wrongful Motives

In James 4:1–3 we learn that the sinful words and actions common to conflict are merely symptoms of deeper problems: "What causes fights and quarrels among you? Don't they come from your desires that battle within you? You want something but don't get it. You kill and covet, but you cannot have what you want. You quarrel and fight. You do not have, because you do not ask God. When you do ask, you do not receive, because you ask with wrong motives, that you may spend what you get on your pleasures."

As James warns, it is not good enough to identify and repent of sinful words and actions. To maintain peace and make needed changes, you must also deal with the attitudes, desires, and motives that prompt you to do what you do. Jesus taught that sinful thoughts, words, and actions come "out of the heart" (Matt. 15:19; cf. Rom. 1:24). In fact, he compared the heart to a tree that produces fruit (Luke 6:43–45). He explained that good behavior comes out of a good heart, and sinful behavior comes out of a bad heart (Luke 8:11–15; cf. Prov. 4:23). Therefore, to achieve lasting changes in the way we live, real change must first occur in our hearts (see Eph. 4:22–24).

The word *heart* is used in the Bible to describe more than just feelings. It often refers to our whole inner life, including thoughts and attitudes (Heb. 4:12). Thus, when the Bible talks about changing our heart, it is calling for changes in feelings, desires, beliefs, expectations, thoughts, and attitudes. A supernatural transformation of your heart takes place when you accept Christ as your Savior, and then God works in you to continue the process of change. God promises: "I will cleanse you from all your impurities and from all your idols. I will give you a new heart and put a new spirit in you; I will remove from you your heart of stone and give you a heart of flesh" (Ezek. 36:25b–26; cf. Heb. 8:10).

As the above passage indicates, one aspect of getting a new heart is to be cleansed of our idols. An idol is not simply a statue of wood, stone, or metal; it is anything we love and pursue in place of God (see Phil. 3:19), and can also be referred to as a "false god" or a "functional god." In biblical terms, an idol is something other than God that we set our hearts on (Luke 12:29; 1 Cor. 10:6), that motivates us (1 Cor. 4:5), that masters or rules us (Ps. 119:133), or that we serve (Matt. 6:24).

Even genuine Christians struggle with idolatry. Although we believe in God and say we want to serve him only, at times we allow other influences to master us. We allow our lives to revolve around the deceitful desires of our hearts rather than around God and his revealed purposes. Listed below are a few of the idols, or functional gods, that slip into our lives, draw us away from the Lord, and contribute to conflict.

1. Improper desires for physical pleasure—lusts of the flesh (1 John 2:15–17; cf. Gal. 5:16–21; Eph. 4:19). This kind of idol is often characterized by an aversion to disciplining one's mind, spirit, or body. Lusts of the flesh can include sexual unfaithfulness, gambling, overeating, or the abuse of drugs or alcohol, which in turn can cause marital or employment problems. The pursuit of pleasure can also lead to laziness, which often results in financial distress.

2. Pride and arrogance. It is also idolatrous to be preoccupied with one's own wisdom, accomplishments, power, abilities, reputation, or possessions (Prov. 8:13; 2 Cor. 5:12; James 3:14; 1 John 2:15–17). Pride can make us reluctant to admit our wrongs, which leads to excessive defensiveness and an obsession with self-justification. It can also cause us to dominate discussions or insist on getting our own way because we believe we know all the answers. Proud people are often reluctant to seek or listen to the counsel of others and may even resent offered advice. This can contribute to unwise decisions and a tendency to blame others for problems that arise.

3. Love of money (or other material possessions) (1 Tim. 6:10). Greed is specifically referred to as idolatry (Eph. 5:5). This kind of false god can also appear as envy, an excessive desire for financial security, boasting about what we possess, or an unhealthy delight in possessing something (Matt. 6:24; Luke 12:16–21; 27–31; Acts 5:1–3). "Love of money" can cause us to lie, break contracts, do shoddy work, mistreat employees, violate copyright laws, or compulsively pursue unnecessary things. It can also make it difficult to forgive debts or show mercy.

4. Fear of man. This can take many forms. Sometimes it involves an actual fear of what others can do to us (Prov. 29:25; Luke 12:4–5), but it is most commonly seen as an excessive concern about what others think about us. This can lead to a preoccupation with acceptance, approval, popularity, personal comparisons, self-image, or pleasing others (John 9:22; 12:42–43; Gal. 1:10; 1 Thess. 2:4). This idol can make us reluctant to confront serious sin. The constant desire for approval and acceptance can cause us to gossip or keep us from speaking out on moral issues. It can also make us do things we really know are not right, eventually leading to guilt and resentment. Furthermore, if we fear what others may think of us, we may also be reluctant to admit our wrongs or ask for help, which often prolongs conflict.

5. Good things that we want too much. Some of the most difficult idols to deal with are good *desires* that we elevate to *demands*. These most subtle idols include love, happiness, good health, companionship, children, success, prosperity, recreation, goodwill, influence, status, a good image, or even spiritual power (Luke 12:27–34). These things, while beneficial in themselves, can become idols if we want them for the wrong reasons, if our thoughts and actions revolve around them, or if our failure to have them is a major source of discontent. An obsessive longing for love and happiness can lead to an abandonment of family and professional commitments. Conversely, the desire for a notable reputation can result in workaholism, a prime contributor to marital disputes.

Idols—the things of the world—can motivate or master us. They influence what we think about, where we invest our time, how we handle our rights and resources, and how we deal with other people. Many of these idols are hard to identify because their influence is sporadic. We may follow God faithfully most of the day, and then, when momentarily faced with a single decision, we may serve an idol rather than God. This is especially true when we are involved in conflict. Although we may have every intention of behaving in a godly way, when we actually come face to face with our opponent, we suddenly say and do things we never planned. This behavior often indicates that there are some idols we need to root out of our hearts. (In the next chapter, we will see how this can be done.)

Summary and Application

Whenever you are involved in a conflict, it is important to consider if you may be contributing to the problem, either directly or indirectly. In some cases, you may have caused the controversy. In others, you may have aggravated a dispute by failing to respond to another person in a godly way. Therefore, before focusing on what others have done wrong, it is wise to carefully examine the way you have been thinking, speaking, and acting. In particular, you should try to identify the desires and motives (idols) that are leading you to behave in a sinful manner. With God's help, you can see where your ways do not line up with his purposes. That realization is the first step toward repentance, which opens the way for confession, personal change, and the restoration of genuine peace.

If you are presently involved in a conflict, these questions will help you to apply the principles presented in this chapter.

1. As you have talked to and about others in this situation, have you been guilty of any of the following kinds of speech? If so, describe what you said.
   Reckless words
   Grumbling and complaining
   Falsehood
   Gossip
   Slander
   Worthless talk
     Hurtful or destructive words
     Harsh or abusive speech

Hurtful criticism

Backbiting

Spreading rumors

Speculating on other's motives

2. Are you guilty of any of the following sins in this situation? If so, describe what you did or failed to do.

Uncontrolled anger

Bitterness

Vengeance

Evil or malicious thoughts

Sexual immorality

Substance abuse

Laziness

Defensiveness

Self-justification

Stubbornness

Resistance to godly advice

Greed

Deficient work

Withholding mercy and forgiveness

Improper concessions

Compulsive behavior

Breaking your word

Misusing authority

Rebelling against authority

3. Have you failed to respond to opportunities to do good to others in this situation? How?

4. Have any of the following idols influenced your behavior in this situation? How?

Lusts of the flesh

Pride

Love of money

Fear of others (or excessive concern about what others think of you)

Good things you want too much (desires elevated to demands)

5. How have your sins contributed to this conflict?

6. Whom have you offended by your sinful thoughts, words, or actions?
7. What do you intend to do about your sins?
8. Go on record with the Lord by writing a prayer based on the principles taught in this chapter.

6

Free Yourself from Sin

He who conceals his sins does not prosper,
but whoever confesses and renounces them finds mercy.

Proverbs 28:13

Once you begin to see how your wrongs have contributed to a problem, it is good to know that God has provided a way to obtain forgiveness, clean up the past, and change undesirable habits. This process involves three basic steps: repentance, confession, and personal change.

Repentance Is More Than a Feeling

Repentance is the first step in gaining freedom from sin. Contrary to popular belief, repentance does not simply mean feeling uncomfortable. Nor does it involve a mere apology. To repent literally means to change the way you think. Thus, repentance is sometimes described as "coming to our senses" (Luke 15:17; 2 Tim. 2:25–26). As this expression indicates, the first step is to wake up to the fact that you have been deceiving yourself and that your ideas, attitudes, values, or goals have been wrong. This realization leads to a change of mind that involves a renouncing of sin and a turning to God (Ezek. 14:6; Acts 3:19). This process is described in Isaiah 55:7–8: "Let the wicked forsake his way and the evil man his thoughts. Let him turn to the LORD, and he will have mercy on him, and to our God, for he will freely pardon. 'For my thoughts are not your thoughts, neither are your ways my ways,' declares the LORD."

Although repentance is often accompanied by sorrow, simply feeling bad does not prove that one is repentant. In fact, there is a world of difference between mere remorse and genuine repentance. As Paul explained to the Corinthians, ". . . I am happy, not because you were made sorry, but because your sorrow led you to repentance. . . . Godly sorrow brings repentance that leads to salvation and leaves no regret, but worldly sorrow brings death" (2 Cor. 7:9–10).

"Worldly sorrow" means feeling sad because you got caught doing something wrong or because you must suffer the unpleasant consequences of your actions, such as financial loss, a broken marriage, a damaged reputation, or merely nagging guilt. Any normal person will feel regretful when faced with these circumstances. Before long, however, worldly sorrow dies away, and most people begin to behave just as they did before. Instead of changing their thinking and conduct, they simply try harder not to get caught again. This kind of limited remorse leads only to further grief.

In contrast, *godly* sorrow means feeling bad because you have offended God. It means sincerely regretting the fact that what you did was morally wrong, regardless of whether or not you must suffer unpleasant consequences. It involves a "change of heart"—which is possible only when you understand that sin is a personal offense against God himself (2 Chron. 6:37–39; cf. Jer. 31:19). Godly sorrow will not always be accompanied by intense feelings, but it implies a change in thinking, which should lead to outward changes in behavior.

When Paul said that repentance "leads to salvation," he was not only referring to eternal salvation, but to the fact that the penitent would be delivered from sinful habit patterns (2 Cor. 7:10). The fact that genuine repentance should lead to changed behavior is confirmed elsewhere in Scripture. For example, John the Baptist warned people to "produce fruit in keeping with repentance" (Matt. 3:8). Similarly, throughout his missionary journeys, Paul preached that people should "turn to God and prove their repentance by their deeds" (Acts 26:20).

The Seven A's of Confession

Confession, the second step in dealing with sin, is one of the most liberating acts in life. Unfortunately, many people do not experience the freedom that comes through confession because they have never learned how to confess their wrongs to others honestly and unconditionally. Again and again, I have heard words like these: "I'm sorry if I hurt you." "Let's just forget the past." "I suppose I could have done a better job." "I guess it's not all your fault." These token statements may temporarily pacify someone who has been offended, but they seldom encourage genuine forgiveness and reconciliation. Fortunately, the Bible provides clear and specific guidelines for an effective confession. I call them the Seven A's:

1. Address Everyone Involved

As a general rule, you should confess your sins to every person who has been directly affected by your wrongdoing. Since all sins offend God by violating his will, all sins should be first confessed to him (see Ps. 32:5; 41:4). In fact, until you are reconciled to God through confession, you will have a very difficult time being reconciled to others.

Whether a sin should be confessed to other people as well as to God depends on whether it was a "heart sin" or a "social sin." Since a heart sin takes place only in your thoughts, it does not directly affect others and needs to be confessed only to God. For example, if you have felt envy or jealousy toward a co-worker but did not act on those feelings, it is unnecessary (and may actually be unwise) to tell that person what you were thinking. The same would be true if you had considered how to violate a law, hurt someone's reputation, or steal something. As long as your thoughts did not give rise to sinful actions, confession need not be made to other people.

The truth is, however, that heart sins often give rise to social sins that actually affect other people. Some social sins involve acts of commission, such as slandering, stealing, or lying. They may also involve acts of omission, such as failing to help someone in need, ignoring a person, giving the cold shoulder, or withholding forgiveness. Social sins must be confessed to those who have been affected by them.

If your sins have wronged only one person, that person is the only one to whom you need to confess. But if several people have been hurt by your behavior, you should confess your sin to *each* one. It is usually wise to talk to each person privately, since this allows for personal feedback and discussion and facilitates forgiveness and reconciliation. At times, however, it is appropriate to confess to an entire group at one time (e.g., Luke 19:8; Acts 19:18). Whatever the case, repentance should be expressed to every person who has felt the impact of your wrongdoing.

2. Avoid If, But, and Maybe

The best way to ruin a confession is to use words that shift the blame to others or that appear to minimize or excuse your guilt. For example, a public official in my state was forced to resign because he had apparently misused his authority to secure a job for a woman he was dating. When the incident was first reported, he vehemently denied any wrongdoing. The governor's office and the news reporters kept digging, however, and eventually the evidence against him was overwhelming. He finally made a public "admission," but his choice of words robbed it of any real meaning: "It's entirely possible that I sent the wrong signals. If I sent the wrong signal and made a mistake, then I'm sorry." He should not have been surprised that his statement failed to pacify anyone. He neither admitted that he had done anything wrong nor committed himself to behaving differently in the future. As a result he failed to obtain forgiveness and lost a job he might otherwise have held for years.

Too many wrongdoers lose the chance for reconciliation by using a watered-down confession. I have heard dozens of people try to smooth over a conflict by saying, "I'm sorry if I've done something to upset you." Such a statement does little to encourage forgiveness. The word *if* is particularly damaging, because it implies that you do not know whether or not you did wrong. The message you are communicating is: "Obviously you're upset about something. I don't know that I have done anything wrong, but just to get you off my back I'll give you a token apology. By the way, since I don't know whether I have done anything wrong, I certainly don't know what I should do differently in the future. Therefore, don't expect me to change. It's only a matter of time before I do the same thing again."

Clearly, that is no confession at all. It is a superficial statement designed to get someone to stop bothering you or to transfer responsibility for breaking a relationship. Small wonder that genuine forgiveness rarely follows such words. Similarly, notice how the following so-called confessions are diluted by the words in italics.

"Perhaps I was wrong."

"Maybe I could have tried harder."

"Possibly I should have waited to hear your side of the story."

"I guess I was wrong when I said those critical things about you;
   I only did it because you made me so angry."

"I shouldn't have lost my temper, *but I was tired."*

Each of these statements would have value if the italicized words were left out. These words neutralize the rest of the confession and ensure that they will probably do little to soften the heart of someone who has been offended.

The word *but* is especially harmful because it has the strange ability to cancel all the words that precede it:

"I'm sorry I hurt your feelings, *but* you really upset me."

"I should have kept my mouth closed, *but* she asked for it."

"I know I was wrong, *but* so were you!"

Whenever statements like these are made, most people sense that the speaker believes the words following the "but" more than those that precede it. Thus, a confession containing a "but" rarely leads to reconciliation. The same is true when you use "however," "if," "maybe," or any other word indicating reluctance to accept full responsibility for what you have done. Therefore, make it a point to strike such words from your vocabulary anytime you need to make a confession.

3. Admit Specifically

The more precise you are when making a confession, the more likely you are to receive a positive response. Specific admissions help to convince others that you are honestly facing up to what you have done, which makes it easier for them to forgive you. In addition, being specific will help you identify clearly the behavior you need to change. For example, instead of saying, "I know I'm not much of an employee," you might say: "I know I've had a very negative attitude the last few months, which has led me to be critical of others and to disrupt the operation of this office. In particular, I admit I was wrong to criticize your work yesterday."

As you strive to be specific in your confessions, make it a point to deal with attitudes as well as actions. As we saw in the previous chapter, many conflicts arise because of pride, selfishness, ingratitude, envy, jealousy, bitterness, resentment, self-righteousness, disloyalty, insensitivity, and stubbornness. If you explicitly identify your wrongful attitudes, others are more likely to believe that you are genuinely repentant, and you will have a better idea of where change is needed.

It is often wise to admit specifically that what you did violated God's will. Jesus demonstrated this point in his parable of the prodigal son. When the son returned home, the first thing he said was, "Father, I have sinned against heaven and against you" (Luke

15:21). These words show that the lost son had come to grips with the moral implications of what he had done; he did not try to gloss over his sins by treating them as minor indiscretions or errors in judgment. By acknowledging that he had violated God's will, he communicated his repentance in an effective way and made it clear that there was no going back to that kind of behavior. One of the most convincing ways to show that you realize you have been morally wrong is to identify specifically the biblical principles you have violated. Here are a few examples of how this can be done:

> "My critical comments have not only hurt you, but they have offended God as well. I have disobeyed his command to not slander others."
>
> "I've finally realized that I have completely failed to be the kind of husband God wants me to be. In Ephesians, he says I should love you as Christ loved his church, but I haven't even come close to living up to that standard."
>
> "Last night I spent quite a while studying what the Bible says about employment relationships, and I realize that I have not treated you the way God wants me to. In particular, I violated Ephesians 6:9 when I threatened you."

Such statements demonstrate to the other person that you know your behavior was wrong. They also help you focus on the principles you need to take more seriously in the future, which will help you make the changes needed to avoid similar wrongdoing.

4. Apologize

If you want someone to respond positively to a confession, make it a point to apologize for what you have done. An apology is an expression of sorrow or regret for hurting another person's feelings or interests. To be most effective, it will show that you understand how the other person felt as a result of your words or actions. Here are two examples of how this can be done:

113

"You must have been terribly embarrassed when I said those
things in front of everyone. I'm very sorry I did that to you."
"I can see why you were frustrated when I didn't deliver the parts
on time. I'm sorry I failed to keep my commitment to you."

You may first have to ask the other person how he or she felt
as a result of your behavior. This is especially wise when you sus-
pect that the other person was deeply hurt by your conduct but
is reluctant to tell you so. Although you should not encourage
unhealthy introspection, you should allow people you have
offended to share their feelings candidly. Another way to make a
confession meaningful is to describe a similar experience from
your own life and explain how it made you feel. For example:

"I can imagine how you feel. I was falsely accused by an
employer, too, and it was one of the worst experiences of my
life. I'm sorry I have put you through the same thing."
"I'm sure you were hurt by what I did. I remember when a
close friend of mine failed to keep a promise to help me with
a business I was just starting. I worked for months, but without his help it just wouldn't work. I was really hurt by what
he did. I'm sorry I failed you in a similar way."

Although you should not dwell excessively on feelings, it is
important to show that you understand how other people feel
and to express genuine regret for hurting them. Once their feelings have been acknowledged and they see that you regret what
you have done, most people will be willing to move ahead with
forgiveness.

5. Accept the Consequences

Sometimes it is helpful to accept explicitly the consequences of
your actions. Otherwise, the person you have wronged may
assume that you are simply trying to be released from your responsibilities. The prodigal son demonstrated this principle. After
acknowledging that he had sinned against God and his father, he

decided to say, "I am no longer worthy to be called your son; make me like one of your hired men" (Luke 15:19).

Similarly, if you have repeatedly violated an employer's trust, you may need to say, "You have every right to fire me because of what I have done, and I wouldn't blame you if you did." Or, if you damaged someone's property, you may need to say, "It will take me some time to earn the extra money, but I will see that your property is repaired or replaced as quickly as possible." (It was a statement like this that made Zacchaeus's confession so credible; see Luke 19:8.) Or, if you helped to spread false information about someone, you may need to say, "Beginning this evening, I will call every person I talked to and admit that my statements were not true." The harder you work to make restitution and repair any damage you have caused, the easier it will be for others to believe your confession and be reconciled to you. Moreover, your very willingness to accept the consequences of your actions may encourage others to behave in a similar manner.[1]

6. Alter Your Behavior

Another way to demonstrate sincere repentance is to explain to the person you offended how you will alter your behavior in the future. I saw this fruit of repentance in a conciliation case involving a man who had been fired from his job for poor work habits and insubordination. During our first conciliation meeting, the employer and the employee began to see how they had each contributed to the problem. When we met a second time, the employer admitted that she had failed to provide her employee with reasonable and consistent instructions, and that she had seldom spoken to him in a constructive manner regarding his work deficiencies. She then presented the draft of a manual she had written the previous evening. It set forth a detailed job description for each position in her business and guidelines for regular job-performance reviews. Finally, the manual established a process for informing employees of work deficiencies and helping them to improve their performance. After showing the mediators and her former employee what she had written, the employer said,

"If I had taken the time to write this two years ago, a lot of unnecessary conflict could have been avoided and you would probably still be working for me. If you are willing, I'd like you to come back to work so we can both have another chance to do things right."

Her confession hit home with her former employee, who responded by admitting that his poor work habits and open criticism of her decisions had justified his termination. Thanking his employer for her offer, he agreed to come back to work. He pledged himself to serve her more faithfully in the future and offered to work overtime to make up for the time he had wasted during the previous months. The changes each person made produced even more fruit in the following months. The employer's new guidelines benefited other workers, and the reinstated employee's example helped to create a new atmosphere of respect and cooperation throughout the office.

The employer's explanation of *how* she was going to change her behavior and policies in the future added greatly to the credibility of her confession. When the employee saw the time and effort she had invested in that plan, he knew she was serious about changing the practices that had created so much turmoil in the past. Because he responded by explaining what he would do differently in the future when he returned to work, the employer's doubts about his sincerity were greatly reduced. The two of them were able to be reconciled more rapidly than anyone would have dreamed.

A written plan for change has other practical benefits. Listing specific goals and objectives helps to remind you what you have committed yourself to, and it provides a standard by which your progress can be measured. It is often helpful to ask the person you have wronged to suggest how you can change. Write those suggestions down and check back with that person periodically to see whether he or she believes you are following through on your commitments. By doing so, you will be able to chart your progress more objectively, and your actions will continue to demonstrate that your confession was genuine.

7. Ask for Forgiveness and Allow Time

If you follow the six steps described above, many people will readily offer to forgive you. If the person to whom you have confessed does not express forgiveness, however, you may ask, "Will you please forgive me?" This question is a signal that you have done all that you can by way of confession and that the responsibility for the next move has shifted to the other person. This will often help the offended person to make and express the decision to forgive you. (The details of forgiveness will be discussed in chapter 10.)

Be careful, however, not to use this question as a means to pressure someone into a decision he or she is not ready to make. Some people can forgive an offense almost instantaneously, while others need some time to work through their thoughts and feelings. My wife is like this. Sometimes, when I have deeply hurt her and later confessed, she needs a while to think and pray. If I press her to say "I forgive you" too quickly, I add to her burdens by introducing feelings of guilt, which can give rise to resentment and bitterness. On the other hand, if I respect her need for some time, she usually comes back to me fairly soon and willingly expresses her forgiveness.

If you sense that the person to whom you confessed is simply not ready to forgive you, it may be helpful to say something like this:

> "I know I have deeply hurt you, and I can understand why you would have a hard time forgiving me. I hope that you will soon be able to forgive me, because I want very much to be reconciled. In the meantime, I will pray for you. Also, I will repair the damage I caused as quickly as possible and, with God's help, I will work to overcome my temper. If there is anything else I can do to make this right, please let me know."

Time alone will not always lead to forgiveness. In some cases, forgiveness is inhibited because a confession was inadequate. Therefore, when forgiveness is delayed, you may need to go back and thoroughly check the elements of confession. For example, you may not have explained adequately how you intend to repair the damage you have done. Or you may have failed to understand and express regret for the way you hurt the other person. If you probe sensitively, you can often discover what is blocking forgiveness and then take care of it. If someone withholds forgiveness even after you have been patient and have covered each of these steps to the best of your ability, you may need to talk with the person again, saying something like this:

> "Bob, I want you to know that I was sincere when I apologized last week, and I am doing all I can to make things right. It doesn't seem like you have forgiven me yet, and I am concerned about our relationship. I'm also worried about the way this may be eating you up. Therefore, I ask again that you will forgive me. If there is anything I can do to make it easier for you to forgive me, please let me know what it is."

If forgiveness is still not offered, you have a few options. If the person is a Christian who apparently doesn't understand what forgiveness means, you may offer a pamphlet or book dealing with forgiveness (see chapter 10). Another possibility would be to encourage the person to talk over the problem with a pastor or a mature Christian friend. If none of these efforts work after a reasonable period of time, you may need to enlist the pastor to help bring about reconciliation. If these avenues are unavailable or ineffective, prayer and the steps outlined in chapter 12 will be your last resort.

Not every confession will require all seven steps. Minor offenses can often be handled with a fairly simple statement. The more serious the offense, however, the wiser it is to make a thorough confession, using all of the Seven A's of Confession.

Before I leave the topic of confession, I must offer an important warning. Any time we use a formula (like the Seven A's), we can turn it into a meaningless ritual and completely miss what God wants us to do (see Mark 7:5–13; Luke 11:42). This usually happens when we start to use the formula for our own benefit instead of seeing it as a means to glorify God and serve other people. I have caught myself going through the Seven A's simply to get a burden off my shoulders and minimize the consequences of my sin. In the process, I heaped greater burdens on the person I had already wronged. (Since I had "fulfilled my duty," the other person felt coerced to forgive me, even though he or she sensed that my confession was mechanical and insincere.)

Ask God to keep you from falling into this sin. When you go to confess a wrong, remember that you are there to serve the other person and not to gain comfort for yourself. Focus on pleasing God and ministering to the person you have harmed. And regardless of his or her response, strive earnestly to fulfill your commitment to repair any damage you have caused and to alter your choices in the future. This is the fastest road to genuine peace and reconciliation.

You *Can* Change

The third step in dealing with sin is to work with God to change your future behavior. This requires renouncing sinful attitudes and conduct and turning away from *everything* that is contrary to God's will (Prov. 28:13; Ezek. 14:6; 18:30; Dan. 4:27). This process fulfills the third opportunity of peacemaking, namely, becoming more Christ-like.

Growing to be like Christ is not optional for a Christian, since the Bible repeatedly *commands* us to imitate Christ, not just in "religious" things, but in the normal activities of everyday life. "Be imitators of God, therefore, as dearly loved children, and live a life of love, just as Christ loved us . . ." (Eph. 5:1–2). "Whoever claims to live in him must walk as Jesus walked" (1 John 2:6; cf. Luke 6:36; Eph. 4:32; 1 Peter 1:15–16).

Godly change is so important that the writers of the New Testament devoted a great deal of attention to it. In one epistle after another, the apostles described the qualities God wants us to develop, and they used the strongest possible language to urge us to do so. One of my favorite passages is 2 Peter 1:4–8:

> . . . [God] has given us his very great and precious promises, so that through them you may participate in the divine nature. . . . For this very reason, make every effort to add to your faith good-

119

ness; and to goodness, knowledge; and to knowledge, self-control; and to self-control, perseverance; and to perseverance, godliness; and to godliness, brotherly kindness; and to brotherly kindness, love. For if you possess these qualities in increasing measure, they will keep you from being ineffective and unproductive in your knowledge of our Lord Jesus Christ.

This passage and many others make it clear that developing a godly character is a vital part of a believer's life.[2] God wants us increasingly to reflect the character of Christ in our lives. This is why Paul encouraged the Thessalonians to "please God" and "love all the brothers . . . more and more" (1 Thess. 4:1, 10).

Change will be difficult at times, but God does not command us to do impossible things. He always provides us with the grace and guidance we need to carry out his purposes (Phil. 2:13). One of the most important points I wish to make is that *people can change*. The human personality is fluid. No matter how many bad habits you (or your adversary!) are struggling with today, by God's grace they can be replaced by better qualities. With God's help, you can change and enjoy a much better life in the days ahead (see 1 Cor. 6:9–11; Col. 3:5–11). Meaningful change does not come about simply by *not* doing what is wrong. Real change is positive—it requires *replacing* our sinful behavior with godly habits (Eph. 4:22–32). There are four basic ingredients of personal change:

Prayer

Prayer is the starting point for all meaningful change. The qualities that God wants us to develop in our lives are sometimes referred to as "the fruit of the Spirit" (Gal. 5:22–23). A farmer cannot grow apples and oranges without the seed, sunshine, and water that God alone provides. Likewise, a Christian cannot cultivate spiritual fruit apart from God's active assistance (John 15:4–5). Prayer is the means by which we seek that assistance (Ps. 139:23–24; Phil. 1:9–11; Col. 1:9–12).

Focusing on the Lord

As we saw in the previous chapter, sinful actions come out of sinful hearts, which is why James wrote, "Wash your hands, you sinners, and purify your hearts, you double-minded" (James 4:8b). The only way to purify your heart is to get rid of your idols. Paul teaches that this is not a passive process: "Therefore, my dear friends, flee from idolatry" (1 Cor. 10:14). "Flee the evil desires of youth, and pursue righteousness, faith, love and peace, along with those who call on the Lord out of a pure heart" (2 Tim. 2:22).

"Flee" is a strong word. It means to escape by running away. This calls for deliberate, strenuous, and prolonged action. By using this word, Paul is warning us that we will not free ourselves from our idols by accident; nor will we escape them by casually wishing to be better people. Moreover, he is warning that we will never be free of an idol as long as we think we can safely go back and indulge it "just for a while." A Christian who flirts with idols is every bit as foolish as a man who walks back into the den of a lion from which he has just escaped.

So how does one flee from an idol? First, through prayer, the study of God's Word, and the counsel of mature Christian friends, you must identify the deceitful desires that motivate and rule over you. Second, you need to confess your idolatry to God and ask for his assistance in overcoming it. If you are dealing with attitudes and desires that have a particularly strong grip on you, you may also need to seek pastoral help in breaking free.

Finally, you must consciously and deliberately *change the focus* of your affections and your thoughts: ". . . set your hearts on things above, where Christ is seated at the right hand of God. Set your minds on things above, not on earthly things" (Col. 3:1–2). You can set your heart and mind on Jesus by studying his Word and meditating on his promises, trusting him, heeding his warnings, praising and thanking him for all he is and all he has done, serving others as he did, and worshiping with other believers and enjoying their fellowship. As you invest more of your time, thoughts, and energies in the Lord, he will reign over your heart more fully. As he promised, "For where your treasure is, there your heart will be also" (Matt. 6:21). The more you make Jesus the treasure of your heart, the less room there will be in your life for idols.

As you focus on Jesus, you will discover that he truly can provide what idols may promise but can never deliver. Only Jesus gives genuine joy, peace, and happiness (1 Peter 1:8; cf. Eccles. 2:26). As his friend, you can let go of pride, comfortably admit your limitations, and find confidence in his wisdom and power (2 Cor. 12:9–10). As you set your heart on his kingdom, he will give you all the material resources you need, plus contentment to enjoy them (Matt. 6:25–34; Phil. 4:12–13). If you are confident that Jesus is pleased with you, you will not have to worry about what others think of you (1 Cor. 4:3–4). Moreover, when you desire and pray for good things, you can be at peace, knowing that he will give or withhold those things according to his perfect timing and plan (Matt. 7:9–11; Luke 1:5–25; 2 Cor. 12:7–10).

God's promise to fulfill you is beautifully stated in Psalm 37:4: "Delight yourself in the LORD and he will give you the desires of your heart." This is not a game in which you go through mere outward motions to get God to satisfy your cravings. Rather, as you truly focus your attention on him and learn to love him with all your mind, heart, soul, and strength, he purifies your heart and fills it with desires that he is eager to satisfy (Matt. 5:3–12). And out of that new heart and those pure desires, he will bring forth the fruit of a godly character.

Study

The Bible frequently emphasizes the close connection between transformed thinking and personal change (Rom. 8:6–8; 12:1–2; 1 Cor. 2:9–16; Eph. 1:17–19; 4:22–24; Phil. 1:9–11; Col. 1:9–12). Wisdom, knowledge, and understanding—all involving our minds—are important prerequisites to spiritual fruitfulness. God does not mysteriously infuse our minds with these qualities; rather, as we carefully study his Word, he helps us understand his principles and his ways so that our minds are truly "made new."

Bible study is especially important when we are trying to develop a Christ-like character and deal with the challenges of conflict. Regular time spent in God's Word helps to identify and guard against the idols and worldly motives that compel us to behave in destructive ways. In particular, study helps us recognize and resist the world's ideas on how to deal with those who oppose us: Look out for number one. Don't get mad, get even. Never forget a friend, and never forgive an enemy. Just give him what he deserves. You'll look weak if you admit you're wrong.

Unbiblical ideas seem especially appealing in the face of conflict, but they will steadily erode our judgment and character unless we work to counterbalance them with the truths set forth in Scripture. Bible study also helps us learn which character qualities are conducive to peace and provides practical advice on how to develop and enhance those qualities.

The study needed to bring about real change in character can take place in many ways. Thoughtful reading of the Bible passages cited in this book would be a profitable beginning. Once you have identified a particular fruit of the Spirit you want to develop, you can learn more about it by using a Bible concordance to find other passages which discuss that quality. Some of the most profitable instruction in this area is set forth in vivid narrative stories, which describe how Jesus and other people in the Bible responded to many of the same problems we face today. The best way to expose yourself to these narratives is through a program of regular Bible reading. The more you study the Bible, carefully absorbing what you learn there, the more you can be conformed to the image of Christ.

Practice

Prayer, a new heart, and study prepare you for the final ingredient of personal change, which is to "put on the new self" (Eph. 4:24). This means you must put into practice what you are learning (Phil. 4:9). In one way or another, every situation that God places us in is an opportunity to practice something worthwhile. Unfortunately, many of us come onto the field and don't even know there's a game in progress. No wonder the Coach calls us back time after time.

Because Paul knew that we can "put on" a Christ-like character only through dedicated practice, he compared that work to the rigorous athletic training needed to win in the Greek Olympic contests (1 Cor. 9:24–27; Phil. 3:14; 2 Tim. 4:7). This teaches us that desirable character qualities are developed in the same way as any other skill—by God's grace we practice the desired action over and over until we have overcome our weaknesses, mastered the proper techniques, and made that behavior both natural and automatic.

This is not a casual process. Paul commanded Timothy to "pursue righteousness, faith, love and peace" (2 Tim. 2:22). *Dioko*, the Greek word translated "pursue," is a strong one. It means to strive after, track down, or hound, and could be used to describe a hungry lion chasing its prey. Paul is telling us that our efforts to put on a new character should be characterized by persistence, dedication, and serious effort.

Practice should be both planned and spontaneous. This principle is illustrated by the Glenn Cunningham story. Glenn's legs were severely burned when he was a young boy. Although he was told that he would never walk again, he developed a rigorous training program of stretching, walking, and running exercises that he followed faithfully in spite of constant and severe pain. In addition, as his legs healed, he began to look for opportunities to run even more. If a letter needed to be mailed, Glenn ran to the post office. If his mother needed flour, he ran to the grocery store. If his father needed nails, Glenn ran to the hardware store. Tasks that other boys grumbled at were viewed by Glenn as opportunities to rebuild his body. His hard work paid off; in 1934, Glenn set a new world record for running a mile! Through a combination of planned training and spontaneous exercise, Glenn overcame seemingly impossible handicaps and achieved the goal he had set his heart on.

With God's help, you can use the same approach to change your character and develop the fruit of the Spirit. First, you should plan how to work at changing specific character qualities. Just as you consciously choose your clothing every morning, you can regularly and deliberately decide to exercise a particular character quality. As Paul said, "Clothe yourselves with compassion, kindness, humility, gentleness, and patience" (Col. 3:12).

Many of the character qualities that you can develop in a planned way can help to prevent or resolve conflict. For example, you can decide to humble yourself and confess a wrong you did the previous day. Or, if you have made it a point to think and say only positive, thankful, and encouraging things, you might plan ahead to respond gently and patiently to a co–worker who invariably aggravates you during coffee breaks. Or you might cultivate perseverance by going to talk with an estranged relative one more time. If you focus on one or two areas and keep at them until you see consistent results, with God's help you can change.

Second, like Glenn Cunningham, you can speed your progress by using unforeseen opportunities to spontaneously exercise a needed fruit of the Spirit. For example, as soon as you sense that an argument is developing, you can give close attention to controlling your tongue. If you are sure you are right, you can make a special effort to be kind and patient with a person who is wrong. When your needs or desires clash with another's, you can recall Jesus' example and willingly submit. Or, if you have been offended, you can ask God to help you resist resentment and forgive as he has forgiven you.

As you practice, do not let failures and setbacks discourage you. Remember, developing spiritual fruit is something like mastering a sport or a musical instrument. No matter how many failures you experience (like saying hurtful things or allowing bitterness to overwhelm you for a time), remind yourself that you can change, ask for God's help once more, and try again. If you really want to make the most of the lessons you are learning, keep a spiritual journal. Record what you learn from both your mistakes and your progress. This discipline will generally facilitate the development of a more godly character.

Whether your goal is patience, wisdom, meekness, or self-control, keep at it until you see results. This is the formula that gets people into the Olympics or onto the stage at Carnegie Hall. Training is also the route to spiritual maturity (Heb. 5:14). With God's help and faithful practice you can develop a Christ-like character, which will demonstrate your repentance and enable you to enjoy the benefits of peace.

Summary and Application

To be an effective peacemaker, deal honestly with your own faults. As Paul told Timothy, "If a man cleanses himself from [sin], he will be an instrument for noble purposes, made holy, useful to the Master and prepared to do any good work" (2 Tim. 2:21). This cleansing process takes place only through repentance, confession, and personal change. The more faithfully you pursue these steps, the more useful you will be to your Master. At the same time, after you get the log out of your own eye, you will be better prepared to help others.

If you are presently involved in a conflict, these questions will help you apply the principles presented in this chapter.

1. As you look back at the way you have handled this conflict, do you see a need for repentance?
2. Write an outline for your confession.
   (a) *Address everyone involved.* To whom do you need to confess?
   (b) *Avoid if, but, and maybe.* What excuses or blaming do you need to avoid?
   (c) *Admit specifically.* What sins have you committed? What biblical principles have you violated?
   (d) *Apologize.* How might others feel as a result of your sin?
   (e) *Accept the consequences.* What consequences do you need to accept? How can you reverse the damage you have caused?
   (f) *Alter your behavior.* What changes do you intend to make, with God's help, in the way you think, speak, and behave in the future?
   (g) *Ask for forgiveness.* What might make the person whom you have wronged reluctant to forgive you? What can you do to make it easier for that person to forgive you?

3. What idols do you need to flee from? How can you do this? In particular, what character quality or promise of God can you focus on to help you overcome these idols?
4. Pick one character quality you wish to develop. Specifically, what steps will you take to practice that quality? How can you practice that quality even while you are working to resolve this conflict?
5. Go on record with the Lord by writing a prayer based on the principles taught in this chapter.

Part 3

Go and Show Your Brother His Fault

"If your brother sins against you, go and show him his fault, just between the two of you. If he listens to you, you have won your brother over."

Matthew 18:15

Once you have identified God's concerns and taken responsibility for your contributions to a conflict, it may be necessary to talk to others about *their* shortcomings. Many people do not like to confront others. This is especially true in modern society, where the accepted rule is "you mind your business and I'll mind mine." Although we should be willing to overlook minor offenses, there are some problems that will only grow worse if they are not dealt with in a straightforward way. Janet, a friend of mine, recently learned this lesson when friction between her and Larry, a fellow teacher, got out of hand.

Larry seemed to irritate almost every person in the school. He continually made fun of other people, often in embarrassing ways. He was quick to criticize others, but was easily offended when someone found fault with him. For some reason, he seemed to pick more on Janet than on anyone else. Whenever she walked into the teachers' lounge, Larry would look up and immediately say something sarcastic to or about her, so Janet found herself avoiding the lounge whenever she thought he might be there.

Janet, who had been a Christian for several years, was especially troubled by the fact that Larry openly claimed to be a Christian. She was particularly distressed by the effect Larry's behavior was having on Carol, a teacher to whom Janet had been witnessing for over a year. The more Carol was repelled by Larry's behavior, the less open she was to Christianity. "If that's what it means to be a Christian, no thanks," she said to another teacher one day. "The people I meet at the bar are more decent than he is!"

Janet had already confronted Larry several times about his conduct. Unfortunately, since she always did it without thinking, usually after he had just offended her, her words were usually angry and sarcastic. This only made Larry defensive and always led to an argument, after which they would both walk away fuming.

Finally realizing the damage that was being done by their open conflict, Janet asked me for advice on how to deal with the problem. After discussing ways that she could please and honor the Lord through this situation, we considered where she had been at fault. Then we carefully planned how she could talk with Larry in a more constructive manner. We prayed that the Lord would give both Janet and Larry grace to resolve their differences in a way that would please and honor him.

The next morning, Janet arrived at school early enough to talk with Larry before any of his students arrived. After telling him that she was concerned about the argument they had had earlier that week, she asked if he would have some time later that day to talk. With some hesitancy, he agreed to meet her in a spare office at 3:30.

When they met later in the office, Larry was obviously nervous and defensive. Janet put him at ease by explaining what she hoped to accomplish through their meeting. She also admitted that she had behaved poorly and asked his forgiveness for losing her temper and saying hurtful things to him. He said, "That's okay. I know I can be sort of abrasive at times."

Instead of settling for this superficial repentance, Janet graciously went on to tell Larry how his conduct was affecting her, other people, and their Christian witness. Larry became defensive again and tried to excuse his behavior. Having already planned how to respond to that tactic, Janet was prepared to give him specific examples of sinful words he had said. She also appealed to him with regard to his Christian witness. Instead of getting angry or harsh, she kept her voice under control and continued to express her concern for Larry and her desire to do what would please and honor the Lord. While they talked, she continued to pray silently that God would help Larry to see the truth about himself.

After forty-five minutes of tense conversation, Larry began to soften. He admitted that his behavior was sinful and agreed that he needed to change. He went on to tell Janet that he had always had trouble getting along with people and that being sarcastic was his way of getting attention. Janet responded with understanding and shared some similar struggles in her own life. They then discussed several ways that they could help each other to overcome some of their harmful habit patterns. They also agreed to meet once a week for five minutes of prayer before school and decided to ask another Christian teacher to join them.

Finally, after recognizing how his behavior had affected Carol, Larry decided that he needed to go to her and ask for forgiveness. When he did so later that day, Carol was astonished. Her wonder increased over the following weeks when she saw how much better Larry and Janet were getting along. As of this writing, Carol has not yet become a Christian, but her interest in talking about Christ has noticeably increased. Janet's decision to confront her Christian brother in love not only won him over but also cleared the way for others to learn about the peace that comes through Christ.

7

Restore the Sinner Gently

Brothers, if someone is caught in a sin, you who are spiritual should restore him gently.

Galatians 6:1

A s we saw in chapter 1, conflict often presents opportunities to serve others. If we show genuine concern for the well-being of others and use our resources to help meet their needs, our Master will consider us to be "faithful and wise servants" (Matt. 24:45–51; cf. Luke 12:42–48). Therefore, even when we are in the midst of a conflict, we should be stewards on the lookout for ways to serve others. This can be done by helping others resolve material issues, by carrying burdens they are unable to bear, by introducing them to Christ, and by teaching and encouraging by our example.

We also need to be open to the opportunity to serve others by helping them learn where they have been wrong and need to change. Although many offenses can and should be overlooked, some problems are so serious that they must be addressed, or they will damage valuable relationships and result in unnecessary harm to other people. In this chapter we will consider several principles that will help you to decide whether an offense should be overlooked or confronted. In chapter 8 we will examine the ingredients of a biblical confrontation. Then, in chapter 9, we will discuss what to do if a private confrontation does not resolve a problem.

When Someone Has Something against You

If you learn that someone has something against you, God wants you to take the initiative in seeking peace—even if you do not believe you have done anything wrong. If you believe that another person's complaints against you are unfounded, or that the misunderstanding is entirely the other person's fault, you may naturally conclude that you have no responsibility to take the initiative in restoring peace. This is a common but false conclusion, for it is contrary to Jesus' specific teaching in Matthew 5:23–24: "Therefore, if you are offering your gift at the altar and there remember that your brother has something against you, leave your gift there in front of the altar. First go and be reconciled to your brother; then come and offer your gift." Note that this command is not limited to situations where the other person has *something justifiable* against you. Jesus said to be reconciled if your brother has *something* against you, implying that the obligation exists whether or not you believe his complaint is legitimate.

There are several reasons why you should initiate reconciliation even if you do not believe you are at fault. Most importantly, Jesus commands you to go. Also, as was discussed previously, peace and unity among believers significantly affects the way other people will receive the gospel message. Seeking peace with an alienated brother enhances your Christian witness, *especially* if he is the one who has done the wrong (Luke 6:32–36).

In addition, you can have greater peace of mind if you have honestly faced any complaints someone might have against you. Only by carefully listening to others can you discover sins of which you were not aware or help others realize that their complaints are unfounded. Either way, you will gain a clear conscience which is an essential ingredient of internal peace and a close relationship with God.

Finally, you should initiate reconciliation out of love for your brother and concern for his well-being. Just before Jesus' command to seek reconciliation, he warned of the danger of unresolved anger: "You have heard that it was said to the people long ago, 'Do not murder, and anyone who murders will be subject to judgment.' But I tell you that anyone who is angry with his brother will be subject to judgment. . . . anyone who says, 'You fool!' will be in danger of the fire of hell" (Matt. 5:21–22).

Bitterness, anger, and unforgiveness are serious sins in God's eyes. If your brother indulges these feelings, they will separate him from God and expose him to judgment (Eph. 4:30–31; cf. Isa. 59:1–2). In addition, these feelings can eat away at your brother's heart like an acid and leave him spiritually, emotionally, and physically scarred (Ps. 32:1–5; 73:21–22; Prov. 14:30). Since this damage can occur even if someone is mistaken in believing you have done something wrong, out of love you should go to the person and do everything within your power to resolve the matter. This may require either confessing your own wrongs or helping that person realize that there is no basis for the complaint. Although you cannot force someone to change his or her mind about you, make every effort to "live at peace" by clearing up misunderstandings and removing obstacles to reconciliation (Rom. 12:18; cf. 14:13–19). This may require repeated attempts and great patience, but the benefit to both of you makes it well worth the effort.

I recall one Sunday when I visited a small ranching community and preached a message on Matthew 5:21–24. After church a friend took me out to lunch. Partway through our meal, a man I had seen in church that morning walked into the restaurant. Seeing me, he came over to our table, smiling from ear to ear.

"I have to tell you what just happened," he said. "Your sermon really shook me up, because I've got a neighbor who hasn't talked to me for two years. We had an argument about where to run a fence. When I wouldn't move it to where he thought it should be, he just turned his back on me and stomped away. Since I thought I was in the right, I've always figured it was up to him to make the first move at being friends again. This morning I saw that the Lord wants *me* to be the one to seek reconciliation, so right after church I drove over to his house to talk with him. I told him I was sorry for being so stubborn two years ago and that I wanted to be friends again. He just about fell over. He said he felt bad all along for stomping away that day, but he didn't know how to come talk with me. Boy, was he glad I came to talk with him!"

When Someone's Sins Are Too Serious to Overlook

Another time you should go and talk to someone about a conflict is when that person's sins are too serious to overlook. This is why Jesus said, "If your brother sins, rebuke him, and if he repents, forgive him" (Luke 17:3). It is sometimes difficult to decide whether a sin is serious enough to call for confrontation. Below are a few of the situations that may warrant this kind of attention.

Is It Dishonoring God?

Sin is too serious to overlook if it is likely to bring significant dishonor to God (e.g., Matt. 21:12–13; Rom. 2:23–24). If someone who professes to be a Christian is behaving in such a way that others are likely to think less of God, of his church, or of his Word, it may be necessary to confront that person and urge him or her to change behavior. This doesn't mean that we should call attention to every minor offense, for God himself is patient and forbearing with much of what we do wrong. But when someone's sin becomes open enough to obviously and significantly affect a Christian witness, it needs to be confronted.

For example, I once talked with a man named Joe who believed that a local businessman had been dishonest with him. Although Joe was willing to overlook the offense, he was troubled by the fact that Fred held himself out to the community as a Christian. Realizing that Fred might also be treating other people dishonestly,

135

causing them to think less of Christians and therefore of Christ, Joe thought it might be necessary to talk with Fred about his business dealings. I agreed, and Joe went to see Fred that afternoon. Although Fred was defensive at first, he eventually began to listen to Joe's concerns and made a commitment to change some of his future business practices. A week later, Joe received a note from Fred that said, "Thanks for taking the time to talk with me. I am trying to be more careful about how I run my business."

Is It Damaging Your Relationship?

As a general rule, you should not overlook an offense that has significantly damaged your relationship with another person. If you are unable to forgive an offense—that is, if your feelings, thoughts, words, or actions toward another person have been altered for more than a short period of time—the offense is too serious to overlook. Anything that has disrupted the peace and unity between two Christians must be talked over and made right.

Even a minor wrongdoing can damage a relationship if it is repeated. Although it may be easily forgiven the first few times, eventually frustration and resentment can build up. When this happens, it may be necessary to bring the matter to the other person's attention so that the offensive pattern can be broken.

Is It Hurting Others?

An offense or disagreement is also too serious to overlook when it results in significant harm to you or others. This can happen in various ways. The offender may be hurting or imperiling others in a direct way (e.g., child abuse or drunken driving). The person may also be setting an example that will encourage other Christians to behave in a similar manner. Knowing that "a little yeast works through the whole batch of dough," Paul commands Christians to confront serious and open sin quickly and firmly to save other believers from being led astray (1 Cor. 5:1–13; cf. 2 Tim. 4:2–4; Prov. 10:17). An offense can also adversely affect others if it is made public and other Christians take sides. When the peace and unity of the church are threatened in this way, the underlying problem needs to be addressed before it causes serious division (Titus 3:10).

Is It Hurting the Offender?

Finally, sin needs to be confronted when it is seriously harming the offender, either by direct damage (e.g., alcohol abuse) or by impaired relationships with God or other people. Looking out for the well-being of other Christians, especially those in your own family or congregation, is a serious responsibility. Unfortunately, because many Christians have adopted the world's view that everyone should be allowed to "do his own thing," some believers will do nothing, even when they see a brother or sister ensnared in serious sin. This is not the kind of love Jesus demonstrated, nor is it consistent with the clear teaching of Scripture:

> "Do not hate your brother in your heart. Rebuke your neighbor frankly so you will not share in his sin" (Lev. 19:17).
>
> Rescue those being led away to death; hold back those staggering toward slaughter. If you say, "But we knew nothing about this," does not he who weighs the heart perceive it? Does not he who guards your life know it? Will he not repay each person according to what he has done? (Prov. 24:11–12).
>
> Better is open rebuke than hidden love. Wounds from a friend can be trusted, but an enemy multiplies kisses (Prov. 27:5–6; cf. 9:8; 19:25; 28:23).
>
> "If your brother sins against you, go and show him his fault, just between the two of you. If he listens to you, you have won your brother over" (Matt. 18:15).
>
> Brothers, if someone is caught in a sin, you who are spiritual should restore him gently. But watch yourself, or you also may be tempted (Gal. 6:1).
>
> My brothers, if one of you should wander from the truth and someone should bring him back, remember this: Whoever turns a sinner from the error of his way will save him from death and cover over a multitude of sins (James 5:19–20).

These verses certainly endorse constructive confrontation, but they are not a license to be a busybody. The Bible repeatedly warns us not to be eagerly looking for opportunities to point out the faults of others (e.g., 2 Thess. 3:11; 1 Tim. 5:13; 2 Tim. 2:23; 1 Peter 4:15). In fact, anyone who is *eager* to go and show a brother his sin is probably disqualified from doing so. Such eagerness is often a sign of pride and spiritual immaturity, which cripple our ability to minister effectively to others (Gal. 5:22–6:2). The best confronters are usually people who would prefer not to have to talk to others about their sin but will do so out of obedience to God and love for others.

At the other extreme from the busybodies are those who are reluctant to confront sin under any circumstances. They often point to Matthew 7:1——"Do not judge, or you too will be judged"—and say that the Bible forbids us to pass judgment on how others live. However, when studied in light of the verses quoted above, which specifically tell us to evaluate and talk to others about their behavior, Matthew 7:1–5 cannot be interpreted as forbidding confrontation. Rather, the entire passage explains *when* and *how* confrontation should occur. Jesus is saying that if you follow his instructions properly, "you will see clearly to remove the speck from your brother's eye" (Matt. 7:5). This unquestionably implies his approval of properly done confrontation.

Some people refuse to confront others because of another passage: "Do not resist an evil person. If someone strikes you on the right cheek, turn to him the other also" (Matt. 5:39). This passage does not forbid personal confrontation. Rather, it forbids people to take the law into their own hands and to seek *vengeance* against those who wrong them.[1] This verse teaches that Christians should be willing to endure personal injury without retaliation when that injury comes as a direct result of their Christian witness (cf. 1 Peter 1:6–7; 2:12–3:18; 4:12–19). In the normal disagreements of daily living, however, Christians have the responsibility to confront serious sin, especially when it is found in a fellow believer.

Others avoid confrontation by saying, "Who am I to tell someone else what to do?" While it is true that we have no right to force our *personal opinions* on other people, we do have a responsibility to encourage fellow believers to be faithful to *God's truths*, contained in Scripture. Thus, if you believe that the Bible contains authoritative instruction from God, and if you have a genuine love for God and for your brother, you will not shirk your responsibility to confront that brother in appropriate ways to help him keep his life in line with God's standards (e.g., Rom. 15:14; Col. 3:16; 2 Tim. 2:22–24).

Another way to avoid confrontation is to say, "Isn't it *God's* job to show people where they are wrong?" It is true that God is the only one who can convict people of sin and change their hearts, which he does through the power of the Holy Spirit. But God often uses another person to speak the words that a sinner needs to hear to see the need to repent (e.g., 2 Sam. 12:1–13; 2 Tim. 2:24–26). We cannot change people on our own, but through loving confrontation we can be used by God to help people see where they have a problem with sin.

A Christian's responsibility to help others deal with serious sins can be understood more clearly by studying two particular words used in Galatians 6:1. In this passage Paul told the Galatians to restore a brother who is "caught in a sin." The Greek word that is translated as "caught" *(prolambano)* means to be overtaken or surprised. Thus, the brother who needs our help is one who has been ensnared by a trespass when he was off guard. He is like a fisherman who wasn't paying attention and got entangled in his net as it was going overboard, and now he is in danger of being drowned. Both the fisherman and the man caught in sin have the same need—their problems have become so serious that they may not be able to save themselves. They need someone else to step in and sever the cords that entangle them. Just as you would not stand by and watch a fisherman drown while tangled in his net, neither should you stand by and watch another Christian be destroyed by his sin.

It also helps to understand what Paul told the Galatians to do with a brother caught in sin. Instead of ignoring or throwing him out, the Galatians were instructed to "restore him gently." The word translated as "restore" *(katartizo)* means to mend, repair, equip, complete, or prepare. This word is used several times in the New Testament—to describe fishermen *mending* and *preparing* their nets (Matt. 4:21), Paul's *supplying* what is lacking in the Thessalonians' faith (1 Thess. 3:10), Jesus' *equipping* believers with every-thing good for doing his will (Heb. 13:21), and God's *restoring* those who have suffered and making them "strong, firm and steadfast" (1 Peter 5:10). Each of these activities has the goal of making some-thing or someone useful for its intended purpose. For example, just as nets are designed to serve people in a specific way, we are designed to serve God in a specific way. Thus, we can see that the goal of *katartizo*, as used in Galatians 6:1, is to mend broken people and restore them to usefulness in God's kingdom.

Understanding these two words will help you decide whether an offense is too serious to be overlooked. First, keep the picture of being "caught" in mind. If a sin does not appear to be doing serious harm to a brother, it may be best simply to pray that he will see his need for change without being confronted. On the other hand, if the sin appears to be dragging your friend under, you should try to help him. Second, remember the *katartizo* prin-ciple. Has that person's sin significantly hurt his spiritual health and reduced his usefulness to God (as a large hole would limit the usefulness of a fishing net)? If so, there may be a need for "mend-ing," which might be accomplished through loving confrontation. For a look at how this can happen, read once more the story that preceded this chapter.[2]

Special Considerations

Confronting Non-Christians

Since the principles discussed above generally apply to non-Christians as well as to fellow believers (see Rom. 12:18; Gal. 6:10), even if a person does not trust in Christ you may need to con-front him or her regarding harmful conduct. In fact, loving con-frontation may be a key factor in helping that person see your concern, which may lead the sinner to acknowledge a need for Christ. Although you will have to adjust your words according to one's spiritual condition and may not be able to appeal openly to Scripture or to Christian concerns, you may use most of the prin-ciples described in this and other chapters in your effort to resolve a conflict and help a non-Christian see where he or she needs to change.

Confronting a Person in Authority

Your right and responsibility to confront someone caught in sin does not vanish just because that person is in a position of authority over you (e.g., an employer or a church elder). Since these people are as human as you are, they will also sin (see 1 Tim. 5:19–20). Of course, you may need to exercise special care in choosing your words when you confront such a person. Speak in a respectful manner and do all you can to affirm your regard for that person's authority (e.g., Dan. 1:11–14). In doing so, you may not only encourage needed changes but also increase that person's respect for you (cf. 1 Sam. 25:23–35).

Go Tentatively and Repeatedly

It is wise to remember that many differences and so-called offenses are the result of misunderstanding rather than actual wrongs. Therefore, when you approach the other person, do so in a *tentative* manner. Unless you have clear, firsthand knowledge that a wrong has been done, give the other person the benefit of the doubt and be open to the possibility that you have not assessed the situation correctly. A cautious, fair-minded manner will usually promote a more relaxed atmosphere and encourage honest dialogue rather than defensive rebuttals.

Be prepared for the fact that your first meeting may not be successful. Since the other person may doubt your sincerity or may not be accustomed to dealing with differences in such a direct and honest way, your initial attempt at reconciliation may do nothing more than plant seeds that you will need to cultivate in following days. The Greek verb used in Matthew 18:15 implies a *continual* action. If you don't succeed at first, try to discern what went wrong (perhaps by reviewing portions of this book), seek appropriate counsel, and correct your mistakes. Give the other person time to think (and give God time to work), then go again to show the person his or her fault. You should continue seeking to resolve the matter privately until the other person firmly refuses to talk any further. Only then should you consider whether it would be wiser to overlook the matter entirely. If doing so is inappropriate, you will need to seek help from others, which will be discussed in chapter 9.

After the Log Is out of Your Eye

Confronting other people about their sins can be difficult if you also have contributed to a particular conflict. As we saw in part two, you must confess your sins before you point out what others have done wrong. Your confession *may* encourage another person to freely admit sins, but not everyone will respond so cooperatively. In some cases the other person will acknowledge little or no responsibility for the problem, which will put you in an awkward position. If you proceed to confront that person, he or she may conclude that your earlier confession was merely a token and that you actually want to blame others for the problem. On the other hand, if you do not point out a wrong, that person may not come to grips with the need for change. So what do you do? Generally speaking, there are four possible courses to follow:

1. You may simply overlook the offense. Then you forgive the other person and get on with your life. This route will be appropriate if the other's sin is not too serious and has not noticeably affected your relationship. It will also be appropriate if your fault in the matter far outweighs the other person's, in which case you should devote your attention to the changes you need to make instead of saying anything about another's fault.

2. You may build on a superficial confession. Your confession may encourage the other person to make some form of admission, even if it is incomplete or halfhearted. (For example: "I guess I sort of lost my temper, too." "Well, it wasn't all your fault." "I can see why you were frustrated.") Sometimes it is appropriate to pick up on another's words and reflect them back in more detail. Below are some examples of what you might say.

"I appreciate your admitting that you lost your temper, Bob. May I explain how that made me feel?"

"I appreciate your saying that. What do you think you did wrong?"

"Why do you think I was frustrated?"

3. You may need to confront now. This will be appropriate when the conflict is so serious or the other person's attitude and behavior is so bad that the situation must be dealt with immediately or further problems are likely to occur. If you do proceed to confront the other person, plan your words carefully so you will reduce the likelihood that he or she will question your motives. For example:

"Bill, I appreciate your forgiveness, and I will really work at controlling what I say in the future. In fact, I'd appreciate it if you would let me know if you ever hear me talking like that again. In the same way, I believe there are some things you could do differently in the future that might help to avoid similar problems. May I explain what I mean?"

"Linda, there's no question that my careless words contributed to this problem, and I really am sorry for aggravating you. At the same time, I'm not sure you realize how you contributed to this problem. As much as I would like to drop the matter, I'm afraid we'll have similar problems again unless we get all of our concerns on the table. May I explain how I see your conduct in this matter?"

4. You may postpone confrontation. This will be appropriate if the matter is not urgent and if immediate confrontation is not likely to be productive. If you genuinely repent of your wrongs and sincerely work at changing your attitude and behavior, several things may result. First, you may eventually decide that the other person's wrongs were actually insignificant, in which case you may never need to bring them up. Second, the effort you make to change and to restore your relationship with the other person may convict him or her, in which case the offender may later come to you and admit past wrongs. Third, if the offense is repeated later, you will be in a better position to confront the offender if you have made an obvious effort to deal with your faults. Since your repentance and changed conduct will make it more difficult for the other person to shift the blame, he or she may finally start to face up to the misbehavior.

If you know you need to confess your wrongs to another person, pray and think carefully beforehand about whether or not it will be wise to confront the person with his or her wrongs during the same conversation. Although you will often not be able to make a final decision on the matter until you see how that person responds to your confession, it is wise to have a tentative plan in mind even before you meet. This will help you to avoid careless words and respond constructively to what the other person says.

Summary and Application

Although it is often best simply to overlook the sins of others, there will be times when doing so only prolongs alienation and encourages them to continue acting in a hurtful manner. If you know that someone has something against you, go to that person and talk about it even before you worship God. Moreover, if another person's sins are dishonoring God, damaging your relationship, hurting others, or hurting that person, one of the most loving and helpful things you can do is to lovingly show that sinner where there is a need for change. With God's help and the right words (including your own confession), such a conversation will often lead to restored peace and stronger relationships.

If you are presently involved in a conflict, these questions will help you to apply the principles presented in this chapter.

1. Do you have any reason to believe that someone else has something against you? If so, why?
2. How has the other person sinned in this situation?
3. Would it be better to overlook the offense against you or to go and talk with the other person about it? What would be

144

the probable benefits and drawbacks of each course of action?

4. Is the other person's sin too serious to overlook? More specifically:

   Is it dishonoring God? How?

   Is it damaging your relationship? How?

   Is it hurting others? How?

   Is it hurting that person? How?

   Is it making that person less useful to the Lord?

5. Which of the other's sins do you need to confront?

6. Do you need to confess any of your sins before you confront the other person? If so, what will you do if the other person does not freely confess the sins?

7. Go on record with the Lord by writing a prayer based on the principles taught in this chapter.

8

Speak the Truth in Love

Speaking the truth in love, we will in all things grow up into him who is the Head, that is, Christ.

Ephesians 4:15

Words play a key role in almost every conflict. When used properly, words promote understanding and encourage agreement. When misused, they usually aggravate offenses and drive people further apart. If your words seem to do more harm than good when it comes to resolving disagreements, don't give up. With God's help you can improve your ability to communicate constructively. In this chapter, we will look at what the Bible says about three basic communication skills and explore practical ways to use them, especially in the midst of conflict.

Speak Only to Build Up Others

As we saw in chapter 5, there are several types of words that cause or aggravate conflict. Therefore, if you want to be an effective peacemaker, make a conscious effort to avoid reckless words, falsehood (e.g., hearsay, speculation, exaggeration, partial truths), gossip, slander, and other forms of worthless talk. A good way to avoid these types of speech is simply to talk less about others. As Proverbs 10:19 teaches, "When words are many, sin is not absent, but he who holds his tongue is wise" (cf. Prov. 10:10; 11:12).

Another way to avoid worthless talk is to get in the habit of talking *to* people with whom you are having a problem rather than *about* them. Check yourself whenever the tone of a conversation about a third party has become negative or critical. Unless further discussion is likely to produce positive solutions to specific problems, it may be wise to end the conversation. A friend of mine did this one day simply by saying, "What good will it do to keep talking this way? Instead of dwelling on what Joe is doing wrong, let's pray for him." The same statement is effective if you change "Joe" to the name of a denomination, politician, or company.

Chapter 6 explained that the best way to squeeze a bad habit out of your life is to replace it with a good habit. This is especially true when it comes to the tongue—the best way to get rid of worthless talk is to train yourself to say only those words that will help to build up others. One way to begin this process is to memorize Ephesians 4:29: "Do not let any unwholesome talk come out of your mouths, but only what is helpful for building others up according to their needs, that it may benefit those who listen." This command does not forbid confrontation, but it does require that confrontation be constructive rather than hurtful.

Another passage that helps us guide and filter our words is Ephesians 4:15, where Paul instructs us to speak "the truth in love," a practice that is appropriate with enemies as well as with friends. Peter wrote, "Do not repay evil with evil or insult with insult, but with blessing, because to this you were called so that you may inherit a blessing" (1 Peter 3:9; cf. Luke 6:27–28; Rom. 12:14: 1 Cor. 4:12–13). To bless *(eulogeo)* means "to speak well of" or "to invoke blessings upon a person." Thus, these passages command us to say good things about others and to ask for good things to happen to them, even if they are opposing or mistreating us (e.g., Luke 23:34; Acts 7:59–60).

147

It is important to remember that other people cannot read your mind. Therefore, they will not know you are speaking to them "in love" unless you make a conscious effort to communicate a genuine concern for their well-being. The best time to do this is long before confrontation becomes necessary. You can do this by speaking positively to and about people you deal with on a daily basis. Thank them for what they do for you, acknowledge their efforts, and praise their accomplishments whenever appropriate. If most of what you say to another person is constructive and positive, that person will be less likely to doubt your motives when you must occasionally say something critical. To put it another way, do all you can to prevent someone from saying, "All you ever do is criticize me!"

When the time comes to actually confront someone, you can demonstrate love and humility by speaking with patience and gentleness, qualities that can add great weight to your words. "Through patience a ruler can be persuaded, and a gentle tongue can break a bone" (Prov. 25:15; cf. Gal. 6:1). If you approach others in a gracious way, expressing concern for them, they will often be more willing to listen to what you say. Therefore, try to use statements like these when you approach someone confrontationally:

> "John, I am concerned about the wall that seems to be growing between us these days. I love you and I want our marriage to be a happy one. Could we take some time this evening to talk about this?"
>
> "Alice, I've noticed that you don't seem to be enjoying your work lately. You are an important part of this department, and we miss your wholehearted support. I'd like to talk with you to see how I might be able to help solve any problems you are having."

A gentle and loving approach will generally make your words more palatable, which can have a direct influence on how others respond to you. Others will generally treat you as you treat them. If you are aggressive and overbearing, don't be surprised if an argument develops. On the other hand, if you are patient and gentle, others will usually respond in a similar manner.

Of course, there are times when you must speak to others in a very firm or even blunt manner, particularly if they have refused to pay attention to a gentle approach and are persisting in sinful behavior. Even so, it is wise to take a gentle approach first and get firmer only as necessary. Strong words are more likely to evoke defensiveness and antagonism, and once a conversation takes on this tone, it is difficult to move to a friendlier plane.

The best way to test your words is simply to ask yourself, "Is what I am saying or about to say likely to please and honor God?" If you can answer that question affirmatively, you can proceed with confidence.

Be Quick to Listen

The second element of effective communication is the ability to listen carefully to what others are saying. Probably because this is not a skill that comes naturally to most of us, James gave this warning to the early church: "My dear brothers, take note of this: Everyone should be quick to listen, slow to speak and slow to become angry" (James 1:19).

This idea is particularly important when it comes to resolving conflict. Good listening will enable you to gather more complete and accurate information, which will improve your understanding of a problem and make possible more suitable solutions. Careful listening can send important messages that words alone often fail to communicate. Quiet, patient listening can demonstrate genuine humility. It shows that you realize you do not have all of the answers, and it tells the other person that you value his or her thoughts and opinions. Giving another person your time and undivided attention is one of the most powerful ways in the world to demonstrate genuine love and concern. Listening also shows sincerity and good faith. Even if you cannot agree with everything a person says or does, your willingness to listen indicates that you accept him or her as a person and have not automatically or lightly dismissed the concerns expressed. Creating an atmosphere of mutual respect will often allow dialogue to continue even when there is disagreement. The following are several of the listening skills you can develop to facilitate effective communication.

Waiting

One of the fundamental elements of effective listening is simply *waiting* patiently while others talk. Waiting is often difficult work, especially when you have limited time or strongly disagree with what others are saying. But unless you learn to wait as others talk, you will seldom get to the root of problems and may complicate matters with inappropriate reactions. As Proverbs 18:13 and 15:28 teach: "He who answers before listening—that is his folly and his shame," and "The heart of the righteous weighs its answers, but the mouth of the wicked gushes evil."

To improve your waiting ability, focus on four common problems:

1. Try not to jump to premature conclusions. Even if you think you know where the other person is going with words, don't allow yourself to arrive there before he or she does. If you do, you may miss much of what is being said and read into words intentions that are not actually there.

2. Discipline yourself not to interrupt others while they are speaking. This is a basic application of Jesus' teaching to treat others as you want them to treat you. Even when someone says something you strongly disagree with, restrain yourself and keep listening until the other person has fully expressed his or her position.

3. Learn to be comfortable with silence. If the other person pauses for a moment to think, resist the temptation to immediately fill the void with your words. Give the other person a while to resume, and if you have any doubt as to whether it's appropriate for you to speak, say something like, "May I respond to that, or would you like to say something more?"

4. Do not offer solutions to every problem others bring to you. I learned this lesson the hard way. Sometimes Corlette would pour out her frustrations or concerns to me, and before she was finished I was telling her how to solve her problems. Afterward, I couldn't understand why she wasn't more grateful for all the "help" I gave her.

It took me a while to realize that she often already knew the solution to a particular problem—what she wanted most from me was understanding, compassion, and tenderness. Even when she wanted answers, my advice didn't mean much to her until she was convinced that I cared about what she was going through. Then one of the best ways for me to help her was not to suggest a solution but to ask questions that encouraged her to analyze her situation and find her own solution. This isn't the fastest way to get potential solutions on the table, but it often produces more satisfactory and enduring results, and is the more loving way to help.

Attending

The human mind can think at least four times faster than a person can talk. Therefore, even when you are listening to someone, your mind is often searching for something more to do. If you allow your mind to wander, you may miss much of what others are saying. Moreover, others can usually tell when you are distracted, which discourages them in their efforts to communicate.

Instead, you need to keep your mind fully present and concentrating when others are talking. Communication experts call this *attending*, which requires discipline and practice for most people. The only way to develop this skill is to focus your attention deliberately and persistently on another's words.

Even when you keep your thoughts on a conversation, you may struggle with the tendency to be rehearsing your response while others are talking. This, too, will reduce your ability to really hear and understand others. Moreover, since it is not hard for others to sense when you have been merely monitoring their words instead of truly listening, rehearsing responses usually discourages open dialogue. Here again the solution is obvious: When others are talking, give them your full attention and make every effort to understand what they are saying and feeling. If you need a moment to collect your thoughts when they are finished, simply say so.

Attending also involves letting the other person know that you are paying attention to what is being said. You can do so with both words and actions. Maintain regular eye contact. Avoid negative body language, such as folding your arms, tapping your foot, or looking around. Eliminate distractions as much as possible—turn off the television, close a door to reduce noise, and sit where you will not be tempted to glance away frequently. Leaning forward slightly usually shows interest, as do warm and responsive facial expressions. Nod your head occasionally to show that you understand what the other person is saying or feeling. These actions may seem unimportant, but experts agree that well over half of what we communicate can come through such nonverbal expressions.

You can also show interest and understanding by various verbal cues. Occasional responses like "hmmm," "uh-huh," "I see," and "oh" tell others that their words are getting through to you. They also encourage others to continue talking, which will allow you to get as much information as possible before you respond further.

Clarifying

A third listening skill that plays a key role in resolving conflict is *clarifying,* the purpose of which is to make sure you understand what the other person is thinking. This requires using questions and statements, such as:

"Are you saying . . . ?"
"Tell me more about. . . ."
"Can you give me an example?"
"I'm confused about. . . ."
"Let me see if I understand. . . ."

Words like these show that you are hearing and thinking about what is being said. Because they also show your interest in getting further information, they encourage the other person to share emotions and perceptions more fully. If he or she responds to that

152

invitation, you can often get beyond the surface issues and discern more clearly underlying concerns, motives, and feelings.

When you use questions, keep in mind that those requiring "yes/no" answers usually produce less information than open-ended ones (i.e., "who, what, when, where, why, and how?"). Also remember that questions should be used to clarify matters, not to embarrass or entrap another person. This is another principle I learned the hard way. As a result of my legal training, I sometimes "cross-examined" my friends when we disagreed on something. Consequently, some of them became defensive and reluctant to talk whenever I started asking questions, because they felt they were being backed into a corner. When I guard against this destructive habit, people are much more willing to talk with me.

Reflecting

A fourth listening skill that improves communication is *reflecting,* or "paraphrasing." This involves summarizing the other person's main points in your words and sending them back in a constructive way. Reflecting may deal with both the *content* of what the other person has said as well as the associated *feelings.* For example:

"You believe I didn't take time to hear you out."
"From your perspective, I was wrong when I said that about you."
"The way you see it then is . . . ."
"This situation has created a lot of problems for you and your family."
"You seem to believe I was being dishonest about . . . ."
"You must really care about this project."
"I get the impression I've really disappointed you."
"You were really hurt by my comment about you in front of the class."
"It sounds like you are upset because I gave John the job instead of you."

Reflecting does not require that you agree with what the other person says; it simply reveals whether or not you are comprehending another person's thoughts and feelings and thereby opens the way for further dialogue even when major disagreements remain. Another person's perceptions are real, even if they are not based on fact. Therefore, if someone says, "You don't even care about how this has affected me," it usually does little good to respond, "That's not true." Instead, even if you believe the other person's perceptions are wrong, take them seriously and use clarifying and reflecting responses to gain more insight and to show that you are getting the message. Only then will you be able to deal with the behavior that contributed to the perceptions and change things at their root.

Reflecting, as well the other listening skills, serves valuable purposes. It proves that you are paying attention and shows that you are trying to understand what the other person is thinking and feeling. As soon as that person is convinced you are getting the message, the need for repetition or a loud voice diminishes. Reflecting also helps to clarify what the other person is saying and allows you to focus the discussion on a specific topic rather than having to deal with several concerns simultaneously. Moreover, it can slow down the pace of a conversation, which is especially beneficial when emotions are high and words may be spoken in haste. Finally, reflecting what others are saying can make them more willing to listen to what you want to say.

Reflecting requires deliberate concentration and a willingness to be patient with your agenda. To be effective, a reflecting statement should be brief and not divert attention from the speaker. It is also important that these paraphrases be conveyed in an appropriate tone of voice and be accompanied by suitable body language; otherwise they will seem insincere and contrived. Matching your responses to what another person says takes extra work, but it is generally worth the effort: "A man finds joy in giving an apt reply—and how good is a timely word!" (Prov. 15:23).[1]

Agreeing

The fifth and often the most powerful listening response is *agreeing* with what another person says. This doesn't mean you should abandon your beliefs, but rather that you should acknowledge what you know is true before going to points of disagreement. Agreeing with the person who is speaking will often encourage him or her to talk openly and to avoid unnecessary repetition.

Agreeing is especially important when you have been in the wrong. For example, responses like these can make the difference between an argument and a meaningful dialogue:

"You're right. I was wrong when I said. . . ."

"You know, a lot of what you just said is true. I do need to deal with my attitude."

"I can understand why you would be upset with my being late again."

Agreeing with others, especially when they are pointing out your faults, is not easy, but it can play a crucial role in peacemaking. When you are talking with another person, first listen for the truth, resisting the temptation to defend yourself, blame others, or focus on points of disagreement. Ask yourself, "Is there *any* truth in what he or she is saying?" If your answer is "yes," acknowledge what is true and identify your common ground before moving to your differences. Doing so is a sign of wisdom and spiritual maturity. "Let a righteous man strike me—it is a kindness; let him rebuke me—it is oil on my head. My head will not refuse it" (Ps. 141:5). "He who listens to a life-giving rebuke will be at home among the wise" (Prov. 15:31; cf. 15:5; 17:10; 25:12). By agreeing with the other person whenever possible, you can quickly resolve certain issues and then focus profitably on matters that deserve further discussion.

One reason we are sometimes reluctant to admit being wrong on one issue is that we fear it will seem like we are accepting responsibility for the entire problem. The best way to overcome this hurdle is to agree with others in *specific* terms. For example:

"Now that I've heard you, I can see that part of this problem really is my fault. I was wrong not to fulfill my part of the agreement, and then I made things even worse when I complained about you to others. What else do you believe I did wrong?"

"I agree that I was wrong not to follow through on my commitment, and I need to be more faithful in the future. I believe there is more to this problem than just that, however. But before we talk about what you have done, I want to hear you out. Would you please be more specific about how my actions hurt you?"

These kinds of responses require genuine humility and also call for keeping a tight rein on your emotions. But they are worth the effort, for a controlled *response* will usually do more for peace than will an emotional *reaction*. The more quickly you agree with what is true and accept responsibility for your own actions, the more open the other person may be if you later say, "Okay, we've agreed on some things I did wrong. How do you think *you* contributed to this problem?" To the degree that both of you begin to focus primarily on personal faults, your conversation can move in a constructive direction.

Heal with Wise Communication

The third communication skill that is often needed to resolve conflict is the ability to confront others in a clear, constructive, and persuasive manner. Proverbs 12:18 is particularly relevant to this task: "Reckless words pierce like a sword, but the tongue of the wise brings healing." Below are a few of the things to do before and during confrontation.

Choose the Right Time and Place

Timing is an essential ingredient of effective confrontation. If possible, do not discuss sensitive matters with someone who is tired, worried about other things, or in a bad mood. Nor should you confront someone about an important concern unless you will have enough time to discuss the matter thoroughly.

Likewise, give careful thought to where you will talk. Unless it is necessary, do not confront someone in front of others. Try to find a place that is free of such distractions as television, other people, and loud noises. If the person you need to talk with is likely to be nervous or suspicious, it may be wise to select a place where he or she will feel relatively secure, perhaps at home. On the other hand, if the person is known to have a temper, you may want to have your conversation in a restaurant, where there may be less inclination to make a scene.

Believe the Best about Others

Another way to enhance confrontation is to believe the best about people until you have facts that prove otherwise. Paul's observation that "love always trusts" (1 Cor. 13:6) doesn't require that you ignore distasteful facts, but rather that you do not think negatively of people until there is a real basis for doing so. If you fail to heed this principle, people will often sense that you have already made up your mind about them and that it is pointless to talk with you. This hardly leads to productive confrontation. On the other hand, confrontation is more likely to succeed if you give someone the benefit of the doubt, put things in the best possible light, avoid backing the person into a corner, and indicate that you really are open to hearing his or her side of the story.

Talk in Person Whenever Possible

As a general rule, communication is most effective if done face to face rather than by a telephone conversation because both people can see facial expressions and communicate with body language as well as with words. In contrast to a letter, oral communication allows you to see how the other person is taking your words, to clarify places where there may be some misunderstanding, and to get feedback before moving to other issues. These advantages can prevent you from making incorrect assumptions that would lead you to write things that give unnecessary offense.

On the other hand, there are times when other forms of communication are helpful. For example, people in our society are not accustomed to having someone drop by their home for an important conversation without giving advance notice. Therefore, it is usually wise to telephone to arrange for a personal conversation. If delicate issues are involved, do not go into extended explanations over the phone. Instead, indicate your desire to meet as soon as it is convenient for the other person.

Letters can sometimes serve a useful purpose. If the other person has refused to respond positively to telephone calls or personal conversations, a brief letter may be the only way to get one to reconsider a stubborn position. If you must resort to communicating by letter, be as personal and gracious as possible. Generally avoid making numerous Bible references or you will seem to be preaching. Also, at least during initial communications, you usually should not try to explain or justify your conduct, because it will probably be misunderstood. If time allows, set the letter aside for a day or two. When you reread it, you may catch words that will do more harm than good. It may be wise to ask a close friend to read the letter as well, because an objective reader may be able to identify needed changes. (If the letter contains personal or confidential information about someone else, however, you may need to delete that information before allowing anyone else to see your letter.)

The advantage of a letter is that it can be read and reread. Even if the other person doesn't like your words at first, they may seem more reasonable as the letter is read again later. The disadvantage of a letter is that it cannot change in response to the other person's reaction. Therefore, although letters are often useful, personal conversations are usually superior when it comes to reconciling people and resolving problems.

Plan Your Words

I cannot overemphasize the importance of planning your words when you know you must confront someone. In delicate situations, careful planning can make the difference between restored peace or increased hostility. The discipline of planning is highly

15

commended in Scripture: "Those who plan what is good find love and faithfulness" (Prov. 14:22b). When you are dealing with important issues or sensitive people, you should think in advance about what you will say. In many cases it will be wise to actually write out several things, such as:

The issues that you believe need to be addressed. (Define the problem as narrowly as possible so you can focus on the central issues and not get distracted by minor details.)

Words and topics that do not need to be included in your discussion and should be avoided because they are likely to offend the other person.

Words that describe your feelings (e.g., concerned, frustrated, confused, disappointed).

A description of the effect the problem is having on you and others.

Your suggestions and preferences for a solution to the problem.

The benefits that will be produced by cooperating to find a solution.

As you plan what to say, make every effort to use words that are gracious, clear, and constructive. It is helpful to write down some of the words you will use when discussing issues that are especially sensitive or likely to arouse strong differences of opinion. Although you cannot write a script for your entire conversation, planning some of your opening comments can help a conversation begin positively. Here are two examples of how to begin a conversation:

Telephone call: "Jim, this is Dave. I'm sorry for what I said last Friday, and I know I was wrong to cut you off. If you have some time in the next day or two, I'd like to stop by so I can apologize in person and see how you would like to finish this project. Would that be all right with you?"

Face to face: "Thank you for taking time to talk with me. Lately I've had the feeling that you are disappointed with my work. If I have done something wrong or if there are specific ways I could improve my work, I would really like to hear about them. Could we sit down together and talk sometime soon?"

These kinds of opening statements clearly indicate that you do not want to continue an argument, but rather that you are seeking positive dialogue. Remember that *asking* for a meeting is less threatening than *telling* someone there will be a meeting. This approach will normally encourage the other person at least to give you an opportunity to talk.[2]

In addition to planning your opening remarks, it is often wise to think of two or three ways the other person may respond to your words, and then plan how you will handle each scenario. Even if the other person says something you had not anticipated, your preparation will generally make it easier to respond. For example, you may anticipate that the person to whom you are going to talk could lose his or her temper. Here is a possible response:

> "Ted, I can understand how frustrating it must be to have so much financial pressure. I can also see why you are upset about having to make a repair on the car so soon after I sold it to you. I'm trying to figure out what I should do about it, and it would help if I knew a little more about what went wrong with the engine. However, I think we could understand each other better if we talked in person, so could I stop by some evening this week?"

In responding to an angry reaction, remember that "a gentle answer turns aside wrath, but a harsh word stirs up anger" (Prov. 15:1). Respond to anger with a gentle voice, relaxed posture, and calm gestures. Communicate in every way that you take the other's expression of anger seriously and want to help resolve the problems that prompt it. Plan ahead how to respond to possible objections and deal with them specifically and reasonably.

If you believe that the other person may refuse to meet with you, you may plan this kind of response:

> "Ted, I need to tell you that according to our contract I do have the legal right to take the car back, keep your deposit, and let you

worry about paying the repair bill. I'd rather not do that. I would still like to work this out in a way that is satisfactory to both of us. Would you at least be willing to think about what I'm suggesting, and I'll call you back in a couple of days?"

Again, don't depend on the other person to follow your script. You will need to be flexible in responding to new developments. Generally speaking, however, if you are prepared when you begin a conversation, you will feel more confident and will be able to deal with developments more constructively. In fact, if you are concerned about your ability to make yourself understood, ask a close friend to role-play with you, so you can practice what you have planned to say. This may seem unusual, but it often pays great dividends, especially for people who have difficulty thinking clearly in tense situations.

Use "I" Statements

One of the most helpful skills Corlette has taught me is how to use "I" statements, which give information about yourself rather than attack the other person—as is the case when you make statements like, "You are so insensitive," or "You are irresponsible." A typical formula for an "I" statement is: "I feel [ ] when you [ ], because [ ]. As a result [ ]."

The following examples fill in the blanks:

> "I feel hurt when you make fun of me in front of other people, because it makes me feel stupid and foolish. As a result, I am getting reluctant to go places with you when others may be around."
>
> "I feel frustrated when you fail to keep your commitments, because you play a key role in this department. As a result I'm finding it difficult to depend on you or work with you."
>
> "I am confused by your saying that I never listen, because two days ago I sat here for over an hour while you shared several deep concerns with me. I really don't know what to do differently."

As these examples illustrate, "I" statements can accomplish three things. First, they tell the other person how his or her conduct is affecting you. By bringing yourself into the picture, you can reduce defensiveness and encourage concern in the person you are addressing. Second, an "I" statement identifies what the other person has done that you are concerned about. By defining the problem *specifically* and not bringing in unrelated issues, you further reduce the chance of threatening the other person. Third, an "I" statement can explain why this issue is important to you and why you would like to discuss it. The more the other person understands your concerns and the effect the behavior is having on you (and possibly others), the more motivated and willing he or she may be to discuss and deal with the problem.

Be Objective

When you are confronting another person, try to keep your remarks as objective as possible. While an expression of personal perceptions and feelings may help someone fully understand a problem (see above), if you emphasize subjective opinions and judgments too much, you are likely to convey condescension or condemnation. Therefore, use facts whenever you can.

Along the same line, make an effort not to exaggerate when you are confronting someone. Words like "you always," "you never," and "every time" reduce the likelihood that others will take the rest of what you say seriously. Here are some illustrations of these principles:

Say: "You were late for work five times in the last two weeks," rather than: "You are *always* late for work."

Say: "John's grades have dropped in three classes," rather than: "Don't you see that your son's performance in school is a *mess?*"

Say: "The fact is, I have gotten to the point that I prefer not to work on committees with you," rather than: "*Nobody* likes to work with you."

Use the Bible Carefully

It is often helpful, if not necessary, to refer to the Bible as a source of objective truth when you have a disagreement with another Christian. If this is not done with great care, however, it will alienate people rather than persuade them. Here are a few basic principles to keep in mind when you use the Scriptures as part of a discussion:

Keep Ephesians 4:29 in mind. Don't quote the Bible to tear others down, but only to build them up in the Lord.

Make sure you are using a passage for its intended purpose. Don't pull a verse out of context and try to make it say something other than its clear meaning.

If possible, encourage the other person to read the passage from his own Bible; then ask, "What do you think that means?" This often achieves better results than imposing your interpretation on others.

Know when to stop. If the other person appears to be getting irritated by your references to Scripture, it may be wise to back off and give him or her time to think about it. (Backing off would not be appropriate if formal church discipline is under way and the person is clearly trying to avoid clear biblical warnings and admonishments.)[3]

Ask for Feedback

When talking to another person, one of your primary goals should be to match impact with intent. In other words, you want to make sure that what you meant to say has actually gotten across to the other person completely and accurately. If the other person responds by clarifying, reflecting, or agreeing with what you say, you will have a fairly good idea whether or not he or she is getting your message.

In many cases, however, it will be difficult to tell what impact your words are having on the other person. Therefore, you will sometimes need to ask the other person to give you some feedback. Here are some ways you can do so:

163

"I'm not sure I've said this clearly. Would you mind telling me what you think I've said?"

"Have I confused you?"

"Have I explained myself clearly enough?"

"What are you thinking about the meeting?"

"What have I said that you would agree with? What would you disagree with?"

Asking questions will promote dialogue and give you an opportunity to measure how well you are communicating as well as how the other person is responding to you. As you take that information into account, you can clarify where needed and adjust what you say to suit developments. As a result, your subsequent words will normally be more relevant and productive.

Offer Solutions and Preferences

Since the twofold goal of confrontation is to help people change and to solve problems, be prepared to offer solutions to the specific problems you have identified. If you can show a person a reasonable way out of a predicament, he or she may be more inclined to listen to you. Hope is a key ingredient in promoting repentance and change.

At the same time, as previously mentioned, try not to give the impression that you have *all* the answers. Make it clear that your suggestions are just a starting point and offer to discuss any ideas the other person has. It may be helpful to tell the other person about your preferences and encourage an exchange of preferences. Here are some examples:

"I would prefer to renegotiate the contract rather than abandon it, but I'm open to suggestions. What would you prefer?"

"My first choice would be to get the whole family together to discuss Dad's will in person. What do you think?"

Again, the more you can promote dialogue and reasonable thinking, the less likely people will be to remain entrenched in one position. If you give them creative ways to deal with a situation and set an example of openly weighing various options, the discussion can result in real progress.

Recognize Your Limits

Finally, whenever you must confront someone, remember that there are limits to what you can accomplish. You can raise concerns, suggest solutions, and encourage reasonable thinking, but you cannot force change. God may use you as a spokesperson to bring certain issues to the attention of another person, but only God can actually penetrate the other person's heart and bring about repentance. Paul clearly describes this division of labor in 2 Timothy 2:24–26: "And the Lord's servant must not quarrel; instead, he must be kind to everyone, able to teach, not resentful. Those who oppose him he must gently instruct, *in the hope that God will grant them repentance leading them to a knowledge of the truth,* and that they will come to their senses and escape the trap of the devil, who has taken them captive to do his will" (emphasis added).

As we have seen throughout this book, be concerned with faithfulness, not with results. If you speak the truth in love and do all you can to confront the other person effectively, you will have succeeded in God's eyes regardless of how others respond (see Acts 20:26–27). God will take it from there—in his time your words will produce exactly the results he wants.

Summary and Application

Ron Kraybill, a respected Christian mediator, has noted that "effective confrontation is like a graceful dance from supportiveness to assertiveness and back again."[4] This dance may feel awkward at first for those who are just learning it, but perseverance pays off. With God's help, you can learn to speak the truth in love by saying only what will build up others, listening responsibly to what others say, and using principles of wisdom. As you practice these skills and make them a normal part of your everyday conversations, you will be well prepared to use them when conflict breaks out. In developing the skills of loving confrontation, you can see for yourself that "The tongue of the wise brings healing."

If you are presently involved in a conflict, these questions will help you to apply the principles presented in this chapter.

1. When you talk to or about your opponent, what might you be tempted to say that would be harmful or worthless?
2. How can you bless or build up your opponent with your words?
3. What can you say that would clearly communicate your love and concern for your opponent?
4. How can you demonstrate humility in this situation?
5. Which listening skills do you have a hard time with: waiting, attending, clarifying, reflecting, or agreeing? Write down some things you will do or say to overcome these weaknesses.
6. What is the best time and place to talk with your opponent?
7. How can you demonstrate to your opponent that you believe the best about him or her?
8. Would it be wiser to communicate in person, on the phone, or by means of a letter? Why?
9. Write a brief summary of what you need to say or avoid saying, including:
    The issues that you believe should be addressed.
    Words and topics to avoid.
    Words that describe your feelings.
    A description of the effect the dispute is having on you and others.
    Your suggestions and preferences for a solution.
    The benefits that will be produced by cooperating to find a solution.
10. Plan your opening statement. What are three ways that your opponent may react to this statement? How could you respond constructively to each of these reactions?
11. Write some of the "I" statements you could use.

12. How can you show that you are trying to be objective?
13. How can you refer to Scripture in a helpful manner?
14. How will you ask for feedback?
15. Go on record with the Lord by writing a prayer based on the principles taught in this chapter.

9

Take One or Two Others Along

"But if he will not listen, take one or two others along, so that 'every matter may be established by the testimony of two or three witnesses.'"

Matthew 18:16

I f you follow the peacemaking principles set forth in Scripture, you should be able to resolve most conflicts by talking in private with your opponent. However, when peace is not restored through personal peacemaking, it may be appropriate to involve one or more respected friends, church leaders, or other neutral individuals who can help to restore peace. Jesus himself commands us to seek such help when we cannot resolve a conflict privately:

"If your brother sins against you, go and show him his fault, just between the two of you. If he listens to you, you have won your brother over. But if he will not listen, take one or two others along, so that 'every matter may be established by the testimony of two or three witnesses.' If he refuses to listen to them, tell it to the church; and if he refuses to listen to the church, treat him as you would a pagan or a tax collector.

"I tell you the truth, whatever you bind on earth will be bound in heaven, and whatever you loose on earth will be loosed in heaven. Again, I tell you that if two of you on earth agree about anything you ask for, it will be done for you by my Father in heaven. For where two or three come together in my name, there am I with them" (Matt. 18:15–20).[1]

In this passage, Jesus teaches us how to minister to a fellow Christian caught in sin. Since unresolved conflict violates Jesus' call for peace and unity, these verses are also applicable to resolving differences between Christians. (The apostle Paul probably had this process in mind when he instructed Christians to resolve their legal disputes with the help of fellow Christians rather than in secular courts [see 1 Cor. 6:1–8].)

The Resolution Process

Although this book is written primarily as a guide to personal peacemaking, I will briefly explain the other steps described in Matthew 18.[2]

Step One: Overlook Minor Offenses

Before we talk about involving others in a conflict, it is wise to review the steps that you should take to resolve a dispute in private. To begin with, you should carefully evaluate how you can use the situation as an opportunity to glorify God, serve others, and grow to be like Christ (see chapters 1 through 3). Then you should seriously consider resolving the dispute unilaterally by overlooking minor offenses and giving up certain personal rights (see chapter 4).

Step Two: Talk in Private

If you need to confess a sin (see chapters 5 and 6), if the other person's sin is too serious to overlook, or if the material issues are too significant to walk away from, you should go to the other person and seek to resolve the matter through discussion and negotiation. In such meetings your purpose should be to *win others over* not to win over them (see chapter 7). Therefore, you should make every effort to communicate in a wise and loving manner (see chapter 8). If repeated efforts to resolve the matter in private fail, and if the matter is too serious to overlook, you may then ask one or more other people to intervene.

Step Three: Take One or Two Others Along

If a dispute cannot be resolved in private, Jesus tells us to ask other people to get involved. "But if he will not listen, take one or two others along, so that 'every matter may be established by the testimony of two or three witnesses'" (Matt. 18:16). At first these people may simply serve as mediators, improving communication and offering advice. If necessary, however, they may serve as arbitrators and provide a binding decision on how to resolve the matter (see 1 Cor. 6:1–8). There are two ways that outside people can become involved in a dispute.

By mutual agreement. If you and your opponent cannot resolve a dispute in private, you can suggest that the two of you ask one or more neutral persons to meet with you in an effort to facilitate more productive dialogue. These neutral persons may be mutual friends, church leaders, respected individuals in your community, or even trained peacemakers, such as you would find through the Institute for Christian Conciliation (a division of Peacemaker Ministries). For the purposes of this discussion, I will generally refer to all of these persons as "conciliators."

Conciliators do not have to be professionally trained to be of service to you. Rather, they should be wise and spiritually mature Christians who are worthy of your respect and trust (1 Cor. 6:5; Gal. 6:1). If your dispute involves technical issues, it is also helpful if one or more of the conciliators has experience in that area. For example, if your dispute involves alleged defects in the construction of a building, an experienced architect or builder might serve as a conciliator. Likewise, when legal issues are at stake, it is wise to include an attorney.

Some of the best conciliators are people who are personally acquainted with you or your opponent, or better yet, who know both of you quite well. Such familiarity is not recommended in secular mediation out of fear that it will allow partiality. But if you are dealing with spiritually mature conciliators, this potential for bias should be more than offset by their commitment before God to do what is just and right. In fact, my experience has shown that someone who knows you well will have freedom to be honest and frank, and that is exactly what you need in a conciliator.

If your opponent balks at your suggestion to involve others, carefully explain why doing so would be beneficial. If the person is a Christian, you can refer to Matthew 18 and 1 Corinthians 6 as the biblical basis for your suggestion. Whether or not you are dealing with a fellow Christian, you can describe the practical benefits of involving others: saving time, money, and energy (when compared to more formal processes); avoiding publicity; receiving the benefit of others' experience and creativity. (Appendix B describes some of these benefits in detail.) You may also share materials produced by Peacemaker Ministries or encourage your opponent to talk personally with a Christian conciliator. If you give sufficient information and enough time to think about it, the other person may eventually agree to work with conciliators.[3]

On your own initiative. While mutual agreement is always preferable, it is not actually required if your opponent professes to be a Christian. Matthew 18:16 indicates that you may seek help from conciliators even if your opponent doesn't want it. Before you take this step, however, it is wise and often beneficial to warn your opponent what you are about to do. For example, you might say, "Bob, I would prefer to resolve this matter just between the two of us. Since that has not happened and because this involves issues that are too important to walk away from, my only other option is to obey what the Bible commands, which means asking some people from our churches to help us out. I would prefer that we go together to get that help, but if you will not cooperate, I'll ask for it by myself."

I have seen many cases where a statement like that has helped "Bob" to change his attitude. If he is aware of the fact that he is somewhat or substantially at fault in the matter, he may not want someone from his church to get involved; therefore he may suddenly become more willing to work with you in private. On the other hand, he may at least decide to participate in selecting the conciliators, if for no other reason than to keep you from gaining some sort of advantage.

If your Christian opponent does not agree to cooperate, you may enlist the help of conciliators in any of several ways. If you can get the help of someone whom your opponent is likely to respect and trust, you and that conciliator may personally visit your opponent and ask to talk. If you have good reason to believe that your opponent would be seriously offended by the first approach, you may ask that conciliator to talk to your opponent individually in an effort to set up a meeting with you and the conciliator later. You may contact your opponent's church and ask for help from one of its leaders. Depending on the circumstances, a pastor or elder may either go with you or talk to your opponent privately in an effort to facilitate a joint meeting.

Regardless of how you enlist the help of conciliators in achieving your opponent's participation, make every effort not to give them unnecessary details about the conflict. Simply explain that you and the other person are at odds and need their help. If you go into detail with the conciliators, the other party might naturally conclude that they have already been biased in your favor. Even worse, doing so may encourage you to slander or gossip. Only when you and the other person are both present should you give a detailed explanation of your perceptions. In some situations, it may be wiser to make your request for assistance by letter and send a copy to your opponent, so he or she will know what you have said—and not said. Here is an example of such a letter:

Dear Pastor Smith,

I am involved in a dispute with John Jones, who I believe is a member of your church. John and I have not been able to resolve this matter in private. Therefore, in the light of 1 Corinthians 6:1–8 and Matthew 18:15–20, I would deeply appreciate it if you or another leader in your church would be willing to arrange a meeting between us and help us come to an agreement. In fairness to John, I will not go into any detail about the dispute in this letter, other than to say that it involves John's purchase of a business from me. I will wait until he and I are with you so you can hear both of our perspectives at the same time.

If you or one of the elders in your church would be willing to help us resolve this matter, I would be able to meet with you and John any evening during the next few weeks. One of the elders from my church would be willing to meet with us as well.

I know you have many other things to do, and I regret having to burden you with this request. In the interest of peace and unity among Christians, however, I don't feel I can leave matters unresolved between John and me. I will deeply appreciate your assistance. (By the way, I have sent a copy of this letter to John so he knows what I have communicated to you.)

If initial attempts to arrange a meeting are unsuccessful, the conciliators should make repeated attempts to talk with or write to your opponent. They should not give up until the opponent adamantly refuses to listen. If that happens, the church may have to move to a more formal process, which we will discuss later in this chapter.

What do conciliators do? Conciliators can play a variety of roles in a conflict. Their primary role is to help you and your opponent make the decisions needed to restore peace. At first they may simply facilitate communication by encouraging both sides to listen more carefully to each other. They may also help to determine the facts by listening carefully themselves, by asking appropriate questions, and by helping you and the other person obtain additional facts.

As implied by Matthew 18:17 and 1 Corinthians 6:1–8, the conciliators may also give advice on how to deal with the problem. They may encourage repentance and confession on either or both sides by pointing out any behavior that has been inconsistent with what is taught in the Bible. They may also facilitate biblical solutions to material issues by directing you to relevant principles and examples in Scripture. Finally, they may draw on their own knowledge and experience to propose practical solutions to specific problems.

If you and your opponent want them to, the conciliators may also help to resolve a deadlock. You may jointly ask the conciliators to suggest an appropriate solution to the problem. (Wise conciliators make sure that every effort has been made to reach a voluntary solution before they give an advisory opinion, however.) In fact, even before you begin to discuss any issues with the conciliators, you and your opponent may agree that if you are not able to reach a voluntary agreement you will abide by the conciliators' counsel, provided it does not require you to violate principles taught in Scripture. If you want to, you may make that agreement legally binding, which means that the conciliators will serve as arbitrators and render a decision that is enforceable by a civil court. Although decisions imposed by others are often less satisfactory than voluntary agreements, they are normally preferable to litigation, which can drag on for months or years, at great financial, emotional, and spiritual expense.[4]

Finally, if either you or the other person refuses to resolve material issues or to be reconciled, the conciliators may serve as "witnesses" to report to your respective churches what they have observed during conciliation efforts (Matt. 18:16). This information may help your church(es) discern the reason for the deadlock and assist them in deciding how to resolve the matter.

Step three may be followed even when your opponent claims to be a Christian but is not acting like one. In fact, this step is specifically designed to help professed believers get their actions back in line with their words.

What if my opponent is not a Christian? The basic principles of step three can also be applied when the other person does not profess to be a Christian. Some modifications may be needed, of course. Formal church involvement will not be possible, and you will not be able to hold the other person to the biblical standards you must follow. Furthermore, your opponent must voluntarily consent to conciliation and may need to be persuaded that the conciliators can offer objective and helpful advice. In spite of these limitations, conciliation can still be beneficial and productive, especially if you keep in mind the principles discussed elsewhere in this book.

Step Four: Tell It to the Church (Church Discipline)

If your opponent professes to be a Christian and yet refuses to listen to the conciliators' counsel, and if the matter is too serious to overlook, Jesus commands you to "tell it to the church" (Matt. 18:17). This does not mean standing up in a worship service and broadcasting the conflict to church members and visitors alike, since unwarranted publicity is totally inconsistent with the tenor of Matthew 18. Instead, you should inform the leadership of the other person's church (and probably yours as well) of the problem, and, pursuant to 1 Corinthians 6:1–8, request their assistance in resolving the matter.[5]

Church leaders may consult with the conciliators and confirm their counsel (especially if one of the conciliators is a member of that church) or they may conduct an entirely independent investigation and issue different counsel. As in secular arbitration, the church's opinion is intended to be binding on its own member, whether the party likes it or not. As Matthew 18:18–20 teaches, the church speaks with the authority of Christ himself when it acts pursuant to its biblical mandate to deal with sin (cf. Matt. 16:18; Heb. 13:17). First Corinthians 6:1–8 indicates that this authority extends not only to personal issues but also to material issues. The only time a Christian may properly disobey his church is when its instructions are clearly contrary to what the Scriptures themselves teach (see Matt. 23:1–3; Acts 4:18–20; 5:27–32).

If the other party's church gives advice that you will not follow, then your church must work in conjunction with the other church until a satisfactory solution is obtained. If either you or the other party adamantly refuses to listen to the advice of a respective church, other members of the church may need to be informed in a discreet and appropriate way so that they may also encourage the stubborn party to face up to sin and to be reconciled to the opponent. Instead of associating with a stubborn brother (or sister) as though nothing were wrong, Christian friends should gently but firmly remind him that he has important business to take care of before he can properly worship God and take part in fellowship (2 Thess. 3:6, 14–15; 1 Cor. 5:9–11). If that does

175

not resolve the problem, the church should proceed with step five.[6]

Step Five: Treat Him as a Nonbeliever

As we have seen throughout this book, Christians are required to act justly, seek peace, and be reconciled with other Christians. If a Christian refuses to do these things, he is violating God's will. If he refuses to listen to his church's counsel to repent of this sin, Jesus says the church should "treat him *as* you would a pagan or a tax collector" (Matt. 18:17, emphasis added). Jesus' use of the word *as* is significant. Since only God can know a person's heart (1 Sam. 16:7; Rev. 2:23), the church has no power to decide whether a person *is* a believer. Instead, the church is called only to make a functional decision: if a person behaves like a nonbeliever would—namely, by disregarding the authority of Scripture and of Christ's church—he is to be treated as a nonbeliever.

Treating someone as a nonbeliever serves three important purposes. First, by revoking the person's privileges in the church, it protects the Lord from being dishonored by someone who acts in a shameful and rebellious way and yet retains his good standing in a Christian church (Rom. 2:23–24). Second, other believers are protected from being led astray by a bad example (Rom. 16:17; 1 Cor. 5:1–6). Third, it may help the rebellious person to realize the seriousness of his or her sin, turn from it, and be restored to God. This objective is often overlooked. Treating others as nonbelievers is not intended to injure them, but rather to help them see the truth about their sin and their need for repentance. Jesus loved pagans and tax collectors enough to warn them of their sinful condition and its consequences and to urge them to repent (e.g., Mark 2:17; John 4:1–18). The church should do no less.[7]

In other words, the church should not pretend that things are all right with people who refuse to listen to God as he speaks through the Scriptures and the church. Treating unrepentant people as unbelievers is sometimes the only way to help them understand the seriousness of their sin. This is accomplished by depriving them of certain Christian privileges (such as communion) and by evangelizing them at every opportunity. (If the person is behaving in a way that disrupts the peace of the church, it may also be appropriate to exclude him or her from church property.) This treatment is designed to bring conviction to stubborn people, with the purpose of leading them to turn from their sinful ways and to be restored to fellowship with God and fellow believers. (This appears to have been the result of the discipline administered in the Corinthian church. Compare 1 Cor. 5:1–13 with 2 Cor. 2:5–11.)[8]

Many Christians balk at this teaching. Some churches ignore or refuse to implement Matthew 18:17, even though the Bible teaches that God views discipline as both an act of love and an important means to restore his wandering sheep and protect his people from being led astray by sinful examples (Heb. 12:1–13; 1 Cor. 5:6). By ignoring this teaching, a church is not only disobeying Jesus' specific commands, but is failing to face up to the seriousness of sin and its consequences (see Ezek. 34:4, 8–10).

Consider this analogy. When a patient has cancer, it is not easy for his doctor to tell him about it, because it is a truth that is painful to hear and difficult to bear. Even so, any doctor who diagnoses cancer but fails to report it to a patient would be guilty of malpractice. After all, a patient can be properly treated only after the disease has been identified. Sin works in the same way; left undiagnosed and untreated, it causes increasing grief and spiritual deterioration (Prov. 10:17; 13:18; 29:1; Rom. 6:23). The church has a responsibility both to promote peace and unity and to help believers disentangle themselves from the terrible effects of sin (Gal. 6:1–2). Church discipline is a serious and painful step, but it is also an act of obedience to God and a loving remedy for the person caught in sin.

This truth was powerfully illustrated in one of my earliest cases. A man had told his wife that he was filing for divorce and moving in with another woman. When the wife was unable to dissuade him, she went to their pastor for advice. He gave her several suggestions on how to persuade her husband to change his mind or at least to come in for counseling. Nothing she said to her husband during the next few days had any apparent impact, and he began to pack his things.

In desperation, she returned to her pastor and asked him to talk with her husband. At first, the pastor declined to take such an active role, saying that he "did not want to scare him away from the church." The wife asked the pastor how he could take such a position in the light of Matthew 18:15–20, Galatians 6:1–2, and many related passages. After a long and heated discussion, the pastor finally realized that he was neglecting his responsibilities as a shepherd.

As a result, he went to visit the husband that evening and offered to help him work out his marital problems. When the husband adamantly refused to change his course, the pastor pleaded with him to change his mind and offered all of the resources of the church to help solve the problems in his marriage. When even that did not dissuade the husband, the pastor finally said, "I can't stop you from filing for divorce, but I must tell you that you will face church discipline if you deliberately violate Scripture as you are planning to do." After he got over his initial shock, the husband asked the pastor what he meant by "church discipline." When the pastor explained, the husband said, "You mean I'll be kicked out of the church for divorcing my wife?"

"Under these circumstances," the pastor replied, "yes." Hearing this, the husband lost his temper and ordered the pastor out of his home. Early the next morning, however, the pastor received a phone call from the husband, who wanted to talk with him again. They met an hour later, and by 10:00 A.M. the husband was on the telephone telling "the other woman" that he would not be moving in with her. Later that afternoon, the pastor began counseling with this couple, and together they started to work out the deep problems that had brought them to this crisis. Ten years later, they are still raising their family together and thanking God for a pastor who cared enough to get involved the way Jesus commanded.[9]

178

Is It Time to Go to Court?

When this resolution process is followed faithfully, one of two things should happen. Preferably, you and your opponent will listen to the counsel of your conciliators or your church leaders and resolve your dispute in a godly manner. Alternatively, if one of you refuses to listen to the church, the church should obey Jesus' command to respond to this rebellion by treating the person as a nonbeliever. As a result, 1 Corinthians 6:1–6, which applies only to disputes between Christians, is no longer applicable to your situation. In other words, once you have exhausted your remedies through the church, you may treat your opponent like any other person, which means you may consider turning to the civil courts to resolve your conflict.[10]

There are two other conditions you must satisfy before proceeding with a lawsuit. In addition to exhausting your church remedies, be sure that the rights you are seeking to enforce are biblically legitimate. As we saw in chapter 4, some of the legal "rights" and remedies available through civil courts today are contrary to Scripture. For example, some of the actions that employees can legally bring against their employers undermine the authority that God has delegated to employers through Scripture. Conversely, some of the things employers can legally do are biblically wrong. As Justice Scalia has noted, exercising such "rights" is clearly wrong in the eyes of God. Before proceeding with a lawsuit against anyone, you should make sure that the rights you are about to assert are consistent with Scripture.

The third condition for bringing a lawsuit is to make sure that your action has a righteous purpose. As we have seen from our study of 1 Corinthians 10:31–11:1, never assert your rights if doing so is likely to dishonor God, to harm other people, or to draw you away from Christ and deplete your ability to serve him. Therefore, do not file a lawsuit unless you are confident that it will somehow (1) advance God's kingdom (e.g., by promoting justice or providing a positive Christian witness to those who observe the action); (2) benefit your opponent (e.g., by invoking the power of the state to force him or her to bear the consequences of wrong

179

behavior, which may help the opponent to behave more responsibly in the future [Rom. 13:1–7]); and (3) enhance your ability to know and serve Christ (e.g., by preserving rights and resources needed to minister to others or to provide for those who depend on you).

When considering this final condition, it is important to realize that litigation often takes a much higher personal toll than most people anticipate. The financial, emotional, and spiritual demands of the adversarial process can be enormous, and they can even outweigh any gains made because of a favorable judgment. That is why Abraham Lincoln gave this advice to a class of law students over a century ago: "Discourage litigation. Persuade your neighbors to compromise whenever you can. Point out to them how the nominal winner is often a real loser in fees, expenses, and waste of time."

As this warning indicates, you should be very cautious about filing a lawsuit. If the three conditions described above are satisfied, however, you may appeal to the civil courts to resolve a conflict. Although this is not the preferable way to settle disputes, it is one that God can and does use to restrain wrongdoers, to protect the weak, and to promote justice, all of which are necessary for peace and the preservation of society.

Summary and Application

It is important to emphasize that each step of this process must be done in Jesus' name (Matt. 18:20). This means much more than simply saying three words. It means doing everything the way that Jesus himself would do it. Thus, each step must be accompanied by diligent prayer, careful investigation, proper application of Scripture, a loving concern for other people, and *above all else* a sincere desire to please and honor God. I have been encouraged by seeing that most conflicts between Christians can be resolved simply by following the first two steps (Matt. 18:15–16). As Supreme Court Justices Burger and Scalia have indicated, civil judges would be more than happy to see Christians resolving their disputes in the church rather than in court. More importantly, such faithfulness honors God, promotes just settlements, and helps to preserve relationships that need not be lost.

If you are presently involved in a conflict and have not been able to resolve it privately, these questions will help you to apply the principles presented in this chapter.

1. Are the personal or material issues in this conflict too serious to overlook or walk away from? Why?
2. Why do you think your efforts to resolve this dispute in private have failed? Is there anything you could still do to resolve it in private?
3. If you must seek outside help to resolve this dispute, are there any persons who would likely be trusted and respected by both you and your opponent?
4. What will you say to your opponent to encourage him or her to allow other people to meet with the two of you to help resolve this dispute? In particular, how would you describe the advantages of getting outside assistance?
5. If your opponent refuses to work voluntarily with others, would it be better to drop the matter or to ask the church to get involved? Why?
6. If all other avenues have failed to resolve this matter and you are considering filing a lawsuit, have you satisfied these three conditions:
   (a) Have you exhausted church remedies? How?
   (b) Are the rights you are seeking to assert biblically legitimate? What makes you think so?
   (c) Is there a righteous purpose for your lawsuit? In particular, what good will a lawsuit do for God? For your opponent? For you?
7. Go on record with the Lord by writing a prayer based on the principles taught in this chapter.

Part 4

Go and Be Reconciled

"First go and be reconciled to your brother; then come and offer your gift."

Matthew 5:24b

Reconciliation is the final step in resolving a conflict. To be reconciled means to replace hostility and separation with peace and friendship. Normally, two things must happen for complete reconciliation to occur. First, the personal offenses that separated the opponents must be laid to rest through confession and forgiveness. Second, the material issues of the conflict must be resolved by negotiating a mutually satisfactory agreement. Sometimes the material issues must be substantially resolved before forgiveness can take place. At other times forgiveness will precede agreement on the material issues. This will allow negotiations to move more quickly, which is what happened when a certain couple asked me to mediate a divorce settlement.

When I first met with Brian and Julie, all they wanted was to resolve some legal issues and finalize their divorce as quickly as possible. Before I would discuss those issues, however, I wanted to know why they had decided to end their marriage. The surface reason was readily apparent. Julie had recently discovered that Brian had been unfaithful. Although Julie had initially been willing to seek joint counseling to try to save their marriage, her subsequent behavior had convinced Brian that there was no hope of repairing the damage he had done. Therefore, they decided to proceed with a divorce.

Sensing that there had to be deeper reasons for this decision, I continued to ask questions. Brian was obviously struggling with feelings of tremendous guilt. He admitted to me that what he had done was a sin and that he had been pleading with God to forgive him. After a long discussion, it was evident to me that Brian had truly repented of his sin, so I opened the Bible to show him God's promises of forgiveness. When Brian learned that God had forgiven him, it was obvious that a great weight was lifted from his shoulders.

Sensing a significant change in Brian's attitude, I asked if he would also like to be forgiven by Julie. To my surprise, he said no. Thinking he might have misunderstood my question, I repeated it, but he gave the same answer.

When I asked him why, he said, "I have confessed to Julie in the past, and she said she forgave me. But her forgiveness doesn't mean a thing. Even when I really try to change my ways, she keeps throwing past wrongs in my face. Whenever she doesn't get her way or we get into an argument, she reminds me of something I did months or years earlier. If she couldn't forget those wrongs, there's no way she'll forget this one. I just can't go on living with a person who keeps a record of everything I've ever done wrong!"

I looked at Julie and asked her if this was true. After thinking for a moment, she admitted that it was. "I know it's probably not right to keep throwing those things back in his face," she said, "but I just can't forget all the things he has done that hurt me. Besides, he never seems to try to change."

For the next few minutes, I described biblical forgiveness to them. I showed Brian and Julie that when God forgives us, he promises not to keep a record of our sins. Once we repent, he will never bring up our wrongs again. I then explained that God wants us to forgive each other in the same way and promises to give us the power to do so.

When I ended my explanation, both Brian and Julie were deep in thought. In response to further questions, Brian again confessed that what hc had done was wrong, and once more he said he was sorry for hurting Julie so deeply. In addition, he said he would be willing to get counseling so he could learn how to avoid similar sin in the future. Finally, he turned to Julie and said, "Will you please forgive me and give our marriage another chance?"

When I looked at Julie, it was obvious that she was involved in a tremendous internal struggle. I silently prayed that God would give her grace to understand his forgiveness and to do what was right. Finally she said, "I can see that I have never forgiven Brian in God's way. I have brooded over his wrongs and brought them up any time I wanted to hurt him or win an argument. If God were to forgive me the way I have forgiven Brian, I would be in a lot of trouble."

Turning to Brian, she said, "I do forgive you, and with God's help I promise never to use this against you in the future." They both stood up, and Brian took Julie into his arms. They still had a great deal of work to do before their marriage would be fully healed, but the promise of forgiveness had opened the way for them to solve the other problems in their marriage and to be completely reconciled.

10

Forgive as God Forgave You

Bear with each other and forgive whatever grievances you may have against one another. Forgive as the Lord forgave you.

Colossians 3:13

Christians are the most forgiven people in the world. Therefore, we should be the most forgiving people in the world. As most of us know from experience, however, it is often difficult to forgive others genuinely and completely. We often find ourselves practicing a form of forgiveness that is neither biblical nor healing.

For example, I sometimes hear people say, "I forgive him— I just don't want to have anything to do with him again." This statement always makes me think of the part of the Lord's Prayer that says, "Forgive us our debts, as we also have forgiven our debtors" (Matt. 6:12). Therefore, I will often respond to this kind of statement by asking, "What would happen if God forgave you in exactly the same way you are forgiving this other person? To put it another way, how would you feel if you had just confessed a sin to the Lord and then heard his voice saying, 'I forgive you—I just don't want to have anything to do with you again'?" Most people quickly agree that they wouldn't feel the least bit forgiven.

As Christians, we cannot overlook the direct relationship between God's forgiveness and our forgiveness: "Be kind and compassionate to one another, forgiving each other just as in Christ God has forgiven you" (Eph. 4:32). "Forgive as the Lord forgave you" (Col. 3:13b). God has given us a very high standard to live up to when we have the opportunity to forgive someone. Fortunately, he also gives us the grace and the guidance we need to imitate him by forgiving others as he has forgiven us.

Neither a Feeling, nor Forgetting, nor Excusing

To understand what forgiveness is, we must first see what it is not. First, forgiveness is not a feeling. It is an act of the will. Forgiveness involves a decision not to think or talk about what someone has done, and God calls us to make this decision regardless of our feelings. As you will see later in this chapter, however, that decision can lead to remarkable changes in our feelings.

Second, forgiveness is not forgetting. Forgetting is a *passive* process in which a matter fades from memory merely with the passing of time. Forgiving is an *active* process; it involves a conscious choice and a deliberate course of action. To put it another way, when God says that he "remembers your sins no more" (Isa. 43:25), he is not saying that he *cannot* remember our sins. Rather, he is promising that he *will not* remember them. When he forgives us, he chooses not to mention, recount, or think about our sins ever again. Similarly, when *we* forgive, we must consciously decide not to think or talk about what others have done to hurt us. This may require a lot of effort, especially when an offense is still fresh in mind. Fortunately, when we decide to forgive someone and stop dwelling on an offense, painful memories usually begin to fade.

187

Finally, forgiveness is not excusing. Excusing says, "That's okay," and implies, "What you did really wasn't wrong," or "You couldn't help it." Forgiveness is the opposite of excusing. The very fact that forgiveness is needed and granted indicates that what someone did was wrong and inexcusable. Forgiveness says, "We both know that what you did was wrong and without excuse. But since God has forgiven me, I forgive you." Because forgiveness deals honestly with sin, it brings a freedom that no amount of excusing could ever hope to provide.

Forgiveness Is a Decision

I once heard a joke that reminded me of the couple described at the beginning of this chapter. A woman went to her pastor for advice on improving her marriage. When the pastor asked what her greatest complaint was, she replied, "Every time we get into a fight, my husband gets historical." When her pastor said, "You must mean *hysterical*," she responded, "I mean exactly what I said; he keeps a mental record of everything I've done wrong, and whenever he's mad, I get a history lesson."

Tragically, this story is all too real in many situations. Having never learned the true meaning of forgiveness, many people destroy important relationships by keeping a record of the wrongs of others. At the same time they deprive themselves of the peace and freedom that come through genuine forgiveness.

To forgive someone means to release from liability to suffer punishment or penalty. *Aphiemi*, a Greek word that is often translated as "forgive," means to let go, release, or remit. It often refers to debts that have been paid or canceled in full (e.g., Matt. 6:12; 18:27, 32). *Charizomai*, another word for "forgive," means to bestow favor freely or unconditionally. This word shows that forgiveness is undeserved and cannot be earned (Luke 7:42–43; 2 Cor. 2:7–10; Eph. 4:32; Col. 3:13).

As these words indicate, forgiveness can be a costly activity. When you cancel a debt, it does not simply disappear. Instead, you absorb a liability someone else deserves to pay. Similarly, forgiveness requires that you absorb certain effects of another person's sins and release the person from liability to punishment. This is precisely what Jesus accomplished at Calvary. He secured our forgiveness by taking on himself the full penalty of our sins (Isa. 53:4 6; 1 Peter 2:24–25). Remembering what he did to purchase our forgiveness should be our greatest incentive to release others from the penalties they deserve.

The penalty from which we release people when we forgive is the same penalty that God releases us from when he forgives. Isaiah 59:2 warns, "But your iniquities have separated you from your God; your sins have hidden his face from you, so that he will not hear" (cf. Rom. 6:23). When we repent of our sins and God forgives us, he releases us from the penalty of being separated from him forever. He promises not to remember our sins any longer, not to hold them against us, not to let them stand between us ever again:

> "I will forgive their wickedness and remember their sins no more" (Jer. 31:34b; cf. Isa. 43:25).
> As far as the east is from the west, so far has he removed our transgressions from us (Ps. 103:12).
> If you, O LORD, kept a record of sins, O LORD, who could stand? But with you there is forgiveness; therefore you are feared (Ps. 130:3–4).
> [Love] . . . keeps no record of wrongs (1 Cor. 13:5).

Through forgiveness God tears down the walls that our sins have erected, and he opens the way for a renewed relationship with him. This is exactly what we must do if we are to forgive as the Lord forgives us; we must release the person who has wronged us from the penalty of being separated from us. We must not hold wrongs against others, not think about them, and not punish others for them. Therefore, forgiveness may be described as a decision to make four promises:

> "I will not think about this incident."
> "I will not bring up this incident again and use it against you."
> "I will not talk to others about this incident."

"I will not allow this incident to stand between us or hinder our personal relationship."

By making and keeping these promises, you tear down the walls that stand between you and your offender. You promise not to dwell on or brood over the problem, nor to punish by holding the person at a distance. You clear the way for your relationship to develop unhindered by memories of past wrongs. This is exactly what God does for us, and it is what he commands us to do for others.

Because few people realize that forgiveness involves such marvelous promises, even when they hear the words "I forgive you" they frequently continue to struggle with feelings of guilt and estrangement. Therefore, whenever you forgive someone who may not understand what biblical forgiveness is, make it a point to explain the four promises you have just made. In addition to reassuring that person regarding your intentions, this explanation may help someone to understand for the first time what God means when he says, "I forgive you."

When Should You Forgive?

Ideally, repentance should precede forgiveness (Luke 17:3). As we saw in chapter 4, however, minor offenses may be overlooked and forgiven even if the offender has not expressly repented. Your spontaneous forgiveness in these cases can put the matter behind you once and for all and save you and the other person from needless controversy.

When an offense is too serious to overlook and the offender has not yet repented, you may need to approach forgiveness as a two stage process. The first stage may be called *positional forgiveness,* and the second *transactional forgiveness.* Positional forgiveness is unconditional and is a commitment you make to God (see Mark 11:25; Luke 6:28; Acts 7:60). You promise to strive to maintain a loving and merciful attitude toward someone who has offended you. It is a decision to make the first promise of forgiveness, which means you will not dwell on the hurtful incident or seek vengeance or retribution in thought, word, or action. Instead, by God's grace you will keep yourself in a "position of forgiveness" in which you pray for the other person and are ready to pursue complete reconciliation as soon as he or she repents. This attitude will protect you from bitterness and resentment, even if the other person takes a long time to repent.

Transactional forgiveness is conditional on the repentance of the offender and takes place between you and that person (Luke 17:3–5). It is a commitment to make the other three promises of forgiveness to the offender. When there has been a serious offense, it would not be appropriate to make these promises until the offender has repented (see chapter 6). Until then, you may need to confront the offender or seek the involvement of others to resolve the matter (Matt. 18:16–20; see chapter 7 and 9). You could not do this if you had already made the last three promises. But once the other person repents, you should complete the transaction of forgiveness, closing the matter forever, the same way that God forgives you.

Both stages of forgiveness were vividly demonstrated by God. When Christ died on the cross, he took on the position of forgiveness, maintaining an attitude of love and mercy toward those who put him to death. "Father, forgive them, for they do not know what they are doing" (Luke 23:34). At Pentecost, the Father's answer to Jesus' prayer was revealed. Three thousand people heard Peter's Pentecost message and were cut to the heart when they realized that they had crucified the Son of God. As they repented of their sin, the transaction of forgiveness was completed, and they were fully reconciled to God (Acts 2:36–41). This is exactly the pattern you should follow, "forgiving each other, just as in Christ God forgave you" (Eph. 4:32).

What about the Consequences?

Forgiveness does not automatically release a wrongdoer from all the consequences of sin. Although God forgave the Israelites who rebelled against him in the wilderness, he decreed that they would die without entering the promised land (Num. 14:20–23). Even Moses was not shielded from this consequence

(Deut. 32:48–52). Likewise, even though God forgave David for adultery and murder, God did not shield him from all the consequences that naturally flowed from his sin (2 Sam. 12:11–14; 13:1–39; 16:21–22; 19:1–4). This is not to say that God is unmerciful; he is quick to remove the penalty of separation (2 Sam. 12:13) and often spares us from many of the consequences of our sins. When he does allow certain consequences to remain for a time, it is always to teach us and others not to sin again.

Following God's example, you should remove any walls that stand between you and a repentant wrongdoer. It may also be appropriate to relieve that person from at least some of the consequences of his or her sin (Gen. 50:15–21; 2 Sam. 16:5–10; 19:18–23). For example, if someone negligently damaged your property and is truly unable to pay for needed repairs, you may decide to bear the cost yourself. Such mercy is especially appropriate when the offender is sincerely determined not to repeat that sin.

On the other hand, there may be times when you forgive someone but cannot afford to absorb the consequence of such wrongdoing. Or, even if you could bear the cost, doing so may not be the wisest and most loving thing for an offender, especially one caught in a pattern of irresponsibility or misconduct. As Proverbs 19:19 warns, "A hot-tempered man must pay the penalty; if you rescue him, you will have to do it again." Thus, a treasurer who secretly stole from your church may benefit from having to repay what he or she took. Likewise, a careless teenager may drive more safely in the future if he or she is made to pay for damages. And an employee who repeatedly neglects his responsibilities may need to lose his job to learn needed lessons.[1]

The important thing to remember is that once a person has expressed repentance, it is your responsibility to make the four promises of forgiveness and to remove the penalty of personal separation. Beyond that, you must imitate God's love and mercy and do only what will help to build up the other person. In other words, "forgive as the Lord forgave you."

Overcoming Unforgiveness

The promises of forgiveness are sometimes difficult to make and even harder to keep. Fortunately, God promises to help us forgive others. He gives us this help through the Bible, which provides practical guidance and many examples of forgiveness. He also strengthens us through the Holy Spirit, who gives us the power and will to forgive others. Finally, for those times when we need extra help, he provides counsel and encouragement through pastors and fellow Christians. Here are a few ways to draw on these resources when you are seeking to overcome unforgiveness:

Confirm Repentance

It is difficult to forgive a person who has failed to repent and confess clearly and specifically. When you find yourself in this situation, it may be wise to explain to the person who wronged you why you are having a difficult time forgiving. My wife had to do this with me shortly after we were married.

While we were attending a conference in Colorado, I carelessly criticized her in front of several other people. When we were alone a few minutes later, she let me know that she was upset about what I had said. I hurriedly said, "I'm sorry; that was wrong of me. Will you forgive me?" She said she did, but a few hours later it was obvious that we had not been reconciled. Finally Corlette asked, "I'm having a hard time forgiving you; could we talk about this some more?" When I agreed, she told me that she did not believe I realized how deeply I had hurt her. She then explained why my remarks had been so embarrassing and painful for her. She was absolutely right; I had not understood the effect my words had on her. After hearing her explanation, I finally apologized specifically and sincerely for the effect of my sin, and I made a commitment to be more sensitive toward her in the future. Once I repented and confessed properly, Corlette found it much easier to forgive me.

If you are having a difficult time forgiving someone, you may need to do what Corlette did. She helped me to see where my confession had been deficient (I had completely neglected four of the Seven A's!), and she encouraged me to take repentance more seriously. In doing so, she did me a service and at the same time removed a major hurdle to forgiveness.

Renounce Sinful Attitudes and Expectations

Forgiveness can also be hindered by sinful attitudes and unrealistic expectations. For example, either consciously or unconsciously, many of us withhold forgiveness because we believe the offender must earn or deserve our forgiveness, or because we want to punish the offender and make her suffer. We may also withhold forgiveness because we want a guarantee that such an offense will never occur again.

These attitudes and expectations are utterly inconsistent with the command to forgive as God forgave us. There is no way that we can earn or deserve God's forgiveness, which is why he gives it to repentant sinners as a free gift (Rom. 6:23). We must grant forgiveness just as freely. Likewise, God does not withhold forgiveness to punish people who have repented of their sins. As 1 John 1:9 promises, "If we confess our sins, he is faithful and just and will forgive us our sins" (cf. Ps. 103:9–12).

Furthermore, just as God demands no guarantee from us regarding our future conduct, we have no right to make such a demand of others. This fact is clearly revealed by Jesus' command in Luke 17:3–4: "'If your brother sins, rebuke him, and if he repents, forgive him. If he sins against you seven times in a day, and seven times comes back to you and says, 'I repent,' forgive him.'" Forgiveness is based on repentance, not on guarantees. Therefore, once someone has expressed repentance for an action, we have no right to let our fears of the future delay forgiveness.

Of course, if someone has expressed repentance but continues to behave in a hurtful manner, it may be appropriate to confront the offender about *present* conduct. A pattern of sinful behavior may need to be confronted repeatedly before it is successfully overcome. Even so, we have no right to demand guarantees and withhold forgiveness from a repentant person.

Assess Your Contributions to the Problem

In many situations, your sins may have contributed to a conflict. Even if you did not start the dispute, your lack of understanding, careless words, impatience, or failure to respond in a loving manner may have aggravated the situation. When this happens, it is easy to behave as though the other person's sins more than cancel yours, which leaves you with a self-righteous attitude that can retard forgiveness. The best way to overcome this tendency is to prayerfully examine your role in the conflict and then write down everything you have done or failed to do that may have been a factor. Remembering your faults usually makes it easier to forgive others for theirs.

Recognize That God Is Working for Good

When someone has wronged you, it is also helpful to remember that God is sovereign and loving. Therefore, when you are having a hard time forgiving someone, take time to note how God may be using that offense for good. Is this an unusual opportunity to glorify God? How can you serve others and help them grow in their faith? What sins and weaknesses of yours are being exposed? What character qualities are you being challenged to exercise? When you perceive that the person who has wronged you is being used as an instrument in God's hand to help you mature, serve others, and glorify him, it may be easier for you to move ahead with forgiveness.

Remember God's Forgiveness

One of the most important steps in overcoming your unforgiving attitude is to focus your attention on how much God has forgiven you. The parable of the unmerciful servant vividly illustrates this principle (Matt. 18:21–35). In that story, a servant owed the king an enormous debt. When the king threatened to have the servant and his family sold as slaves to pay the debt, the servant begged for mercy. The king "took pity on him, canceled the debt and let him go" (v. 27). Moments later, the servant saw a man who owed him a much smaller debt. When he demanded payment, the man asked for time to repay it. The servant refused and "had the man thrown into prison until he could pay the debt" (v. 30). When the king heard about this, he summoned the servant and said, "'You wicked servant . . . I canceled all that debt of yours because you begged me to. Shouldn't you have had mercy on your fellow servant just as I had on you?'" (vv. 32–33). Then, "In anger his master turned him over to the jailers to be tortured, until he should pay back all he owed" (v. 34). Jesus concludes the parable with these words, "'This is how my heavenly Father will treat each of you unless you forgive your brother from your heart'" (v. 35).

This parable illustrates an attitude that is all too common among Christians. We take God's forgiveness for granted while we stubbornly withhold our forgiveness from others. In effect, we behave as though others' sins against us are more serious than our sins against God! Jesus teaches that this is a terribly sinful thing to do—it is an affront to God and his holiness, and it demeans the forgiveness that Jesus purchased for us at Calvary. Until we repent of this sinful attitude, we will suffer unpleasant consequences. To begin with, we will feel separated from God and other Christians. We may also experience unusual hardships and lose blessings that would otherwise be ours (e.g., Ps. 32:1–5).[2]

If you are struggling with unforgiveness, take another look at the enormous debt for which God has forgiven you. Turning to the Bible and reminding yourself of God's holiness will help you see more clearly the seriousness of even your smallest sin (see Isa. 6:1–5; James 2:10–11). Make a list of the sins for which God has forgiven you. In particular, ask yourself whether you have ever treated God or others the same way you have been treated by the person you are trying to forgive. Take a long look at this list and remind yourself what you deserve from God because of your sins. Then rejoice in the wonderful promise of Psalm 103:8–11: "The Lord is compassionate and gracious, slow to anger, abounding in love. . . . he does not treat us as our sins deserve or repay us according to our iniquities. For as high as the heavens are above the earth, so great is his love for those who fear him."

The more you understand and appreciate the wonders of God's forgiveness, the more motivation you will have to forgive others.

As Pat Morison notes in his excellent booklet on forgiveness, "We are not called to forgive others in order to earn God's love; rather, having experienced his love, we have the basis and motive to forgive others."[3]

Draw on God's Strength

Above all else, remember that true forgiveness depends on God's grace. If you try to forgive others on your own, you are in for a long and frustrating battle. But if you continually ask for and rely on God's strength, you can forgive even the most painful offenses. God gives us his grace through Scripture, through biblical counseling, and through the Holy Spirit. This grace was powerfully displayed in the life of Corrie ten Boom, who had been imprisoned with her family by the Nazis for giving aid to Jews during World War II. Her father and sister, Betsie, died as a result of the brutal treatment they received in the concentration camps. Corrie survived and after the war traveled throughout the world, testifying to God's love. Here is what she wrote about a remarkable encounter in Germany:

> It was at a church service in Munich that I saw him, the former S.S. man who had stood guard at the shower room door in the processing center at Ravensbruck. He was the first of our actual jailers that I had seen since that time. And suddenly it was all there—the roomful of mocking men, the heaps of clothing, Betsie's pain-blanched face.
>
> He came up to me as the church was emptying, beaming and bowing. "How grateful I am for your message, Fraulein," he said. "To think that, as you say, he has washed my sins away!"
>
> His hand was thrust out to shake mine. And I, who had preached so often to the people in Bloemendall the need to forgive, kept my hand at my side.
>
> Even as the angry, vengeful thoughts boiled through me, I saw the sin of them. Jesus Christ had died for this man; was I going to ask for more? Lord Jesus, I prayed, forgive me and help me to forgive him.
>
> I tried to smile, I struggled to raise my hand. I could not. I felt nothing, not the slightest spark of warmth or charity. And so again

I breathed a silent prayer. Jesus, I cannot forgive him. Give me Your forgiveness.

As I took his hand the most incredible thing happened. From my shoulder along my arm and through my hand a current seemed to pass from me to him, while into my heart sprang a love for this stranger that almost overwhelmed me.

So I discovered that it is not on our forgiveness any more than on our goodness that the world's healing hinges, but on him. When he tells us to love our enemies, he gives, along with the command, the love itself.[4]

Reconciliation and the Replacement Principle

The four promises of forgiveness tear down the wall that stands between you and a person who has wronged you. Forgiveness does not end there, however. After you demolish an obstruction, you usually have to clear away some debris and do some repair work. The Bible calls this "reconciliation," a process involving a change of attitude that leads to a change in the relationship. More specifically, to be reconciled means to replace hostility and separation with peace and friendship. This is what Jesus had in mind when he said, "go and be reconciled with your brother" (Matt. 5:24; cf. 1 Cor. 7:11; 2 Cor. 5:18–20).

Being reconciled does not mean that the person who offended you must now become your closest friend. What it means is that your relationship will be at least as good as it was before the offense occurred. Once that happens, an even better relationship may develop. As God helps you and the other person to work through your differences, you may discover a growing respect and appreciation for each other. Moreover, you may uncover common interests and goals that will add a deeper and richer dimension to your friendship.

Reconciliation requires that you give a repentant person an opportunity to demonstrate repentance and to regain your trust. This may be a slow and difficult process, especially when that person has consistently behaved in a hurtful and irresponsible manner. While you may proceed with some caution, you should not demand guarantees from a person who has expressed repentance. If the person stumbles, the process of loving confrontation, confession, and forgiveness may need to be repeated (Luke 17:3–4). In spite of setbacks and disappointments, for the Lord's sake the process of reconciliation should continue until your relationship has been fully restored.

Although reconciliation can sometimes take place with little or no special effort, in most cases you will need to remember the saying, "If you are coasting, you must be going downhill." In other words, unless a deliberate effort is made to restore and strengthen a relationship, it will generally deteriorate. This is especially true when you are recovering from intense and prolonged conflict. Moreover, unless you take definite steps to demonstrate your forgiveness, the other person may doubt your sincerity and withdraw from you. These problems can be significantly reduced if you pursue reconciliation at three different levels.

In Thought

Even when we say "I forgive you," many of us have a difficult time not thinking about what others have done to hurt us. Try as we might, memories of the offense keep popping back into our minds, and we find ourselves reliving all kinds of painful feelings.

I remember a time when this happened to me. When I woke up one morning, I immediately thought about what Jim (not his real name) had done to me the previous day. Since I had forgiven him, I tried to stop to thinking about it. Within fifteen minutes, however, the same thoughts were rolling through my mind. I pushed them aside once more, but before long there they were again. After wrestling with these painful thoughts several more times, I realized I was stuck in a rut. When I asked God to help me get rid of these thoughts and feelings, these two Bible passages came to my mind:

> "But I tell you who hear me: Love your enemies, do good to those who hate you, bless those who curse you, pray for those who mistreat you" (Luke 6:27–28).

> Finally brothers, whatever is true, whatever is noble, whatever is right, whatever is pure, whatever is lovely, whatever is admirable—if anything is excellent or praiseworthy—think about such things (Phil. 4:8).

"Okay," I prayed, "but I'll need your help, Lord. I sure don't feel like doing any of this." By God's grace, I began to pray for Jim, asking God to be with him and to bless his day. My thoughts then turned to other matters. When I caught myself thinking about the offense an hour later, I prayed for Jim again, this time thanking God for some of Jim's special qualities. This process repeated itself many times during the next two days, and then I discovered something amazing. Whenever Jim came to my mind, my thoughts were automatically positive, and they no longer gravitated toward the offense he had committed.

This was how I learned the *replacement principle*. It is very difficult simply to stop thinking about an unpleasant experience. Instead, we must replace negative thoughts and memories with positive ones. This principle is especially helpful when trying to keep the first promise of forgiveness. Every time you begin to dwell on or brood over what someone has done, ask for God's help and deliberately pray for that person or think of something about the offender that is "true, noble, right, pure, lovely, admirable, excellent, or praiseworthy." At first, you may struggle to come up with even one positive thought, but after you find one good thought or memory, others should come more easily. If you cannot think of a single good thing about the person you are trying to forgive, then use thankful thoughts about God and his work in this situation to replace unpleasant memories (see Phil. 4:4–7).

In Word

As Luke 6:27–28 implies, the replacement principle applies to your words as well as your thoughts. When talking to others about the person who offended you, make it a point to speak well of the person. Express appreciation for things he or she has done and draw attention to redeeming qualities. Do the same when talking to the offender. Praise, thank, or encourage!

Kind words are especially important if the other person is struggling with guilt or embarrassment. When Paul learned that a member of the church in Corinth had recently repented of a serious sin, he commanded the other members of the church to "forgive and comfort him, so that he will not be overwhelmed by excessive sorrow" (2 Cor. 2:7). As you verbally reaffirm your friendship and sincerely build up the other person, both of you should experience improved attitudes and feelings.

In Deed

If you really want to be reconciled to someone, apply the replacement principle to your actions as well (1 John 3:18). As C. S. Lewis noted, "Don't waste time bothering whether you 'love' your neighbor; act as if you did. As soon as we do this we find one of the great secrets. When you are behaving as if you loved someone, you will presently come to love him."[5]

When I first read Lewis's comment, I thought it was rather naive. But then I experienced exactly what he was describing. Corlette and I had quarreled about some petty thing, and I had not really forgiven her. My unhappiness was compounded by her request that I run to the grocery store to "pick up a few small items." (As you can guess, I dislike shopping for groceries.) As I grudgingly pushed my cart down the aisle, I noticed some special coffee that Corlette loves to drink. *If she hadn't been so unkind to me today, I would have surprised her with that.* Even as I thought these words, another part of me wanted to get her the coffee. I wrestled with conflicting feelings for a few moments and then decided to pick up the can, "just to check the price," I told myself. The moment I touched it, my feelings began to change. My resentment melted away, and I was overwhelmed with love for my wife and a desire to see her face light up as I gave her this special gift. Needless to say, we were completely reconciled shortly after I returned home.

Loving actions can do much more than change your feelings; they can also communicate in unmistakable terms the reality of your forgiveness and your commitment to reconciliation. Thomas Edison apparently understood this principle. When he and his staff were developing the incandescent light bulb, it took hundreds of hours to manufacture a single bulb. One day, after finishing a bulb, he handed it to a young errand boy and asked him to take it upstairs to the testing room. As the boy turned and started up the stairs, he stumbled and fell, and the bulb shattered on the steps. Instead of rebuking the boy, Edison reassured him and then turned to his staff and told them to start working on another bulb. When it was completed several days later, Edison demonstrated the reality of his forgiveness in the most powerful way possible. He walked over to the same boy, handed him the bulb, and said, "Please take this up to the testing room." Imagine how that boy must have felt. He knew that he didn't deserve to be trusted with this responsibility again. Yet, here it was, being offered to him as though nothing had ever happened. Nothing could have restored this boy to the team more clearly, more quickly, or more fully.

Summary and Application

This is what reconciliation is all about. By thought, word, and deed, you can demonstrate forgiveness and rebuild relationships with people who have offended you. No matter how painful the offense, with God's help, you can make four promises and imitate the forgiveness and reconciliation that was demonstrated on the cross. By the grace of God, you can forgive as the Lord forgave you.

If you are presently involved in a conflict and have not been able to resolve it privately, these questions will help you to apply the principles presented in this chapter.

1. How has your opponent sinned against you?

2. Which of these sins has your opponent confessed?

3. Which of the unconfessed sins can you overlook and forgive at this time? (Those that cannot be overlooked will have to be dealt with by applying the principles taught in chapters 7 through 9.)

4. Write out the four promises that you will make to your opponent at this time to indicate your forgiveness.

5. What consequences of your opponent's sin will you take on yourself? What consequences will you expect your opponent to bear?

6. If you are having a hard time forgiving your opponent:
    (a) Is it because you are not sure he or she has repented? If so, how could you encourage confirmation of repentance?
    (b) Do you think your opponent must somehow earn or deserve your forgiveness? Are you trying to punish by withholding forgiveness? Are you expecting a guarantee that the offense will not happen again? If you have any of these attitudes or expectations, what do you need to do?
    (c) How did your sins contribute to this problem? Which of these sins will God refuse to forgive? How can you imitate his forgiveness?
    (d) Read Matthew 18:21–35. What is the point of this passage? How does it apply to you?
    (e) How might God be working for good in this situation?
    (f) What has God forgiven you for in the past? How serious are your opponent's sins against you when compared to your sins against God? How can you show God that you appreciate his forgiveness?

7. How can you demonstrate forgiveness or promote reconciliation:
    In thought?
    In word?
    In deed?

8. Go on record with the Lord by writing a prayer based on the principles taught in this chapter.

11

Look Also to the Interests of Others

Each of you should look not only to your own interests, but also to the interests of others.

Philippians 2:4

So far we have focused primarily on how to resolve the personal issues that can arise during a conflict. As we all know, however, conflict may also involve material concerns. Two people may disagree on the cost of repairing damaged property, or two business people may interpret a contract in entirely different ways. A couple may disagree on where to spend a vacation. Neighbors may differ on whether or not a fence needs to be replaced and who should bear the cost. Until these matters are settled, reconciliation will be hindered, even if the related personal issues are fully resolved. In this chapter we will look at five principles that can help us to reach agreements on material issues in a biblically faithful manner.

Cooperative vs. Competitive Negotiation

Many people automatically resort to a competitive style when negotiating material issues. Thus they aggressively pursue the results they desire and let their opponents look out for themselves.

Although this approach may be appropriate when prompt results are needed or when someone is defending important moral principles, it has three inherent weaknesses. First, a competitive approach often fails to produce the best possible solution to a problem. When people work against each other, they tend to focus on surface issues and neglect underlying desires and needs. As a result, they often reach inadequate solutions. Moreover, a competitive approach usually assumes that for one side to get more, the other side must get less. This "fixed pie" attitude discourages the openness and flexibility needed to develop creative and comprehensive solutions.

Second, competitive negotiation can also be quite inefficient. It usually begins with each side stating a specific position, and progress is made by successive compromises and concessions. Because each compromise is typically about half the size of the previous one and takes twice as long, this process can consume a great deal of time and generate significant frustration.

Finally, competitive negotiating can significantly damage personal relationships. This approach tends to focus on material issues rather than on personal concerns, perceptions, and feelings. At best, those involved in the process get the message that these matters are unimportant. At worst, the inherent contest of wills leads to overt intimidation, manipulation, and personal attacks. Many relationships are seriously damaged by this painful process.

Many of these problems can be avoided by negotiating in a cooperative rather than a competitive manner. People who practice cooperative negotiation deliberately seek solutions that are beneficial to everyone involved. By working with our opponents rather than against them, we are more likely to communicate and appreciate underlying needs and concerns. As a result, we are apt to develop wiser and more thorough solutions. When carried out properly, cooperative negotiation is relatively efficient because less time and energy is wasted on defensive posturing. Best of all, because attention is paid to personal concerns, this style of negotiation tends to preserve or even improve relationships.

Cooperative negotiation is highly commended by Scripture, which repeatedly commands us to have an active concern for the needs and well-being of others:

> "'Love your neighbor as yourself'" (Matt. 22:39).
> [Love] is not self-seeking . . . (1 Cor. 13:5).
> "So in everything, do to others what you would have them do to you, for this sums up the Law and the Prophets" (Matt. 7:12).
> Do nothing out of selfish ambition or vain conceit, but in humility consider others better than yourselves. Each of you should look not only to your own interests, but also to the interests of others (Phil. 2:3–4; cf. 1 Cor. 10:24).

Having a loving concern for others does not mean always giving in to their demands. We do have a responsibility to look out for our interests (Phil. 2:4). Furthermore, Jesus calls us to be "as shrewd as snakes and as innocent as doves" (Matt. 10:16). The Greek word *phronimos,* translated "shrewd" in this passage, means to be "prudent, sensible, and practically wise."[1] A wise person does not give in to others unless there is a valid reason to do so. After gathering all the relevant information and exploring creative options, a wise person works toward solutions that honor God and provide lasting benefits to as many people as possible. While this may sometimes lead to unilateral concessions, it usually requires that *both* sides contribute to a solution.

As these passages indicate, cooperative negotiation may be described as a combination of love and wisdom. I have found that this combination generally involves five basic steps, which may be summarized in this simple rule: *When you need to negotiate, PAUSE.* This acronym stands for the following steps:

Prepare
Affirm relationships
Understand interests
Search for creative solutions
Evaluate options objectively and reasonably

The more carefully you follow each of these steps, the more likely you will be to reach mutually beneficial agreements on material issues.

Prepare

Preparation is one of the most important elements of successful negotiation (Prov. 14:8, 22). This is especially true when significant issues or strong feelings are involved. Here are a few things you can do to prepare for negotiation:

Pray. Ask God for humility, discernment, and wisdom as you prepare.

Get the facts. Read relevant documents carefully (e.g., contracts, employment manuals, letters). Talk with key witnesses. Conduct necessary research.

Identify issues and interests. Try to discern the real cause of the disagreement. Carefully list the issues involved. Make a list of your interests as well as the interests of others as you understand them.

Study the Bible. Clearly identify the biblical principles involved and make sure you know how to put them into practice.

Develop options. Do some brainstorming before you talk with your opponent so you can propose a few reasonable solutions to the problem. Be prepared to explain how each option will benefit your opponent.

Anticipate reactions. Put yourself in your opponent's shoes and try to predict a few likely reactions to your proposals. Develop a response to each of those reactions.

Plan an alternative to a negotiated agreement. Decide in advance what you will do if negotiations are not successful.

Select an appropriate time and place to talk. Consider your opponent's possible preferences.

Plan your opening remarks. In particular, plan how to set a positive tone at the outset of the meeting and how to encourage your opponent to enter into the discussion with an open mind.

Seek counsel. If you have doubts about how to proceed with negotiations, talk with people who can give you wise and biblically sound advice.

The Barking Dog. To make this discussion as practical as possible, I will show how the PAUSE approach to negotiation could be followed in an actual conflict. Here is the situation we will consider throughout this chapter.

Jim and Julie Johnson live on a two-acre tract of land outside of town. Their nearest neighbors, Steve and Sally Smith, have a similar acreage. The two houses are located within a hundred feet of each other on adjacent corners of the properties. The Smiths raise border collies as a hobby and a small business. A few weeks ago they acquired a new dog named Molly, who barks sporadically several evenings a week. The annoying barking has been keeping the Johnsons awake at night, and their children are complaining about being tired in school. To make matters worse, the Smiths recently began to exercise and feed Molly at 5:00 A.M. The resulting noise robs the Johnsons of another hour of sleep.

A week or so ago, Jim noticed Sally working in her garden, and he went over to ask if she would do something about the barking. She said she was sorry, and for a few days the barking subsided. Within a week, however, it started again and seemed even worse than before. Yesterday another neighbor told Julie that Steve had called everyone in the subdivision to see whether the dog was bothering them. In the process, he had said some very critical things about Jim.

Julie has conducted her own survey and found out that only a few of her neighbors have been annoyed by Molly's barking. Two neighbors are hard of hearing, and some of the others live in earth homes that block out most sounds. Julie then checked with the county attorney and found out that it is a misdemeanor to keep a dog that disturbs a "considerable number of persons" in a neighborhood. Unfortunately, the county attorney apparently does not believe that the dog has disturbed enough people to justify misdemeanor charges. Therefore, Jim and Julie will need to negotiate a solution without the aid of the authorities.

Since the problem with the barking dog did not need to be resolved immediately, Jim and Julie took several days to prepare to negotiate with the Smiths. Each day they prayed for the Smiths and asked God for wisdom and discernment. They also spent some time discussing how to apply relevant biblical principles to this situation.

To verify their complaint and identify significant patterns, they began to keep a written log of when Molly barked. Jim read the subdivision covenants to see whether there were any rules against barking dogs, but there were not. Julie went to the library and checked out several books on dog training. They made a list of the suggestions that expert trainers gave regarding barking dogs.

Jim and Julie identified two issues that needed to be addressed: (1) Is it reasonable to expect the Smiths to do something about Molly's barking? (2) If it is, what is the best way to moderate her barking? They then made a preliminary list of the interests involved. They decided that *they* had the following interests: a desire for peace and quiet, sufficient rest for their children, a comfortable relationship with the Smiths and with other neighbors. They inferred that *the Smiths* had these interests: an affection for dogs, a need for additional income, possibly a resentment toward "being told what to do." (I will list more interests later in this chapter.)

The Johnsons then put together a preliminary list of options that might solve the problem, including: sell the dog, teach the dog not to bark, get a remote-controlled shock collar for the dog, muzzle the dog, get ear plugs for themselves, and so on. They tried to anticipate how the Smiths would respond to each option and listed the costs and benefits of the more viable ones.

Jim and Julie also spent some time discussing what they would do if the Smiths refused to do anything about the barking. Although they were tempted to find a way to retaliate and make life difficult for the Smiths, they knew that would not please or honor God. Therefore, they decided that if they could not stop the barking right away, they would simply work harder at cultivating a positive relationship with the Smiths. They would do this by inviting them over for meals, taking time to get to know their children, and looking for opportunities to help them or to be kind to them.

Since the Smiths seemed to relax more on Saturdays, Jim and Julie decided that would be a good time to approach them. They also decided that it would be wise to offer to talk at the Smiths' home, which would put them more at ease. They planned to request a meeting by having Jim go over to the Smiths in person and say something like this: "Molly seems to be barking a lot lately, and our children are having a difficult time getting enough sleep. Julie and I would appreciate it if you would be willing to take a few minutes to talk with us about this situation."

Jim and Julie also discussed three ways that Steve and Sally might react to this request, and they planned appropriate responses. Once their preparation was complete, they were ready to approach the Smiths.

Affirm Relationships

A conflict generally involves two basic ingredients: people and a problem. All too often, we ignore the feelings and concerns of the people and focus all our attention on the problems that separate us. This approach often causes further offense and alienation, which only makes conflicts more difficult to resolve. One way to avoid these unnecessary complications is to affirm your respect and concern for your opponent throughout the negotiation process. For example, you may begin a conversation with words like these:

"You are one of my closest friends. No one in town has been more kind or thoughtful toward me. It's because I value our friendship so much that I want to find a permanent solution to this problem."

"I admire how hard you have worked to pay this debt. I also appreciate your efforts to keep me informed about your financial situation. Since you have treated me with respect, I would like to do everything I can to find a workable payment plan."

"I appreciate your willingness to listen to my concerns about this project. Before I explain what they are, I want to make it clear that I will respect your authority to decide this matter, and I will do all that I can to make this project successful."

Obviously, these affirming words must be backed up with comparable actions. If they are not, your opponent will rightfully conclude that you are a flatterer and a hypocrite. Here are a few ways to demonstrate concern and respect during the negotiation process:

Communicate in a courteous manner. Listen respectfully to what others have to say. Use words like "please," "May I explain?" "Would it be all right with you if . . .?" and "I don't think I explained my reasons very clearly."

Spend time on personal issues. Instead of moving directly to material issues, try to understand your opponent's personal concerns. Deal with personal offenses and frustrations as soon as possible.

Submit to authority. Offer clear and reasonable advice, and be as persuasive as possible, but respect the authority of leaders and support their decisions to the best of your ability.

Earnestly seek to understand. Pay attention to what others are thinking and feeling. Ask sincere questions. Discuss their perceptions.

Look out for the interests of others. Seek solutions that really satisfy others' needs and desires.

Confront in a gracious manner. If you must confront someone, use the skills described in chapter 8.

Allow face-saving. Don't back others into a corner. Develop solutions that are consistent with others' values and with God's.

Give praise and thanks. When someone makes a valid point or a gracious gesture, acknowledge it or express your appreciation for it.

If you sincerely and consistently affirm your concern and respect for your opponent, you will generally have more freedom to discuss material issues honestly and frankly. Even if you are not entirely satisfied with an agreement, it is wise to affirm your relationship with the other person at the end of the negotiation process. This protects your relationship from residual damage and may improve your ability to negotiate subsequent issues in a more satisfactory manner.

The Barking Dog. Affirming their relationship with the Smiths was a basic part of the Johnsons' initial request for a meeting with the Smiths. By *asking* for a meeting instead of demanding it, he conveyed courtesy and respect. This process continued during their first meeting with the Smiths the next day. Jim began that meeting by saying: "We really appreciate your willingness to talk with us. In fact, we're hoping that this situation will give us a chance to get to know one another better and to be better neighbors than before."

After allowing Steve and Sally to respond, Julie asked if it would be all right for her to explain some of the Johnsons' concerns. She chose her words carefully and used "I" (or "we") statements as much as possible. She was careful not to accuse the Smiths of deliberately bothering anyone, and she made it clear that she and Jim were assuming the best about them. She then asked Steve and Sally to explain some of their feelings and concerns. As they did so, Jim and Julie asked questions at appropriate times and responded with statements like, "I see," "I didn't realize that," and "That helps me to understand your situation." Although the Smiths were somewhat defensive when the conversation began, they eventually began to relax. As their relationship with the Johnsons was affirmed, they became increasingly willing to talk about the problem that had brought them together.

Understand Interests

The third step in the PAUSE strategy is to understand the interests of those involved in the disagreement. Only then can you properly respond to the command to "look not only to your own interests, but also to the interests of others." In order to identify "interests," it is important to understand how they differ from "issues" and "positions."

An *issue* is an identifiable and concrete question that must be addressed in order to reach an agreement. For example: "Should the Smiths do something to stop Molly's barking?" or "How can the Smiths stop Molly's barking?"

A *position* is a desired outcome or a definable perspective on an issue. For example: "If the dog keeps barking, you should get rid of her," or, "She's my dog, and you have no right to tell me what to do with her."

An *interest* is what motivates people. It is a concern, desire, need, limitation, or something that a person values. Interests provide the basis for positions. Some interests are concrete and easy to identify. For example: "I like breeding and training dogs, and I need the extra income," or, "My kids need sleep." Other interests are abstract, hidden, and difficult to measure. For example: "I don't want my family to think that I can be pushed around," or, "This is the only thing I've ever done that made me feel like a success."

As these examples demonstrate, positions are frequently incompatible; one person's desired result often conflicts with the other person's desired result. While interests may sometimes clash as well, in many situations the parties' primary interests are surprisingly compatible. (For example, both the Smiths and the Johnsons probably want their children to enjoy living in this neighborhood.) Therefore, when people focus on interests rather than positions, it is usually easier to develop acceptable solutions.

The Bible is filled with stories that illustrate the wisdom of identifying and focusing on interests rather than positions. One of my favorite negotiation stories is described in 1 Samuel 25:1–44. David's popularity among the people of Israel had become so great that King Saul became jealous and tried to kill him. David and several hundred of his supporters fled into the desert, where they lived as mercenaries. During this time, they protected the flocks and herds of the local inhabitants from marauders. One of the people who had benefited from David's protection was a wealthy landowner named Nabal. Therefore, when David's provisions ran low, he sent ten young men to ask Nabal for food. In spite of the good David had done for him, Nabal denied the request and hurled insults at the young men. When David learned of this, he was furious. He immediately set out with four hundred armed men, determined to kill Nabal and all of his men.

In the meantime, Nabal's wife, Abigail, learned what Nabal had done. Seeing the danger her husband was in, she set out to negotiate a peace treaty with David. First she loaded a large amount of food on several donkeys and instructed her servants to take it to David. (Very wise preparation!) She then mounted her own donkey and set out to intercept him before he had time to launch his attack. When Abigail met David at the foot of the mountains, she dismounted and bowed down before him. Then she said:

> "My lord, let the blame be on me alone. Please let your servant speak to you; hear what your servant has to say. . . . *[T]he LORD has kept you, my master, from bloodshed and from avenging yourself with your own hands.* . . . Please forgive your servant's offense, for the LORD will certainly make a lasting dynasty for my master, because he fights the LORD's battles. *Let no wrongdoing be found in you as long as you live.* . . . When the LORD has done for my master every good thing he promised concerning him and has appointed him leader over Israel, *my master will not have on his conscience the staggering burden of needless bloodshed or of having avenged himself . . .*" (vv. 24–31, emphasis added).

Abigail clearly affirmed her concern and respect for David. More importantly, instead of lecturing him or talking directly about her own concerns, Abigail focused on David's primary interest in this situation. She had probably heard about King Saul's recent massacre of an entire town of people who had innocently given assistance to David (1 Sam. 22:6–19). She also appeared to know that David had recently passed up an opportunity to kill Saul (1 Sam. 24:1–22). Abigail must have seen that David's clean record and honorable reputation was of great value to him, especially when compared to Saul's bloody record. She apparently realized that if David stained his hands with innocent blood, he would lose God's blessing as well as the love and respect of the people of Israel. David's rage had blinded him to his own interests, but Abigail's brilliant appeal brought him to his senses:

David said to Abigail, "Praise be to the LORD, the God of Israel, who has sent you today to meet me. May you be blessed for your good judgment and for keeping me from bloodshed this day and from avenging myself with my own hands. Otherwise, as surely as the LORD, the God of Israel, lives, who has kept me from harming you, if you had not come quickly to meet me, not one male belonging to Nabal would have been left alive by daybreak. . . . Go home in peace. I have heard your words and granted your request" (vv. 32–35).

This dramatic incident shows that "wisdom is better than strength" (Eccles. 9:16). It also illustrates one of the most important principles of cooperative negotiation: The more fully you understand your opponent's interests, the more persuasive and effective you can be in negotiating an agreement.

Before you attempt to understand the interests of other people, it is wise to make a written list of your own interests. Remembering the three opportunities provided by conflict, you might begin by listing interests related to glorifying God, serving others, and growing to be like Christ. This part of your list is primarily for your own benefit, and it may not be appropriate to reveal these interests to your opponent, especially at the outset of negotiations.

You should also note any personal concerns, desires, needs, or limitations that are not included in one of the categories described above. Your list should include everything that is of value to you or that might be motivating you in this particular situation. Once this list is fairly complete, it often helps to note which interests have the greatest priority. This will help you make wise decisions if you later have to choose between several interests.

You should then try to discern your opponent's interests. Before you meet together, you may analyze information you already have or do some discreet research to develop a list of possible interests. When you are actually talking with your opponent, you should carefully note anything he says and does that reveals hidden interests. Asking "Why?" and "Why not?" and "How?" at appropriate times can provide additional insights.

It is often helpful to get each side's interests out in the open. One way to do this is to take out a sheet of paper and write down all the interests that have already come to the surface. Explain to your opponent what you are doing, and read the items you are listing. Then ask what other concerns, goals, or interests your opponent has. As much as possible, acknowledge them as being reasonable and significant. Ask questions to clarify your understanding. Set a positive tone by drawing attention to similar interests and areas of agreement.

Once you understand each other's interests, it is often helpful to redefine and set priorities for the issues you will need to resolve to reach an agreement. Place the easiest issues at the beginning of your list. If you work on those first, you should see some positive results fairly quickly. This tends to encourage further cooperation and builds momentum as you move on to the more difficult issues.

The Barking Dog. By the time they sat down to talk with the Smiths, Jim and Julie had developed a more thorough list of the interests they thought were involved in this situation. It included the following items:

I. Personal interests that are confidential for now
   A. Glorify God
      1. Trust and obey him.
      2. Overlook minor offenses.
      3. Do all we can to live at peace.
      4. Do what is just and right.
      5. Exercise compassion and mercy.
      6. Speak the truth in love.
   B. Serve others
      1. Teach our children by example what it means to be a Christian.
      2. Do good to the Smiths; try to help them in concrete ways.
      3. Demonstrate and, if possible, describe the difference Jesus has made in our lives, in the hope that the Smiths may be encouraged to follow him (if they are not already Christians).
      4. Help the Smiths see where they may need to change, and give them all the encouragement and help we can.

216

  C. Grow to be like Christ

   1. See our weaknesses more clearly so that we will learn to depend on God more consciously and consistently.

   2. See our sins and idols more clearly so that with God's help we can repent and change.

   3. Practice the character traits we see in our Lord, such as love, joy, peace, patience, kindness, goodness, faithfulness, gentleness, self-control, discernment, wisdom, and perseverance.

 II. Personal interests we should reveal

  A. A desire for peace and quiet (which is the reason we moved to the country)

  B. Sufficient rest for us and for our children

  C. Having a comfortable relationship with the Smiths and with other neighbors

  D. Having our children get along so they can have good playmates nearby

 III. Interests the Smiths may have that we should be sensitive to but should not mention

  A. Tension within their marriage or family that makes them more irritable or less thoughtful toward others

  B. Not enough money to pursue expensive solutions (e.g., building a new kennel)

  C. A resentment toward "being told what to do"

 IV. Interests the Smiths may have that may be mentioned when it seems appropriate

  A. Affection for dogs

  B. A need for additional income

  C. Having a comfortable relationship with their neighbors

  D. Having their children get along with our children.

Shortly after they sat down with the Smiths, Jim and Julie suggested that they write down some of their interests. After the Johnsons explained what an interest is and how this step would help to understand them, Steve and Sally agreed to cooperate in compiling a list. Jim and Julie explained a few of their own interests and then allowed the Smiths to explain some of theirs. This was obviously an unfamiliar process for the Smiths, but they became increasingly open. As the Smiths talked, Jim and Julie learned that their preliminary appraisal of the Smith's interests was fairly accurate, but it was not complete. They learned that the Smiths had these additional interests:

Steve and Sally both came from families that loved dogs and invested a lot of time and energy in them; Molly was descended from one of Sally's father's favorite dogs.

Steve didn't feel very successful in his occupation as an accountant, but he derived a great deal of satisfaction and a sense of accomplishment from his success as a breeder and trainer.

One of the main reasons Steve and Sally valued their dogs so highly was that showing them provided an opportunity for their entire family to work and travel together; furthermore, by having their children take care of the dogs, they were teaching them to be responsible.

When they left town for dog shows or family trips, Steve and Sally worried about their dogs because they had not found anyone they really trusted to take proper care of them.

Their house had been burglarized several years ago, and Sally was fearful of its happening again. Therefore, having a dog that barked at disturbances was very reassuring to her.

As Jim and Julie considered these additional interests, they realized that the Smiths would undoubtedly refuse to get rid of Molly. Solving this problem was going to take some careful thinking.

Search for Creative Solutions

The fourth step in the PAUSE strategy is to search for solutions that will satisfy as many interests as possible. This process should begin with spontaneous inventing. Everyone should be encouraged to mention *any* idea that comes to mind. Imagination and creativity should be encouraged, while evaluating and deciding should be postponed. As you are searching for possible solutions, avoid the assumption that there is only one answer to your problem. The best solution may involve a combination of several options, so feel free to use parts of several ideas to form a variety of choices.

During this stage, make a conscious effort to "expand the pie." Try to bring in additional interests that could be satisfied as part of your agreement. For example, if the primary issue being negotiated is whether your neighbor will replace his broken fence, you might offer to help him remove some diseased trees that threaten to fall on your garage. By focusing on shared interests and developing options that provide mutual gains, you can create incentives for agreement on the more difficult points of contention.

As you begin to identify possible solutions that seem wise to you, you should make an effort to "sell" these options to your opponent. In other words, explain how these solutions would benefit your opponent.

The Barking Dog. After discussing their interests, the Johnsons and the Smiths began to search for some creative solutions to their problem. Here were some of the ideas they came up with:

Teach Molly not to bark at night by using a remote-controlled shock collar.

The Johnsons and their children could get ear plugs, or they could purchase a "white sound" box (a device that makes noise that tends to mask other noise).

Put a fence or row of trees between the houses to muffle the noise.

Exercise the dogs a little later in the morning.

The Johnsons could change their sleep schedule so that they were not in bed when Molly normally barked.

Get an electronic burglar alarm for the Smiths' home.

Move the Johnson children's bedrooms to the far side of the house where they wouldn't hear the barking so much.

Partway through their discussion, Sally suggested that they think for a moment about the times that Molly barked the most. As they compared records, they discovered that most of the nighttime barking occurred when the Smiths were out of town for several days and Molly had not been out of her kennel for any exercise. (The person who took care of the dogs in the Smiths' absence merely came by to give them food and fresh water.) Realizing that Molly was simply getting tired of being confined, Julie offered to have her oldest daughter, Karen, feed and water Molly and take her for a walk each day when the Smiths were gone. Sally knew Karen to be responsible and conscientious, so she was open to the idea and even said that they could pay Karen. However, Steve doubted that Karen could handle the dogs, so he was not willing to agree to this proposal.

Trying to change the focus of the conversation, Sally noted that Molly sometimes barked even when they were at home. Jim then asked, "What do you think Molly is barking at anyway?" Several possibilities came to mind. The one that seemed most likely was that she was barking at people walking along a nearby highway. Jim asked whether Steve would be willing to move the kennel to the other side of his house where Molly couldn't see the highway. Steve rejected the idea because he didn't have time to do the work, and it would be too expensive to hire someone to do it. "Besides," he said, "I'm not convinced that she's barking at people along the road, so moving the kennel may be a total waste of time. Furthermore, there's no shade on that side of the house in afternoon, and I don't want my dogs getting baked by the sun."

After discussing a few more possibilities, Jim sensed that Steve's patience was wearing thin, so he suggested that they take a few days to think about the situation and talk again on Wednesday evening. The Smiths agreed. As they left, Jim and Julie were careful to express their appreciation for the Smiths' willingness to meet with them.

Evaluate Options Objectively and Reasonably

The final step in the PAUSE strategy is to evaluate possible solutions objectively and reasonably so you can reach the best possible agreement. Even if the previous steps have gone well, you may encounter significant differences of opinion when you get to this stage. If you allow negotiations to degenerate into a battle of wills, your previous work will have been wasted. Therefore, instead of relying on personal opinions, insist on using objective criteria to evaluate the options before you. If you are dealing with Christians, refer to relevant biblical principles. Whenever possible, introduce appropriate facts, official rules and regulations, or professional reports. In addition, you may seek advice from experts or respected advisors.

The Book of Daniel contains an outstanding example of an objective evaluation. When Nebuchadnezzar attacked Jerusalem in 605 B.C., he captured many Israelites from the royal family and the nobility. He instructed the chief of his court officials to bring in "young men without physical defect, handsome, showing aptitude for every kind of learning, well informed, quick to understand, and qualified to serve in the king's palace" (Dan. 1:4). Among these were Daniel, Hananiah, Mishael, and Azariah.

When Daniel learned that he and his companions would be provided with food and wine that was ceremonially unclean, he asked the chief official for permission to eat different food (Dan. 1:8). Although the official was sympathetic, he refused Daniel's request, saying, "I am afraid of my lord the king. . . . Why should he see you looking worse than the other young men your age? The king would then have my head because of you" (v. 10). This left Daniel with some interesting choices. He could eat the food and defile himself, or he could refuse to eat and either starve to death or be killed for disobedience. Instead, he chose to PAUSE.

> Daniel then said to the guard whom the chief official had appointed over Daniel, Hananiah, Mishael and Azariah, "Please test your servants for ten days: Give us nothing but vegetables to eat and water to drink. Then compare our appearance with that of the young men who eat the royal food, and treat your servants in accordance with what you see." So he agreed to this and tested them for ten days.
>
> At the end of the ten days they looked healthier and better nourished than any of the young men who ate the royal food. So the guard took away their choice food and the wine they were to drink and gave them vegetables instead (Dan. 1:11–16).

As you can see, Daniel carefully prepared his negotiation strategy. He affirmed his respect for those who were in authority over him. By God's grace, he understood the interests of the people with whom he was dealing. The king wanted healthy and productive workers. The chief official wanted to keep his head. Instead of focusing exclusively on his own interests, Daniel searched for a solution that would meet their interests as well as his own. Then, rather than offering his personal opinions, he suggested a way that the guard could evaluate his proposal objectively. When the test results showed that Daniel's proposed solution was valid and reasonable, a permanent agreement was quickly reached.

In addition to using objective criteria, you should make every effort to negotiate in a reasonable manner. Listen carefully to your opponent's concerns and suggestions, showing respect for his or her values and interests. Try to discern the hidden reasons behind objections and positions. Continue to put yourself in the other person's shoes and try to see things from that perspective. In your responses, build on the other person's ideas and words. Invite specific criticism, alternatives, and advice. Whenever your opponent tries to put pressure on you, move the discussion back to objective principles. Throughout your discussions, treat the other person as you would like to be treated.

If your evaluations result in an agreement, it is often wise to put it in writing. This will help to prevent misunderstandings and subsequent disputes on the details. At the very least, your agreement should cover these items:

What issues were resolved
What actions will be taken
Who is responsible for each action
Dates by which each action should be completed
When and how the results of the agreement will be reviewed

If you are unable to reach an agreement, don't give up too quickly. It may be that you need to return to one of the earlier steps to identify overlooked interests or to invent new options. On the other hand, it may be wise to summarize what you have accomplished and what remains to be done, and then take a few hours or days to think about the matter. If you believe that further private negotiations will be ineffective, you may suggest that the unresolved issues be resolved with the assistance of one or more objective advisors (see chapter 9).

The Barking Dog. When Jim and Julie got home that night, they made sure their windows were open so they could hear Molly the moment she began to bark. Sure enough, an hour later she was going at it. Jim ran outside and saw that two people on bicycles had just ridden by. He kept a journal for the next two evenings and noted three other barking episodes that coincided with people walking or riding by on the highway. He and Julie also prayed and talked some more about possible solutions. As a result, when they met with the Smiths on Wednesday night, they were prepared to offer some objective information and some creative proposals.

First they showed Steve their journal, indicating the relationship between Molly's barking and people passing by on the highway. Steve acknowledged that Molly was probably barking at those people, but he repeated his concerns about the lack of shade and his lack of time to move the kennel. Jim countered by saying, "I've been looking for a way to give my son some experience in construction work. How about if he and I come over next Saturday and help you dismantle and move your kennel? I'll bet it would only take us three or four hours. As far as needing shade, my father-in-law has got dozens of young trees on his land north of town. We could take your pickup truck out there and bring back all the trees you'd need to put in a great shelter belt around the kennel. Dad gets his land cleared, my son learns about carpentry and transplanting trees, and you have a new kennel."

Jim's proposal was so reasonable that Steve couldn't find a way to say no. That's when Julie added her suggestion: "I have an idea about the problem of your going out of town. I talked with Karen, and she said she'd be delighted to take care of your dogs. I can understand your reluctance to trust them to a stranger, so why not have her come over to your house every day for the next week to help you work your dogs? If she proves she can handle them, then maybe you'll feel more comfortable trusting her with them. If not, we can look for another solution. Also, I should tell you that if you let her care for them, she would prefer not to be paid in cash. What she would really like is a puppy out of one of Molly's litters next year."

Once the conversation turned to puppies, Steve's heart really softened. The more he thought about the suggestions Jim and Julie were making, the more he liked them. It took a while to work out all of the details, but later conversations became even easier as the two families learned to cooperate more and more.

Summary and Application

Negotiation does not have to be a painful tug-of-war. If approached properly, many people will respond favorably to cooperative negotiation, which can allow you to find mutually beneficial solutions to common problems. Sometimes all it takes is a willingness to "look not only to your own interests, but also to the interests of others."[2]

If you are presently involved in a conflict, these questions will help you to apply the principles presented in this chapter.

1. Which style of negotiation is most appropriate in this situation: competitive or cooperative? Why?
2. How can you prepare to negotiate a reasonable agreement in this situation?
3. How can you affirm your concern and respect for your opponent?
4. Understand interests by answering these questions:
   (a) Which material issues need to be resolved in order to settle this conflict? What positions have you and your opponent already taken on these issues?
   (b) What are your interests in this situation?
   (c) What are your opponent's interests in this situation?

5. What are some creative solutions or options that would sat-isfy as many interests as possible?
6. What are some ways that these options can be evaluated objectively and reasonably?
7. Go on record with the Lord by writing a prayer based on the principles taught in this chapter.

12

Overcome Evil with Good

Do not be overcome by evil, but overcome evil with good.

Romans 12:21

Most people will respond favorably to the peacemaking principles set forth in Scripture. At times, however, you may encounter someone who simply refuses to be reconciled with you. As a result of bitterness, pride, mistrust, or greed, some people will persistently ignore repentance, reject confrontation, and resist cooperative negotiation. Sometimes a person will even continue to deliberately mistreat you. The natural reaction to such conduct is to strike back, or at least to stop doing anything good to that person. As we have seen throughout this book, however, Jesus commands us to take a remarkably different course of action when we encounter such treatment: "But I tell you who hear me: Love your enemies, do good to those who hate you, bless those who curse you, pray for those who mistreat you. . . . Then your reward will be great, and you will be sons of the Most High, because he is kind to the ungrateful and wicked. Be merciful, just as your Father is merciful" (Luke 6:27–28, 35–36).

From a worldly perspective, this approach seems naive and appears to concede defeat, but the apostle Paul knew better. He had learned that God's ways are not the world's ways. He also understood the profound power of God's principles. When he was subjected to intense and repeated personal attacks, he described his response with these words: "For though we live in the world, we do not wage war as the world does. The weapons we fight with are not the weapons of the world. On the contrary, they have divine power to demolish strongholds. We demolish arguments and every pretension that sets itself up against the knowledge of God, and we take captive every thought to make it obedient to Christ" (2 Cor. 10:3–5).

The divine weapons to which Paul was referring are described throughout his letters. They include: Scripture, prayer, truth, righteousness, the gospel, faith, love, joy, peace, patience, kindness, goodness, faithfulness, gentleness, and self-control (Eph. 6:10–18; Gal. 5:22–23). To many people these resources and qualities seem to be feeble and useless when dealing with "real" problems. Yet, these are the very weapons that Jesus used to defeat Satan and to conquer the world (e.g., Matt. 4:1–11; 11:28–30; John 14:15–17). Since Jesus chose to use these weapons instead of resorting to worldly weapons, we should do the same.

Romans 12:14–21 describes how we should behave as we wield these spiritual weapons, especially when dealing with people who oppose or mistreat us:

> Bless those who persecute you; bless and do not curse. Rejoice with those who rejoice; mourn with those who mourn. Live in harmony with one another. Do not be proud, but be willing to associate with people of low position. Do not be conceited.
>
> Do not repay anyone evil for evil. Be careful to do what is right in the eyes of everybody. If it is possible, as far as it depends on you, live at peace with everyone. Do not take revenge, my friends, but leave room for God's wrath, for it is written: "It is mine to avenge; I will repay," says the Lord. On the contrary: "If your enemy is hungry, feed him; if he is thirsty, give him something to drink.

In doing this, you will heap burning coals on his head." Do not be overcome by evil, but overcome evil with good.

This passage of Scripture shows that Paul understood the classic military principle that the best defense is an effective offense. He did not encourage a passive response to evil. Instead, he taught that we should go on the offensive—not to beat down or destroy our opponents, but to win them over, to help them see the truth, and to bring them into a right relationship with God. As this passage indicates, there are five basic principles that contribute to a victorious offensive. We have already referred to most of these principles in previous chapters, but it is encouraging to see how relevant they are, even in the most difficult conflicts.[1]

Control Your Tongue

The more intense a dispute becomes, the more important it is to control your tongue (Rom. 12:14). When you are involved in prolonged conflict, you may be sorely tempted to indulge in gossip, slander, and reckless words, especially if your opponent is saying critical things about you. But if you react with harsh words or gossip, you will only make matters worse. Even if your opponent speaks maliciously against you or to you, do not respond in kind. Instead, make every effort to say only what is true and helpful, speaking well of your opponent whenever possible and using kind and gracious language. As Peter wrote, "Do not repay evil with evil or insult with insult, but with blessing, because to this you were called so that you may inherit a blessing" (1 Peter 3:9; cf. 1 Cor. 4:12–13).

In addition to preventing further offenses, controlling your tongue can help you to maintain a loving attitude and an accurate perspective of your situation (see chapters 4, 5, and 8). As a result, you are likely to think and behave more wisely and constructively than you would if you indulged in all kinds of critical talk. Instead of undermining further progress, you will be prepared to take advantage of new opportunities for dialogue and negotiation.

Seek Godly Advisors

As Paul says, it is difficult to battle evil alone (Rom. 12:15–16). This is why it is important to develop relationships with people who will encourage you and give you biblically sound advice. These friends should also be willing to correct and admonish you when they see that you are in the wrong (Prov. 27:5–6).

Godly advisors are especially helpful when you are involved in a difficult conflict and are not seeing the results you desire. If a lack of noticeable progress causes you to doubt the biblical principles you are following, you may be tempted to abandon God's ways and to resort to the world's tactics. One of the best ways to avoid straying from the Lord is to surround yourself with wise and spiritually mature people who will encourage you to stay on a biblical course, even when the going is tough.

Keep Doing What Is Right

Romans 12:17 emphasizes the importance of continuing to do what is right even when it seems that your opponent will never cooperate. When Paul says, "Be careful to do what is right in the eyes of everybody," he does not mean that we should be slaves to the opinions of others. The Greek word that is translated "be careful" *(pronoeo)* means to give thought to the future, to plan in advance, or to take careful precaution (cf. 2 Cor. 8:20–21). Therefore, what Paul is saying is that you should plan and act so carefully and so properly that everyone who is watching—including your opponents—will eventually have to admit that what you did was right. Peter taught the same principle when he wrote:

> Live such good lives among the pagans that, though they accuse you of doing wrong, they may see your good deeds and glorify God on the day he visits us. . . . For it is God's will that by doing good you should silence the ignorant talk of foolish men. . . . But do this with gentleness and respect, keeping a clear conscience, so that those who speak maliciously against your good behavior in Christ may be ashamed of their slander (1 Peter 2:12, 15; 3:15b–16).

This principle is dramatically illustrated in 1 Samuel 24:1–22. When King Saul was pursuing David through the desert, intending to murder him, he carelessly entered a cave where David was hiding with his men. David's men urged him to kill Saul, but David refused, saying, ". . . I will not lift my hand against my master, because he is the LORD's anointed" (v. 10b). After Saul left the cave and walked away, David emerged and called after him. When Saul realized that David could have killed him, he was deeply convicted of his sin and said:

> "You are more righteous than I. . . . You have treated me well, but I have treated you badly. You have just now told me of the good you did to me; the LORD delivered me into your hands, but you did not kill me. When a man finds his enemy, does he let him get away unharmed? May the LORD reward you well for the way you treated me today. I know that you will surely be king and that the kingdom of Israel will be established in your hands" (vv. 17–20).

Years later, Saul's prediction came true, and David ascended the throne of Israel. David's determination to obey God and to keep doing what was right helped him to avoid saying and doing things he would have later regretted. As a result, all of his enemies were eventually won over or defeated. Thousands of years later people are still taking note of David's righteousness.

Recognize Your Limits

When dealing with difficult people, it is also important to recognize your limits. Even when you continue to do what is right, some people may adamantly refuse to admit you are right or to live at peace with you. This is why Paul wrote, "If it is possible, as far as it depends on you, live at peace with everyone" (Rom. 12:18). In other words, do all you can to be reconciled to others, but remember that you cannot force others to do what is right. Once you have done everything within your power to resolve a conflict, you have fulfilled your responsibility to God. If circumstances change and you have new opportunities to seek peace with an opponent, you should certainly try to do so. In the meantime, you should not waste time, energy, and resources fretting about someone who stubbornly refuses to be reconciled.

It is easier to accept your limits if you have a biblical view of success. The world defines success in terms of what a person possesses, controls, or accomplishes. God defines success in terms of faithful obedience to his will. The world asks, "What results have you achieved?" God asks, "Were you faithful to my ways?" As we saw in chapter 3, the Lord controls the ultimate outcome of all you do. Therefore, he knows that no matter how hard you try, you cannot always accomplish the results you desire. This is why he does not hold you accountable for specific results. Instead, he asks for only one thing—obedience to his revealed will. "Fear God and keep his commandments, for this is the whole duty of man" (Eccles. 12:13b). If you have done all that you can to be reconciled to someone, you have fulfilled your duty and are a success in God's eyes. Let him take it from there.

One aspect of recognizing your limits is rejecting the temptation to take personal revenge on someone who is doing wrong. Paul reminds us that God is responsible for doing justice and for punishing those who do not repent (Rom. 12:19). Proverbs 20:22 commands, "Do not say, 'I'll pay you back for this wrong!' Wait for the LORD, and he will deliver you" (cf. 24:29). God has many instruments that he can use to deliver you from evil people and to bring them to justice. Among other things, he can use the church (Matt. 18:17–20), the civil courts (Rom. 13:1–5), or even Satan (1 Cor. 5:5; 1 Tim. 1:20) to deal with unrepentant people.

Instead of taking justice into your own hands, respect and cooperate with God's methods for dealing with people who persist in doing wrong. Sometimes this may involve church discipline, and in other cases it may be appropriate for you to pursue litigation (see chapter 9 and Appendix D). In some cases, however, all you may be able to do is to wait for God to deal with people in his own way (see Pss. 37 and 73). Although his results may come more slowly than you desire, they will always be better than anything you could bring about on your own.

Use the Ultimate Weapon

The final principle for responding to a stubborn opponent is described in Romans 12:20–21: "On the contrary: 'If your enemy is hungry, feed him; if he is thirsty, give him something to drink. In doing so you will heap burning coals on his head.' Do not be overcome by evil, but overcome evil with good." Here is the ultimate weapon: deliberate, focused love (cf. Luke 6:27–28; 1 Cor. 13:4–7). Instead of reacting spitefully to those who mistreat you, you are commanded to discern their deepest needs and to do all you can to meet those needs. Sometimes this will call for loving confrontation. At other times there may be a need for mercy and compassion, patience, and words of encouragement. You may even have opportunities to provide material and financial assistance to those who least deserve or expect it from you.

Paul's reference to "burning coals on his head" indicates the enormous power of deliberate, focused love. One of the most powerful weapons of his day was called "greek fire," which was a mixture of pitch, sulphur, and burning charcoal. No soldier could resist this weapon for long; it would eventually overcome even the most determined attacker. Love has the same irresistible power. At the very least, actively loving an enemy will protect you from being spiritually defeated by anger, bitterness, and a thirst for revenge. And, in some cases, your active and determined love for your opponent may be used by God to bring that person to repentance.

This power was vividly demonstrated during World War II by a Catholic priest named Hugh O'Flaherty, who served in the Vatican during the war. As he learned of Nazi atrocities, he became actively involved in efforts to protect the Jews and to hide Allied pilots who had been shot down over Italy. Colonel Kappler, the German SS commander in Rome, eventually learned of O'Flaherty's activities and set out to kill him. Several assassination attempts failed, but Kappler finally succeeded in capturing several of O'Flaherty's associates. Kappler himself ordered the torture and execution of these prisoners, one of whom was O'Flaherty's closest friend.

When the Allied armies invaded Italy and surrounded Rome in 1944, Colonel Kappler was captured. He was sentenced to life imprisonment for his war crimes. In spite of all the wrongs Kappler had committed, O'Flaherty resisted the temptation to delight in his enemy's downfall. Instead, remembering Jesus' teaching and example, O'Flaherty resolved to love his enemy not only with words, but also with actions. Every month, he drove to Gaeta Prison to see the man who had tried so hard to kill him. Year after year he learned about Kappler's needs and did all he could to meet them. Above all else, he demonstrated to Kappler the love, mercy, and forgiveness of God. In March of 1959, after almost 180 visits from the priest, Kappler finally confessed his sins and prayed with the priest to accept Christ as his Savior. He who had tried so hard to overcome others with evil was overwhelmed by the "burning coals" of love that O'Flaherty had poured on his head.[2]

Summary and Application

The principles described in Romans 12:14–21 are applicable at every stage of a conflict, and they are echoed throughout the Bible—Love your neighbor as yourself. . . . Do to others what you would have them do to you. . . . Overlook an offense. . . . If someone is caught in a sin, restore him gently. . . . Speak the truth in love. . . . Look out for the interests of others. . . . Forgive as the Lord forgave you. . . . Do not be overcome by evil, but overcome evil with good. Applying these principles can be difficult, but it is always worth the effort, because God works in and through us as we serve him as peacemakers. Paul promises: "Therefore, my dear brothers, stand firm. Let nothing move you. Always give yourselves fully to the work of the Lord, because you know that your labor in the Lord is not in vain" (1 Cor. 15:58).

As Jesus demonstrated, the peacemaking principles set forth in Scripture provide the most effective and powerful means we could ever find to resolve conflict and restore broken relationships. He also demonstrated that peacemaking is not a passive process. Just as our Lord came to earth to purchase peace for us, we must actively and fervently pursue peace with those who oppose and mistreat us. Jesus said, "Leave your gift there in front of the altar. First go and be reconciled to your brother; then come and offer your gift" (Matt. 5:24). From this command, we can draw a simple and yet profound definition: *A peacemaker is a person who goes.*

If you are presently involved in a conflict, these questions will help you to apply the principles presented in this chapter.

1. Which worldly weapons have you been using, or are you tempted to use, in this situation?
2. Have you been using your tongue to bless your opponents— or to speak critically of them? What will you do differently in the future in this regard?
3. To whom can you turn for godly advice and encouragement?
4. What can you keep on doing in this situation that is right?
5. Have you done everything in your power to live at peace with your opponent? Is it appropriate to turn to church or civil authorities to seek assistance in resolving this dispute?
6. What needs does your opponent have that God may want you to try to meet? In other words, how can you love your opponent in a deliberate and focused way?
7. Go on record with the Lord by writing a prayer based on the principles taught in this chapter.

Conclusion

The Peacemaker's Pledge

As you have learned, peacemaking may require many steps and involve a wide variety of biblical principles. While this may result in a fairly complicated process in some cases, the essential elements of peacemaking may be summarized in four basic principles drawn directly from Scripture. Since every Christian should be committed to following these principles, it seems appropriate to think of them as "The Peacemaker's Pledge."

The Peacemaker's Pledge

As people reconciled to God by the death and resurrection of Jesus Christ, we believe that we are called to respond to conflict in a way that is remarkably different from the way the world deals with conflict (Matt. 5:9; Luke 6:27–36; Gal. 5:19–26). We also believe that conflict provides opportunities to glorify God, serve other people, and grow to be like Christ (Rom. 8:28–29; 1 Cor. 10:31–11:1; James 1:2–4). Therefore, in response to God's love

235

and in reliance on his grace, we commit ourselves to respond to conflict according to the following principles.

Glorify God

Instead of focusing on our own desires or dwelling on what others may do, we will seek to please and honor God—by depending on his wisdom, power, and love; by faithfully obeying his commands; and by seeking to maintain a loving, merciful, and forgiving attitude (Ps. 37:1–6; Mark 11:25; John 14:15; Rom. 12:17–21; 1 Cor. 10:31; Phil. 4:2–9; Col. 3:1–4; James 3:17–18; 4:1–3; 1 Peter 2:12).

Get the Log out of Your Own Eye

Instead of attacking others or dwelling on their wrongs, we will take responsibility for our own contribution to conflicts—confessing our sins, asking God to help us change any attitudes and habits that lead to conflict, and seeking to repair any harm we have caused (Prov. 28:13; Matt. 7:3–5; Luke 19:8; Col. 3:5–14; 1 John 1:8–9).

Go and Show Your Brother His Fault

Instead of pretending that conflict doesn't exist or talking about others behind their backs, we will choose to overlook minor offenses or we will talk directly and graciously with those whose offenses seem too serious to overlook. When a conflict with another Christian cannot be resolved in private, we will ask others in the body of Christ to help us settle the matter in a biblical manner (Prov. 19:11; Matt. 18:15–20; 1 Cor. 6:1–8; Gal. 6:1–2; Eph. 4:29; 2 Tim. 2:24–26; James 5:9).

Go and Be Reconciled

Instead of accepting premature compromise or allowing relationships to wither, we will actively pursue genuine peace and reconciliation—forgiving others as God, for Christ's sake, has forgiven us, and seeking just and mutually beneficial solutions to our differences (Matt. 5:23–24; 6:12; 7:12; Eph. 4:1–3, 32; Phil. 2:3–4).

By God's grace, we will apply these principles as a matter of stewardship, realizing that conflict is an assignment, not an accident. We will remember that success, in God's eyes, is not a matter of specific results but of faithful, dependent obedience. And we will pray that our service as peacemakers brings praise to our Lord and leads others to know His infinite love (Matt. 25:14–21; John 13:34–35; Rom. 12:18; 1 Peter 2:19; 4:19).

I hope and pray that you will use this pledge in three ways. First, use it as a personal commitment and guide for resolving the conflicts God allows in your life. In doing so, you will bring glory to God, serve other people, and grow to be like Christ.

Second, use it as a teaching tool to help others understand and follow the powerful peacemaking principles God has given to us in Scripture. As people learn from you, they too can model and teach these principles, eventually impacting a multitude of people.

Finally, use the pledge as a standard for conflict resolution in your church, ministry, or business. As more and more groups of Christians adopt this pledge, the church as a whole will be able to deal with conflict in a more biblically consistent manner. Such a trend would help to reestablish the church as the effective peacemaking body God intended it to be. Surely this would bring honor to our Lord Jesus Christ, the greatest peacemaker of all.[1]

Appendix A

A Peacemaker's Checklist

Whenever you are involved in a conflict, you may apply the four basic principles of peacemaking by asking yourself these questions:

Glorify God

How can I please and honor the Lord in this situation?

Get the log out of your eye

How have I contributed to this conflict and what do I need to do?

Go and show your brother his fault

How can I help others to understand how they have contributed to this conflict?

Go and be reconciled

How can I demonstrate forgiveness and encourage a reasonable solution to this conflict?

The following checklist summarizing the principles presented in this book is designed to help you answer these four questions.

Glorify God

With God's help, I will seek to glorify him by:

☐ Striving earnestly, diligently, and continually to live at peace with those around me.

☐ Remembering that Jesus' reputation is affected by the way I get along with others.

☐ Guarding against Satan's schemes and false teachings, which are designed to promote selfishness and incite conflict.

☐ Trusting that God is in control and working for my good and the good of others, even when I must undergo suffering.

☐ Giving God praise and thanks for his goodness and his help.

☐ Obeying God's commands, even when doing so is difficult and requires sacrifice.

☐ Using conflict as an opportunity to serve others by: helping them to find godly solutions to their problems; helping to bear their emotional, spiritual, or material burdens; helping them to see where they have been wrong and need to change; encouraging them to put their faith in the Lord Jesus Christ; and teaching and encouraging them by my example.

☐ Cooperating with God as he prunes me of sinful attitudes and habits, and helps me to grow to be more like Christ.

☐ Seeing myself as a steward and managing myself, my resources, and my situation in such a way that God would say, "Well done, good and faithful servant!"

Get the Log out of Your Eye

To decide whether something is really worth fighting over, with God's help I will:

☐ Define the issues (personal and material), decide how they are related, and deal only with issues that are too important to be overlooked, beginning usually with personal issues.

☐ Overlook minor offenses.

☐ Change my attitude by: recalling how much God has for-given me; being gentle toward others; replacing anxiety with prayer and trust; deliberately thinking about what is good and right in others; putting into practice what God has taught me through the Bible.

☐ Carefully consider how much it will cost (emotionally, spiritually, and financially) to continue a conflict instead of simply settling it.

☐ Use my rights only to advance God's kingdom, to serve oth-ers, and to enhance my ability to serve and grow to be like Christ.

Before talking to others about their wrongs, with God's help I will ask myself:

☐ Am I guilty of reckless words, falsehood, gossip, slander, or any other worthless talk?

☐ Have I kept my word and fulfilled all of my responsibilities?

☐ Have I abused my authority?

☐ Have I respected those in authority over me?

☐ Have I treated others as I would want to be treated?

☐ Am I being motivated by: lusts of the flesh, pride, love of money, fear of others, or wanting good things too much?

When I see that I have sinned, with God's help I will:

☐ Repent—that is, change the way I have been thinking so that I turn away from my sin and turn toward God.

☐ Confess my sins by using the Seven A's, namely: addressing everyone I have affected; avoiding *if, but,* and *maybe*; admit-ting specifically what I did wrong; apologizing for hurting others; accepting the consequences of my actions; explain-ing how I will alter my attitudes and behavior in the future; and asking for forgiveness.

☐ Change my attitudes and behavior by: praying for God's help; focusing on the Lord so that I can overcome my personal idols;

studying the Bible; and practicing godly character qualities in a manner that is both planned and spontaneous.

Go and Show Your Brother His Fault

☐ When I learn that someone has something against me, I will go to that person to talk about it, even if I don't believe I have done anything wrong.

A sin is too serious to overlook if it:

☐ Is dishonoring God.
☐ Has damaged our relationship.
☐ Is hurting or might hurt other people.
☐ Is hurting the offender and diminishing that person's usefulness to God.

When I need to confront others, with God's help I will:

☐ Listen responsibly by waiting patiently while others speak, concentrating on what they say, clarifying their comments through appropriate questions, reflecting their feelings and concerns with paraphrased responses, and agreeing with them whenever possible.
☐ Choose a time and place that will be conducive to a productive conversation.
☐ Believe the best about others until I have facts to prove otherwise.
☐ Talk in person whenever possible.
☐ Plan my words in advance and try to anticipate how others will respond to me.
☐ Use "I" statements when appropriate.
☐ State objective facts rather than personal opinions.
☐ Use the Bible carefully and tactfully.
☐ Ask for feedback.

☐ Offer solutions and preferences.

☐ Recognize my limits and stop talking once I have said what is reasonable and appropriate.

If I cannot resolve a dispute with someone in private, and if the matter is too serious to overlook, with God's help I will:

☐ Suggest that we seek help from one or more spiritually mature advisors who can help both of us see things more objectively.

☐ If necessary, ask one or two others to talk with us.

☐ If necessary, seek help from our respective churches and respect their authority.

☐ Go to court only if I have exhausted my church remedies; if the rights I am seeking to enforce are biblically legitimate; and if my action has a righteous purpose.

Go and Be Reconciled

When I forgive someone, with God's help I will make these promises:

☐ I will no longer dwell on this incident.

☐ I will not bring up this incident again and use it against you.

☐ I will not talk to others about this incident.

☐ I will not allow this incident to stand between us or to hinder our personal relationship.

When I am having a difficult time forgiving someone, with God's help I will:

☐ If necessary, talk with that person to address any unresolved issues and to confirm repentance.

☐ Renounce the desire to punish the other person, to make that person earn my forgiveness, or to demand guarantees that I will never be wronged again.

☐ Assess my contributions to the problem.

☐ Recognize the ways that God is using the situation for good.

☐ Remember how much God has forgiven me, not only in this situation but also in the past.

☐ Draw on God's strength through prayer, Bible study, and, if necessary, Christian counseling.

With God's help I will demonstrate forgiveness and practice the replacement principle by:

☐ Replacing painful thoughts and memories with positive thoughts and memories.

☐ Saying positive things to and about the person whom I have forgiven.

☐ Doing loving and constructive things to and for the person whom I have forgiven.

When I need to negotiate an agreement on material issues, with God's help I will PAUSE:

☐ Prepare thoroughly for our discussions.

☐ Affirm my respect and concern for my opponent.

☐ Understand my opponent's interests as well as my own.

☐ Search for creative solutions that will satisfy as many of our interests as possible.

☐ Evaluate various options objectively and reasonably.

When others continue to mistreat or oppose me, with God's help I will:

☐ Control my tongue and continue to say only what is helpful and beneficial to others.

☐ Seek counsel, support, and encouragement from spiritually mature advisors.

☐ Keep doing what is right no matter what others do to me.

☐ Recognize my limits by resisting the temptation to take revenge and by remembering that being successful in God's eyes depends on *faithfulness*, not results.

☐ Continue to love my enemy by striving to discern and meet his or her deepest spiritual, emotional, and material needs.

Appendix B

Alternative Ways to Resolve Disputes

Since the early '80s, a great deal of attention has been devoted to developing alternative ways to settle conflicts. In this appendix, I will describe and compare several of the more common dispute resolution processes, including negotiation, mediation, arbitration, litigation, and Christian conciliation.

Negotiation

Negotiation is a personal bargaining process in which parties seek to reach a mutually agreeable settlement of their differences. Although some people are able to negotiate for themselves, many rely on attorneys or other professionals to advise them or act on their behalf.

Negotiation has several advantages when compared to more formal methods of resolving disputes. It is usually faster, less expensive and less time-consuming, and more private and flexible than arbitration or litigation. Because it is entirely voluntary, negotiation also reduces the likelihood that one party will lose everything while the other party wins.

The primary disadvantage of negotiation is that it sometimes allows a more knowledgeable or powerful person to take advantage of a weaker person, thus resulting in injustice. In addition, if attorneys are involved, negotiation may still cost hundreds or thousands of dollars. Also, some parties may use negotiation to resolve urgent money and property issues without considering the deeper personal problems that may continue to cause conflict and alienation.

Mediation

Mediation is similar to negotiation, except that it involves the addition of one or more neutral mediators who work to facilitate communication and understanding between the parties. The mediator may initially act as an intermediary, but the ultimate goal is usually to arrange a conference at which all of the parties and the mediator are present. A mediator helps the parties explore various solutions to their differences, but the parties retain control of the results and are not obligated to follow the mediator's advice. A mediator may be a paid professional, a respected individual from the community, or a personal acquaintance of the parties who agrees to help them without charge.

The presence of a neutral mediator tends to reduce the possibility that one party will take advantage of the other. Mediation has several other advantages when compared to arbitration and litigation. Because of its informal nature, mediation is relatively flexible, private, inexpensive, and time-efficient. It facilitates understanding and allows parties to maintain their dignity while dealing with sensitive issues. Consequently, it is less likely to damage a relationship than is a more adversarial process. As a voluntary process, it is also likely to allow both parties to win on some of their concerns and arrive at a settlement that both sides will be inclined to preserve.

Mediation does have several disadvantages, however. Either party may refuse to participate in the process. Imbalances of power may still affect the results. The process may become deadlocked, thus wasting the previous investment of time and money. Also, the results of mediation are not legally enforceable unless the parties incorporate their settlement in a legal contract.

Arbitration

In arbitration, the parties agree to present each side of their dispute before one or more neutral arbitrators and, in most cases, to be legally bound by the arbitrator's decision on the matter. Unlike mediators, arbitrators do not attempt to help the parties communicate with each other or assist them in negotiating a settlement; instead, like judges, they gather evidence and render a binding decision. Most states have laws that allow parties to appoint their own arbitrators; these may be unpaid volunteers or trained professionals from organizations like the American Arbitration Association.

The primary advantage of arbitration when compared to negotiation and mediation is that it always produces a resolution to a dispute, even if one or both of the parties do not like it. In contrast to litigation, arbitration is relatively private and informal and is usually less expensive. Also, because most statutes allow only limited grounds for appealing an arbitration decision, arbitration has the capability to produce a final, legally enforceable result more quickly than litigation.

When compared to negotiation and mediation, the primary disadvantage of arbitration is that relationship problems are ignored, which often perpetuates or aggravates personal estrangement. Arbitration has disadvantages when compared to litigation. It is less guarded by procedural rules. Because many arbitrators lack formal legal training, arbitrated decisions are sometimes less consistent and predictable than what would result in court. Also, if one party refuses to abide by the arbitrators' decision, the other party may still need to resort to the courts to enforce it.

Litigation

Litigation utilizes the judges, juries, and procedural rules of the civil court system. Compared to other methods of resolving a dispute, litigation has several advantages. A court has the authority to require all parties to appear and to abide by its decisions. With its foundation of statutes and case law, a court is also able to render more predictable decisions on many issues. In addition, court decisions are a matter of public record, recognized in other jurisdictions, and subject to full appellate review.

Litigation has many disadvantages, however. In addition to being expensive and time-consuming, litigation is constrained by formal procedures, encourages public attention, offers limited remedies (usually money or injunctions), and often allows one party to win completely while the other party loses everything. Court technicalities restrict communication and understanding, often leaving the parties frustrated and angry. A court is usually forced to deal with the symptoms of a problem rather than its real causes, thus leaving the parties in an ongoing state of antagonism. As a result of these factors, litigation is likely to increase bitterness between the parties and further damage any personal relationship they had previously enjoyed.

The side effects of litigation and, to a lesser degree, of the other secular methods of conflict resolution are even more serious when viewed from a spiritual perspective. The more adversarial a process is, the more likely it is to provide a poor witness of Christian love and obedience. The adversarial process aggravates critical attitudes and encourages complaining and self-justification. It obstructs confession and repentance, thus prolonging destructive habit patterns. Moreover, as the parties' hearts are hardened by these factors, they are likely to experience more conflict in the future. This is why Supreme Court Justice Antonin Scalia said: "Judges can also tell you of brothers and sisters permanently estranged by litigation over a will, or of once-friendly neighbors living in undying enmity because of a boundary dispute that is, in financial terms, inconsequential. Whatever the legal rights and wrongs of such matters, these results are not worth it."[1]

As Justice Scalia notes, the spiritual, emotional, financial, and time costs of resolving a dispute through the adversarial process often negate whatever else might be gained. Therefore, whenever possible, a Christian should exhaust the principles of conflict resolution set forth in the Bible before resorting to other means.

Christian Conciliation

Christian conciliation is a process for reconciling persons and resolving disputes out of court in a biblically faithful manner.[2] The process is conciliatory rather than adversarial in nature—that is, it encourages honest communication and reasonable cooperation rather than unnecessary contention and manipulation.

Conciliation may involve three steps. First, one or both parties may receive *individual counseling* on how to resolve the dispute in private. Second, if private efforts are unsuccessful, the parties may submit their dispute for *mediation,* a process in which one or more Christian conciliators meet with them to promote constructive dialogue and to encourage a voluntary and biblically faithful settlement of their differences. Third, if mediation is unsuccessful, the parties may proceed to *arbitration,* which means that one or more arbitrators will hear their case and render a biblical and legally binding decision.

Christian conciliation is more values-oriented than most types of mediation. While secular mediators will work to help the parties come to a voluntary settlement, they will often be reluctant to go beyond this, especially if doing so would require that they evaluate others' attitudes and behavior from a moral perspective. In contrast, Christian conciliators make it a point to draw out the underlying reasons for a dispute, which are sometimes referred to as "matters of the heart." Believing that God has established timeless moral principles that he has recorded in Scripture and written in our hearts, Christian conciliators will draw the parties' attention to attitudes, motives, or actions that appear to be inconsistent with those standards. This will be especially true with parties who profess to be Christians; anyone who claims to be a follower of Christ will be encouraged to obey God's commands and to behave in a manner that will please and honor him.

When compared to secular means of resolving disputes, Christian conciliation has many advantages. It promotes traditional values, preserves relationships, encourages meaningful change, avoids negative publicity, provides a positive Christian witness, and is relatively inexpensive. In addition, when compared to litigation, Christian conciliation is less constrained by rigid procedures and thus allows more creative remedies and faster results. Another benefit is that Christian conciliators have much more flexibility than do civil judges when it comes to hearing testimony or reviewing evidence. Thus, if a dispute involves defects in the construction of a building or the repair of an automobile, a conciliator may personally inspect the building or drive the car. As a result of this flexibility, parties often feel that the facts and issues in the case are given a more thorough review than could occur in a court of law.

People who sincerely want to do what is right and are open to learning where they have been wrong can receive great benefits from the conciliation process. Conciliators can help them to identify improper attitudes or unwise practices, to understand more fully the effects of their decisions and policies, and to make improvements in their lives and businesses that will help them to avoid unnecessary conflict in the future.

Christian conciliation does have limitations, however. Conciliators do not have the same authority as civil judges and therefore cannot force parties to cooperate with conciliation or to abide by its results. (However, signed agreements reached through mediation and arbitration awards can be enforced by a civil court.) Conciliation can be less predictable than litigation, because each case has different conciliators and because the process is less constrained by procedures, statutes, and case precedents. Finally, there are only limited grounds for appealing arbitrated decisions, which means that parties will have little opportunity to have an unfavorable decision reviewed by a higher authority. (On the other hand, this means they will be spared from the expenses and delays inherent in the appeal process.)

In spite of these limitations, Christian conciliation usually provides more thorough and satisfying solutions to conflict than can be obtained through secular processes. As a couple wrote after their dispute was resolved:

> I believe that the most valuable thing we received from [Christian conciliation] was sound advice, seasoned with good Christian ethics and godly wisdom. I really believe that the right answer was attained. Understand please that the answers you gave were not what I came to hear, but I knew that this was right and it was confirmed as the neighbors were pacified. You could not have been more helpful. Our only regret was that we waited much too long to come to you.

Ideally, Christian conciliation should be pursued within a local church with the help of spiritually mature Christians. If this kind of conflict resolution is not available within a church, assistance can be sought from other godly people who are capable of serving in this way. When needed, parties or church leaders may obtain written resources (such as Rules of Procedure or various model forms) and other specialized assistance from a local Christian conciliator or from Peacemaker Ministries (see Appendix E).

Appendix C

Principles of Restitution

Restitution is an important biblical concept. When a person has injured someone else, God says that he "must confess the sin he has committed [and] make full restitution for his wrong" (Num. 5:5–7). This is what Zacchaeus did when he was led to repentance by the Lord Jesus. Zacchaeus did not merely ask for forgiveness and go on about his business. Instead, he stood up in front of Jesus and the people he had wronged and said, "Look, Lord! Here and now I give half of my possessions to the poor, and if I have cheated anybody out of anything, I will pay back four times the amount" (Luke 19:8).

Restitution produces several benefits. As much as possible, it restores the injured party to his or her former position. Restitution also benefits society by making destructive behavior unprofitable. In addition, it gives the offender an opportunity to make amends for sin and to demonstrate by actions that he or she wishes to be restored to the injured person and to society in general.

Much of what the Bible teaches about restitution is given in the form of case law. In other words, instead of presenting a multitude of specific rules to cover every conceivable situation, the Bible provides a few examples from which we can derive general principles that carry over into similar situations. For example, the principles taught in Exodus 21:18–23 apply to all kinds of personal injuries. These principles would also apply to injuries resulting from various forms of negligence, such as failing to install adequate railings on balconies or fences around swimming pools (see Deut. 22:8). Likewise, the principles set forth in Exodus 22:1–15 apply to all types of property damage, such as theft or accidental damage to borrowed property.

According to Exodus 21:19, when a person is deliberately injured, the offender is liable for all actual damages—that is, for medical expenses and for time lost from work. An offender is also liable for actual damages resulting from negligence (Exod. 21:22–35; cf. vv. 28–29). Exodus 21:22 implies that the injured party should assess damages and report them to the offender. If the offender believes the assessment is too high, the matter should be arbitrated by an appropriate authority (cf. 1 Cor. 6:1–8). Apparently, restitution is to be made only for actual damages. There does not appear to be a biblical foundation for restitution for pain and suffering or for intentional infliction of emotional distress. The biblical remedy for these wrongs is confession, repentance, and forgiveness.

When property has been damaged unintentionally, the Bible says that the offender must make "simple restitution," that is, repair or replace the property (Exod. 22:5–6). If the theft or damage was intentional, but the offender has truly repented and was determined to make restitution even before the damage was discovered, the offender must pay for the property plus a penalty of 20 percent (Lev. 6:1–5; cf. Num. 5:5–10). If the offense was intentional and the offender is apprehended along with the undamaged property the offender must return it along with its equivalent value (Exod. 22:4). If the offender is caught after the property has been disposed of, the offender must pay at least four times its value. If the property is difficult to replace, the offender must repay five times its value (Exod. 22:1).[1] These penalties are obviously designed to discourage deliberate wrongs and to encourage prompt repentance and confession.

Some people argue that restitution is not a valid concept in the New Testament age. I disagree. Nothing in the New Testament explicitly repeals the concept (see Matt. 5:17–20). In fact, restitution is implicitly endorsed by Jesus in Luke 19:1–10. Moreover, restitution is a sign of taking responsibility for one's actions, and nothing in the Bible indicates that God wants believers to be less responsible in this age than they were before the advent of Christ.

Furthermore, restitution is not inconsistent with forgiveness. Believers in Old Testament times were called to forgive others' offenses, yet they were entitled to receive restitution (Num. 5:5–8). Forgiving another person's wrong means you will not dwell on it, use it against the person, talk to others about it, or let it stand between you. But being forgiven does not necessarily release the offender from responsibility to repair the damage. Certainly, an injured party may exercise mercy, and in some cases it is good to waive the right to restitution (Matt. 18:22–27). But in many cases making restitution is beneficial *even for the offender*. Doing so demonstrates remorse, sincerity, and a new attitude, which can help to speed reconciliation (Luke 19:8–9). At the same time, it serves to ingrain lessons that will help the offender to avoid similar wrongdoing in the future (see Ps. 119:67, 71; Prov. 19:19).

Therefore, if you have damaged another person's property or physically harmed someone, God expects you to do all you can to make that person whole. If that person decides to release you from your responsibility, you should be deeply grateful for such mercy. On the other hand, if you have been harmed or your property damaged, you should prayerfully consider how badly you need to be made whole, as well as whether making restitution would benefit or unduly burden the offender. As you pray about it, keep in mind that blending mercy with justice is a powerful way to restore peace and glorify God.

Appendix D

When Is It Right to Go to Court?

First Corinthians 6:1–8 specifically limits a Christian's free-dom to sue another Christian in civil court. There is sig-nificant confusion regarding the intent of this passage and the extent of its limitation. In this appendix, I will address a few of the central issues in this passage.

The Scope of 1 Corinthians 6

There are three common views on the scope of 1 Corinthians 6:1–8 (which I will refer to as 1 Corinthians 6). One view holds that this passage forbids lawsuits against both Christians and non-Christians. This view is difficult to support. The passage talks about "one brother [going] to law against another—and this in front of unbelievers!" (v. 6). It also asks if it is possible "that there is nobody among you wise enough to judge a dispute *between believers?*" (v. 5, emphasis added). Moreover, this passage instructs Christians to submit to the "judgment" of the fellow believers within the con-text of the church. Paul would have hardly expected unbelievers to submit to the authority of the church. In fact, earlier in the

255

same letter he had specifically warned the church not to judge unbelievers (1 Cor. 5:12). Therefore, 1 Corinthians 6 should be understood to apply only to disputes between Christians.

Another view of this passage is that it forbids any and all lawsuits between people who profess to be Christians. This view is not supported by the express language of the passage, nor is it consistent with the rest of Scripture, which clearly indicates that God has established civil courts and expects his people to respect their authority and cooperate with them in appropriate situations (see Rom. 13:1–7; 1 Peter 2:13–14; cf. Acts 24:2–4; 25:10–11).

The third view of this passage is that it *forbids Christians to sue persons who are members in good standing of a Christian church that is faithful to Scripture.* I believe this is the most reasonable view of this passage. Paul was upset with the Corinthian Christians because they were suing one another in secular court rather than resolving their disputes with the help of the church. Realizing the terrible witness this was giving to unbelievers (v. 6), he said it would be better to be wronged or cheated than to sue a person who is part of the church—that is, someone who is "among you" (vv. 5, 7). As indicated in 1 Corinthians 5:1–13, however, a person should not be considered to be part of the church if he or she has been removed from the fellowship through official church discipline (see Matt. 18:17). Even if that person claims to be a Christian (1 Cor. 5:11), once he or she has been removed from the protection of the church (v. 5), that person can no longer enjoy the fellowship and privileges that belong to believers (vv. 9–11). Among other things, this means that such an offender no longer qualifies as a "brother" who is "among you." Therefore, 1 Corinthians 6 does not apply to that person, and other Christians are not necessarily forbidden to go to court against him or her.

Exhausting Church Remedies

This view of the scope of 1 Corinthians 6 gives the church a crucial role in resolving conflicts between people who profess to be Christians. If the church obeys Jesus' commands to help resolve disputes between Christians (Matt. 18:15–20), many conflicts will be settled far short of litigation. If your opponent (or you) refuses to listen to the church, and if the church obeys Scripture and disfellowships such a person, the dispute can still be resolved in a righteous manner through the civil courts, if necessary.

If your opponent's church does not carry out its biblical responsibility, it places you in a difficult position, because your opponent will still be a member in good standing of a Christian church. When this happens, I believe you have at least two alternatives. First, you could drop the matter and suffer loss (1 Cor. 6:7). This course would be appropriate if the issues are not very important and if it is likely that a lawsuit would cause others to think less of Christians and of Christ. Second, you could ask the leaders of your church to meet with the leaders of your opponent's church in an effort to persuade them to fulfill their biblical responsibility to help resolve your dispute. If they respond to that appeal, the two churches could cooperate by appointing a panel of peacemakers from both churches who would carry out the responsibilities described in 1 Corinthians 6, with both churches agreeing that they will support the decision of that panel and, if necessary, enforce it through church discipline.

If your opponent's church rejects the appeal of your church leaders, you could again consider dropping the matter. If that would not be wise, your church could declare that since your opponent's church is not acting in a manner faithful to Scripture, it should not be treated as a true Christian church, at least for the purposes of this conflict. As a result, your opponent need not be considered to be a part of a true Christian church. This would make 1 Corinthians 6 inapplicable and allow you to proceed with litigation if the other two conditions discussed in chapter 9 are satisfied.

Of course, your own church may refuse to work with you, and decline to either appeal to your opponent's church or declare that church to be disobedient to Scripture. If your church leaders believe that you do not have a biblical basis to pursue an action against your opponent, in general you should respect that counsel and drop the matter. If, however, your church simply refuses to obey what is taught in Matthew 18:15–20 and 1 Corinthians 6, you should consider moving to a church that is faithful to Scripture.

When you have to stay in your church because there are no Bible-believing churches in your community to move to, you should still avoid deciding for yourself whether you should treat your opponent as a believer and proceed with a lawsuit. Such unilateral conduct would violate the spirit of Matthew 18 and 1 Corinthians 6. Instead, you should turn to several spiritually mature Christians who can objectively evaluate your situation and give you biblical counsel. They may even approach your opponent in one last effort to resolve the conflict biblically. If your opponent still refuses to cooperate, and if these advisors conclude that your opponent is behaving "as a nonbeliever" and that your action is worth pursuing, you can proceed with a lawsuit with a clear conscience.

Before you file an action, however, you should consider once more the other two conditions for bringing a lawsuit, namely, that you are exercising biblically legitimate rights and that your action has a righteous purpose (see chapter 9). If you sincerely believe that you have done all you can to resolve the matter through the church and that these other two conditions are satisfied, then and only then should you proceed with a lawsuit.

Who Has Jurisdiction?

In certain situations, it may be appropriate to pursue legal remedies at the same time you are pursuing church remedies. This may happen in cases where both the church and the state have jurisdiction over a matter and when irreparable harm might occur if legal action is delayed.

God has given the church jurisdiction over the way Christians respond to the commands set forth in Scripture. ("Jurisdiction" means the right or authority to interpret and apply the law.) In other words, the church has *jurisdiction over sinful acts and attitudes,* that is, offenses that are violations of God's revealed will. This is why the church has both the responsibility and the authority to lovingly correct a person who is guilty of sin (Matt. 18:17–20). If a person refuses to respond to the correction of the church, the church may impose a variety of biblically established penalties, the most severe of which is to put that person out of the church and to treat him or her as a non-Christian. This penalty essentially removes the person from the jurisdiction (and protection) of the church and exposes the person to the unfettered attacks of Satan (1 Cor. 5:4–5; 1 Tim. 1:20).

Likewise, God has given civil government jurisdiction over the way people interact with one another in society. *Government has jurisdiction over criminal acts,* that is, offenses that are violations of society's laws (Rom. 13:1–7; 1 Peter 2:13–14).[1] This is why civil government has both the responsibility and the authority to correct a person who is guilty of criminal behavior. This correction may include a variety of penalties, including fines, imprisonment, loss of property, or even capital punishment.

When an offense is a sin but not a crime (e.g., refusing to be reconciled to another person), it comes under the exclusive jurisdiction of the church. When an offense is a crime (e.g., shoplifting), it is also a sin if the violated law is biblically legitimate; therefore, it comes under the jurisdiction of both the church and government. In other words, there are certain acts over which the church and government share *concurrent* or *overlapping jurisdiction.*

First Corinthians 6 indicates that when an offense comes under the jurisdiction of both the church and civil government, those involved should normally turn first to the church for a resolution, especially if there is a possibility that the church may be able to resolve the matter completely. If the church is unable to resolve the matter, those involved may turn to the civil courts for a remedy. For example, if Bob steals groceries from Betty's supermarket, Betty may postpone filing charges while she enlists the help of Bob's church in an effort to resolve the matter. With the help of the church, Bob may be brought to repentance, at which point there would be no need to involve the civil authorities. If Bob refuses to repent and make restitution, the church should treat him as an unbeliever, at which point the church's jurisdiction ends and the jurisdiction of the civil courts may be legitimately invoked. Then Bob would have to face criminal penalties.

On the other hand, if an offense is a *dangerous* crime and others may be seriously injured if the offender is not effectively restrained, it may be appropriate simultaneously to invoke the jurisdiction of the church and the civil government. While the church attempts to deal with the sinful heart condition that prompted the act, the civil authorities may deal with the behavior itself and restrain the offender from harming others. For example, in cases of physical abuse, it may be appropriate to call in the church and the police at the same time, especially when there is an indication that further abuse is likely unless there is effective intervention.

Unusual Situations

Because our society has changed in significant ways since Paul wrote his letter to the Corinthians, there are some situations that do not fit easily into the 1 Corinthians 6 scenario. When this happens, it will be necessary to consider carefully the jurisdictional issue as well as the three conditions for proceeding with a lawsuit. Most of all, it will be important to remember that one of the major concerns behind 1 Corinthians 6 is the potential for a negative witness when Christians sue one another in civil courts.

For example, since the church does not have jurisdiction over civil government or corporate organizations, it is appropriate to resolve in court disputes with these types of bodies, assuming you cannot arrive at a solution through personal and informal means. The same would be true of disputes involving insurance coverage. Since the church does not have jurisdiction over insurance companies, you will need to turn to the courts for a remedy if you are unable to arrive at a settlement. Even so, if the insured person who injured you is a Christian, you need to do all you can to resolve any personal animosity in a biblical manner. Furthermore, it would probably not be appropriate to seek excess damages from that individual (i.e., damages that exceed the coverage of the policy) without involving the church.

There may also be situations in which the only issue in dispute is the interpretation of a point of law. If there is truly no animosity between you and your opponent, and if you both believe that the other person is simply mistaken rather than acting in a sinful manner, it may be appropriate to allow a civil court to resolve relevant legal questions. When going this route, you must both agree that you will accept the court's decision without resentment. Of course, if possible, it would be preferable in many ways for the two of you to submit the legal issue to a respected Christian lawyer or judge who would resolve the matter more informally, perhaps through binding arbitration.

What If Someone Sues You?

The three conditions for filing a lawsuit apply equally well to defending yourself in a lawsuit. If you are sued by a person who professes to be a Christian, you should do all you can to divert the case to a church setting. If your opponent refuses, you should follow the Matthew 18 process, as described in chapter 9. If you exhaust that process (as described earlier in this appendix) and are confident that you are defending biblically legitimate rights and that you have a righteous purpose in defending yourself, you may continue in court with a clear conscience. If you do not satisfy all three conditions, however, you should follow the advice given in Matthew 5:25a: "Settle matters quickly with your adversary who is taking you to court."

Summary

Since every conflict is somewhat unique, it is impossible to address every question that might arise when a matter may be headed toward court. Moreover, as Jesus warned, it is important not to get caught up in a multitude of detailed and legalistic rules. Instead, you should pay attention to the basic principles set forth in Scripture and focus on what our Lord called "the more important matters of law—justice, mercy and faithfulness" (Matt. 23:23; cf. Micah 6:8). One way to apply these principles when you are trying to decide whether or not to go to court is to remember that you are a steward of Christ and to ask yourself, "Would my Master be pleased and honored if I use my time and resources to pursue this matter in court?"

Appendix E

Christian Conciliation Ministries

T he concept of Christian conciliation originated with the
Christian Legal Society in 1977, when several attorneys
began to explore ways to apply biblical peacemaking principles in legal conflicts. Since the establishment of the first
full-time Christian Conciliation Service in 1979, the conciliation network has grown to include individuals and organizations located throughout the United States and in several foreign
countries.

The primary purpose of most conciliators is to help people,
churches, and other organizations settle their differences in a biblically faithful manner (see the last section in Appendix B for a
description of how this process works). Conciliators also provide
advice, support, and assistance to church leaders, lawyers, and
others as they work to help Christians resolve conflicts out of
court. Some conciliation ministries offer training designed to
encourage and equip individual Christians and church leaders to
resolve conflicts according to biblical principles.

In 1987 a group of organizations and individuals committed to
conciliation formed the Association of Christian Conciliation Services (ACCS), which was established to coordinate national pro-

motion, education, and conciliation activities. Two years later Peacemaker® Ministries began serving as the headquarters for the ACCS, and in 1993 the two ministries merged into a single organization. For more information about these resources or about Christian conciliation, contact Peacemaker® Ministries, 1537 Avenue D, Suite 352, Billings, MT 59102; 406-256-1583; e-mail: mail@HisPeace.org; www.HisPeace.org.

Notes

Preface

1. W. H. Lewis, *Letters of C. S. Lewis*, (New York and London: Harvest/HBJ, 1966), p. 203.

Chapter 1: *Conflict Provides Opportunities*

1. My wife, Corlette, has worked as an elementary school teacher and counselor for twenty years, and she has found that children are very receptive to biblical peacemaking principles. She has developed several resources that explain how to teach these principles to children. You may obtain these materials through Peacemaker Ministries at 1537 Avenue D, Suite 352, Billings, MT 59102.

2. Charles R. Swindoll, *Growing Strong in the Seasons of Life* (Portland: Multnomah Press, 1983), pp. 85–86.

3. I have found that many Christians rely more on their own ideas and feelings than they do on the Bible, especially when Scripture commands them to do difficult things. In particular, many people seem to believe they can be sure they are doing what is right if they pray and feel a sense of "inner peace." Nowhere does the Bible guarantee that a sense of peace is a sure sign that one is on the right course. Many people experience a sense of relief ("inner peace") even when they are on a sinful course, simply because they are getting away from stressful responsibilities. Conversely, doing what is right sometimes generates feelings other than peace, especially when we are required to obey difficult commands, die to our own desires, or put others' needs above our own. Since the Bible alone provides absolutely reliable guidance from God, it should always be our supreme source of truth and direction. As the Spirit works to help us understand and obey Scripture, we can enjoy a sense of confidence that we are indeed walking in God's will, even if we don't have a peaceful feeling about it (Mark 14:32–34; Luke 22:43). For more information on how God guides us, see Garry Friesen's book *Decision Making and the Will of God* (Portland: Multnomah Press, 1980).

4. For an excellent description of how the Holy Spirit works in our lives, see J. I. Packer's book *Keep in Step with the Spirit* (Old Tappan: Fleming H. Revell, 1984).

Chapter 2: *Live at Peace*

1. Tim Hansel, *When I Relax I Feel Guilty* (Elgin, Ill.: David C. Cook, 1979), p. 93.

2. For a truly biblical perspective on spiritual warfare, I strongly recommend *Power Encounters: Reclaiming Spiritual Warfare* by David Powlison (Grand Rapids: Baker Book House, 1995).

3. See also Phil. 4:2–9; 2 Thess. 3:11–15; 1 Tim. 6:3–6; 2 Tim. 2:23–26; Titus 3:1–2, 9; Philem. 17–18; Heb. 12:14; James 3:17–18; 1 Peter 3:8–9.

4. Justice Warren Burger, "Annual Report on the State of the Judiciary," American Bar Association Journal (March 1982), p. 68.

5. Justice Antonin Scalia, "Teaching About the Law," Quarterly 7, no. 4 (Christian Legal Society, Fall 1987): 8–9.

6. There has been a dramatic increase of interest in secular negotiation, mediation, and arbitration in recent years. Appendix B describes these dispute-resolution options and compares them to what can be accomplished through the church.

7. There are a few situations when litigation may be necessary and appropriate for a Christian. Chapter 9 and Appendix D discuss this issue and provide guidelines for deciding when it is appropriate for a Christian to go to court.

Chapter 3: *Trust in the Lord and Do Good*

1. John Piper, *Desiring God* (Portland: Multnomah Press, 1986), p. 26.

2. J. I. Packer, *Knowing God* (Downers Grove, Ill.: InterVarsity, 1973), p. 37.

3. J. I. Packer, *Hot Tub Religion* (Wheaton: Tyndale, 1988), p. 35.

4. First Peter was specifically written to encourage Christians who were undergoing severe trials and suffering. If you are presently involved in a difficult conflict, I encourage you to read Peter's letter for its encouragement and guidance.

5. This passage refers to the two dimensions of the will of God. To prevent confusion, I will briefly describe the distinctions between the two. God's sovereign will (also called decretive will) is the ultimate cause of all things, whether God wills to accomplish them effectively and directly, or permits them to occur through the unrestrained actions of people. His sovereign will is not fully revealed to us, but it will always be accomplished (see Isa. 46:9–10). God's revealed will (also called preceptive will) is the pattern of rules that he commands us to follow in order to glorify him and enjoy fellowship with him. His revealed will is completely revealed in Scripture, but it is often disobeyed.

6. The more confidence we have that God is both sovereign and good, the more meek we can be. Meekness is an attitude toward God that causes us to accept all his dealings with us as being good, and thus to be received without resistance or resentment (Rom. 8:28). A meek person is content and thankful no matter what his circumstances (Phil. 4:12–13), because he sees that God has already given him everything he needs in Christ (Matt. 5:5; Rom. 8:31–32). Thus, instead of thinking, "I'm missing out; it's not fair," a meek person thinks about and gives thanks for God's goodness, mercy, power, and provision (Acts 4:23–31; 5:40–42; 7:59–60; John 18:11). Meekness has nothing to do with weakness, for both Moses and Jesus are described in the Bible as being meek (Num. 12:3; Matt. 11:29). In fact, meekness has sometimes been referred to as "power under control." This quality is highly commended throughout Scripture (Ps. 37:11; Matt. 5:5). Meekness has a direct impact on our dealings with other people, especially in the midst of conflict. Knowing that God works for good in all things, a meek person is able to endure mistreatment from others with patience and without resentment or bitterness. (Because this attitude does not come to us naturally, we need to pray that the Holy Spirit will work steadily to help us to become meek.)

7. Elisabeth Elliot, *Through Gates of Splendor* (Wheaton: Tyndale, 1981), pp. 252–54.

8. Ibid., pp. 268–69, 273.

9. Joni Eareckson Tada, "Is God Really in Control?" (Joni and Friends, 1987), pp. 2, 3, 8.

10. Packer, *Knowing God*, p. 145.

11. Marital conflicts are particularly painful and present many difficult questions. If you are trying to understand biblical options for dealing with a difficult marriage, read Jay E. Adams's *Marriage, Divorce, and Remarriage* (Grand Rapids: Zondervan Publishing House, 1980). If you are facing a marital separation, read Gary Chapman's *Hope for the Separated* (Chicago: Moody Press, 1982).

Chapter 4: *Is This Really Worth Fighting Over?*

1. Wayne Mack, *A Homework Manual for Biblical Counseling*, vol. 1 (Phillipsburg, N.J.:

Presbyterian and Reformed Publishing, 1979), p. 12.

2. Justice Antonin Scalia, "Teaching About the Law," Quarterly 7, no. 4 (Christian Legal Society, Fall 1987): 9.

3. See Romans 14:1–15:3, 1 Corinthians 8:1–13, and Philemon for three additional examples of when it is appropriate not to exercise rights to their fullest.

Chapter 5: *Examine Yourself*

1. Although translations of these passages often use the English word slander, somewhat different words and concepts are involved. Blasphemia describes talk that is irreverent, abusive, or evil (Eph. 4:31; Col. 3:8; 2 Tim. 3:2; 2 Peter 2:10, 12). Loidoreo means to subject to verbal abuse or to scold in harsh or insolent language (1 Cor. 5:11; 6:10).

2. One kind of "tearing down" is beneficial. It involves the work of God's Word and the Holy Spirit in our heart to convict us of our sins and to help us to see our need for God and for change (Matt. 5:3; Acts 2:37). Therefore, when we speak the truth in love to people, they may feel broken for a while. This is beneficial if it results in repentance.

3. R. C. Sproul, *The Intimate Marriage* (Wheaton: Tyndale House, 1988), p. 32.

4. In chapter 11, we will look more closely at ways to identify someone else's interests and develop creative ways to help meet those needs and desires in a biblical manner.

Chapter 6: *Free Yourself from Sin*

1. See Appendix C for more specific information on principles of restitution.

2. See also 2 Cor. 13:11; Eph. 4:1–2, 17; Col. 1:9–12; 3:5, 12–15; 1 Tim. 6:11; 2 Tim. 2:22).

Chapter 7: *Restore the Sinner Gently*

1. See Matthew 5:38. Remember that the "eye for eye" principle was to be applied by judges, not individuals (see, for example, Exod. 21:22–24). Moreover, the context for this passage is Jesus' teaching on what his followers must be willing to suffer for the sake of the gospel (Matt. 5:11–12).

2. As a general rule, the closer you are to someone, the more latitude you should have in mentioning your concerns. For example, if one of my close friends sees me saying or doing something that may hurt my marriage, irritate others, or otherwise make me less useful to the Lord, I would want him to point it out to me, even if it's not a terribly serious sin. This kind of loving and constructive confrontation is one of the privileges and blessings of being part of the body of Christ (Ps. 141:5; Col. 3:16; Heb. 10:24–25).

Chapter 8: *Speak the Truth in Love*

1. Reflecting is a valuable listening skill that can substantially improve communication. Unfortunately, if it is not used carefully, reflecting can appear to give approval to unbiblical ideas and undermine the authority of Scripture. While it is often helpful to paraphrase another person's words to show that you understand his or her concerns, you should take care not to give approval, even implicitly, to attitudes or actions that are contrary to the Bible. In other words, once you have shown that you understand someone's thoughts or feelings, you should do all you can to help that person change unbiblical ideas and behave in a way that would please and honor the Lord.

2. Asking questions during a tense conversation is often beneficial as well. Questions generally evoke responses and thus lead to more dialogue. Other examples include, "Would you like me to explain?" and "May I give you an example?"

3. When you refer to God's Word as the basis for your concerns, some people may accuse you of legalism, a term that is often misunderstood and misused. Legalism is the abuse of God's Word, not the faithful use of God's Word. Common forms of legalism include an overfascination with the minute

266

detail of certain laws to the exclusion of "more important matters of the law" (Matt. 23:23; cf. 5:21–48); strict adherence to traditions that are not supported by Scripture (Matt. 15:3–9); and a pattern of holding others to the strictest legal standard but failing to practice it yourself (Matt. 23:1–4). Avoid these abuses of Scripture. Unfortunately, you may be accused of "legalism" even when you are using the Bible properly. Taking the Bible seriously is not legalism. We are clearly called not only to obey God's commands, but also to encourage and exhort one another to do likewise (Matt. 18:15–20; Gal. 6:1). Doing so with humility, patience, gentleness, and love is not legalism—God calls it obedience.

4. Ron Kraybill, Conciliation Quarterly, Mennonite Central Committee, Summer 1987, p. 7.

Chapter 9: *Take One or Two Others Along*

1. Some early manuscripts do not have the words "against you" in the first sentence (v. 15). Thus, this passage is not necessarily restricted to confronting sin that was committed against you personally (cf. Luke 17:3).

2. For more detailed information on the Matthew 18 process, see *Managing Conflict in Your Church*, a risk management manual produced by Peacemaker Ministries.

3. One way to ensure that conflicts related to contract relationships will be resolved in a biblical manner rather than in court is to include a conciliation clause in the contract itself. The Institute for Christian Conciliation recommends using a clause like this: "Any claim or dispute arising out of or relating to this agreement shall be settled by mediation and, if necessary, arbitration in accordance with the *Rules of Procedure for Christian Conciliation* of the Institute for Christian Conciliation; judgment upon an arbitration award may be entered in any court of competent jurisdiction." The legal requirements for the wording and style of these clauses vary from state to state, so you should consult an attorney before using such a clause.

4. The Institute for Christian Conciliation has developed a set of forms, guidelines, and procedures that can be used by church leaders and others when they are serving as conciliators or arbitrators. The ICC also provides training resources and opportunities for individuals who would like to enhance their abilities to serve as peacemakers. See Appendix E for information on how to obtain these materials.

5. You may have already asked the leaders of your church or churches to be involved as conciliators as part of step two, which would have been an informal process. When you ask them to get involved at the level of step three, you are moving into a formal process that invokes the God-given authority of the church to instruct believers how they should live.

6. Although some lawsuits have been filed against churches regarding their exercise of church discipline, the civil courts have generally upheld a church's right to exercise biblical discipline, provided the church was not acting in an arbitrary, capricious, or malicious manner. (See Lynn Buzzard and Thomas Brandon's *Church Discipline and the Courts* (Wheaton: Tyndale House, 1987). Although a church will rarely encounter legal problems if it exercises discipline in a reasonable and consistent manner, it would be wise to contact a knowledgeable attorney, a Christian Conciliation Service, or the Christian Legal Society (703–642–1070) for information on what safeguards may be taken to avoid legal problems.

7. Note that Matthew 18:15–20 immediately follows Jesus' stern warning to repent of sin (vv. 7–9) and his parable of the lost sheep, which emphasizes the church's responsibility to work aggressively to reclaim "wandering" Christians (vv. 10–14). It also is important to note that this passage is immediately followed by a teaching on forgiveness.

8. Don Baker's *Beyond Forgiveness* (Portland: Multnomah Press, 1984) provides a powerful testimony of how a man who was guilty of serious sin was confronted and

restored to usefulness through the faithful application of church discipline.

9. I wish I could say that all interventions turn out this well, but obviously they don't. Even so, I know of many marriages that are together today because of such intervention. More importantly, even in those cases where one party proceeded on a sinful course in spite of church discipline, the churches at least knew that they had been faithful to the Lord. Such faithfulness can significantly increase the respect that church members have for their leaders and for Scripture. At the same time it sends a message that willful sin will not be casually overlooked, which encourages others in the church to work out their problems in a biblically faithful manner.

10. Unfortunately, some churches will not fulfill their responsibilities to resolve disputes involving their members. Appendix D explains how to exhaust your church remedies in such situations. It also discusses unusual conflicts, such as criminal problems and insurance claims.

Chapter 10: *Forgive as God Forgave You*

1. See Appendix C for a detailed discussion of restitution.

2. Some people mistakenly believe that unforgiveness can also cause us to lose our salvation. This belief sometimes results from a misunderstanding of Jesus' words in passages like Matthew 6:14–15, which says: "For if you forgive men when they sin against you, your heavenly Father will also forgive you. But if you do not forgive men their sins, your Father will not forgive your sins" (cf. Matt. 18:35; Mark 11:25; Luke 6:36–37). To understand the true meaning of this passage, we must realize that God forgives us in two different ways because he relates to us in two different ways. God is first of all our Judge. When we repent of our sins and accept Jesus Christ as our Savior and Lord, God forgives us our sins and declares us "not guilty." This process takes place by God's grace through faith, and it does not depend on our works (Eph. 2:8–9; Rom. 3:24–30). Since we are

not saved because of our works, we will not lose our salvation by failing to perform certain works. In other words, God's judicial forgiveness (and our salvation) does not depend on whether or not we forgive others.

God also relates to us as our Father, and his parental forgiveness does depend on our forgiveness of others. When we become Christians, God adopts us into his family and treats us as his children. (Note that Matt. 6:14–15 and the related passages are all addressed to believers because they refer to God as "Father.") And how does a good parent treat a disobedient child? He doesn't kick the child out of the family! He may send a disobedient child to his or her room and isolate the child from the rest of the family until behavior changes. In some cases, the unrepentant child may also receive a spanking or be deprived of certain favors. God treats us in the same way. He does not disown us by taking away our salvation, but he does discipline us. Thus, when we refuse to forgive others, we may suffer afflictions and feel cut off from a close and joyful relationship with God. As Matthew 6:14–15 warns, God will continue to discipline us until we repent of our sin and forgive others as he forgives us.

3. Patrick H. Morison, *Forgive! As the Lord Forgave You* (Phillipsburg, N.J.: Presbyterian and Reformed Publishing, 1987), p. 7.

4. Corrie ten Boom, *The Hiding Place* (New York: Bantam, 1974), p. 238.

5. C. S. Lewis, *Mere Christianity* (New York: Macmillan, 1960), p. 116. Behaving contrary to your feelings is not hypocrisy. If it were, Luke 6:27–28 would essentially command us to be hypocrites. Rather, hypocrisy is pretending to be what you are not, or pretending to act from one motive when you are actually inspired by another motive (Matt. 23:23–32; cf. Gal. 2:11–14). Thus, if you have negative feelings toward someone, it would be hypocritical to act lovingly and pretend that you are motivated by genuine fondness for that person. In contrast, it would not be hypocritical to behave in a kind and gracious manner, even if you don't feel like it, while acknowledging through your words

or actions that you are motivated by your love for God (1 Peter 2:13–25; cf. Acts 7:59–60).

Chapter 11: *Look Also to the Interests of Others*

1. W. E. Vine, *An Expository Dictionary of Biblical Words* (Nashville: Thomas Nelson, 1985), p. 679.

2. For further direction and insight on cooperative negotiation, see *A Fight to the Better End* by G. Brian Jones and Linda Phillips-Jones (Wheaton: Victor Books, 1989) and *Getting to Yes* by Roger Fisher and William Ury (Boston: Houghton Mifflin, 1981). Both of these books provide excellent guidance and practical suggestions on how to negotiate agreements.

Chapter 12: *Overcome Evil with Good*

1. These principles are discussed in greater detail in Jay Adams's book *How to Overcome Evil* (Grand Rapids: Baker Book House, 1979).

2. J. Gallagher, *The Scarlet Pimpernel of the Vatican* (New York: Coward-McCann, 1968), p. 181.

Conclusion: *The Peacemaker's Pledge*

1. "The Peacemaker's Pledge" was developed as part of Peacemaker Ministries Partners in Peacemaking Program. One of the primary goals of this program is to build a consensus within the Christian community on how believers ought to respond to conflict. The program also provides partners with better access to conciliation services and risk management advice, along with savings on educational resources. Please contact the Institute (see Appendix E) for copies of "The Peacemaker's Pledge" and for information on how your church, ministry, or business can join the Partners in Peacemaking Program.

Appendix B: *Alternative Ways to Resolve Disputes*

1. Justice Antonin Scalia, "Teaching about the Law," Quarterly 7, no. 4 (Christian Legal Society, Fall 1987), p. 9.

2. The information in this section is derived from *Guidelines for Christian Conciliation*, a booklet published by Peacemaker Ministries. Used by permission.

Appendix C: *Principles of Restitution*

1. Exodus 22:1 is somewhat difficult to understand. I believe its differing treatment of sheep and oxen shows the need for wisdom and flexibility when determining restitution. Since sheep need only to graze in a pasture to enable them to produce wool, meat, and offspring, they are relatively easy to replace. In contrast, a great deal of training must be invested in an ox before it can perform its draft duties properly. Therefore, replacement involves more than simply buying a new ox and turning it loose in a pasture, as you would with a sheep. Thus, Exodus 22:1 seems to imply that the more difficult something is to replace, the more restitution should be paid to ensure that the owner is in fact made whole.

Appendix D: *When Is It Right to Go to Court?*

1. As the writers of the Declaration of Independence realized, these laws must have as their purpose the protection of "inalienable rights," that is, those things that may not be taken from a person without due process. These things include life (e.g., freedom from assault, battery, rape), liberty (e.g., freedom from unjust imprisonment or intrusions into the raising of one's children), and the pursuit of happiness, which the writers understood to mean primarily the right to own and control private property (e.g., the right to contract, freedom from theft, burglary, and certain torts).

Bibliography

Church Conflict

Adams, Jay E. *Sibling Rivalry in the Household of God.* Denver: Accent Books, 1988.

Dobsen, Edward G., Speed B. Leas, and Marshall Shelley. *Mastering Conflict and Controversy.* Portland: Multnomah Press, 1992.

Fenton, Horace L., Jr. *When Christians Clash.* Downers Grove, Ill.: InterVarsity Press, 1987.

Flynn, Leslie B. *When the Saints Come Storming In.* Wheaton: Victor Books, 1988.

Gangel, Kenneth O., and Samuel L. Canine. *Communication and Conflict Management in Churches and Christian Organizations.* Nashville: Broadman Press, 1992.

Haugk, Kenneth C. *Antagonists in the Church.* Minneapolis: Augsburg, 1988.

Huttenlocker, Keith. *Conflict and Caring.* Grand Rapids: Zondervan, 1988.

Kniskern, J. Warren. *Courting Disaster.* Nashville: Broadman and Holman, 1995.

Martin, Frank. *War in the Pews.* Downers Grove, Ill.: InterVarsity Press, 1995.

Thomas, Marlin E. *Resolving Disputes in Christian Groups.* Winnipeg: Windflower Communications, 1994.

Wecks, John. *Free to Disagree.* Grand Rapids: Kregel Resources, 1996.

Church Discipline

Adams, Jay E. *Handbook on Church Discipline.* Grand Rapids: Zondervan, 1986.

Baker, Don. *Beyond Forgiveness.* Portland: Multnomah Press, 1984.

Buzzard, Lynn, and Thomas Brandon. *Church Discipline and the Courts.* Wheaton: Tyndale, 1987.

Gage, Ken and Joy. *Restoring Fellowship.* Chicago: Moody Press, 1984.

MacNair, Donald J. *Restoration God's Way.* Philadelphia: Great Commissions Publications, 1978.

White, John and Ken Blue. *Healing the Wounded.* Downers Grove, Ill.: InterVarsity Press, 1985.

Forgiveness

Adams, Jay E. *From Forgiven to Forgiving.* Wheaton: Victor Books, 1989.

Morison, Patrick H. *Forgive! As the Lord Forgave You.* Phillipsburg, N.J.: Presbyterian and Reformed Publishing,, 1987.

Marital Conflict

Adams, Jay E. *Marriage, Divorce, and Remarriage.* Grand Rapids: Zondervan, 1980.

Chapman, Gary. *Hope for the Separated.* Chicago: Moody Press, 1982.

Dobson, James. *Love Must Be Tough.* Waco: Word, 1983.

Kniskern, J. Warren. *When the Vow Breaks.* Nashville: Broadman and Holman, 1993.

Talley, Jim. *Reconcilable Differences.* Nashville: Thomas Nelson, 1985.

Wheat, Ed. *How to Save Your Marriage Alone.* Grand Rapids: Zondervan, 1983.

Negotiation/Mediation

Fisher, Roger, and William Ury. *Getting to Yes.* Boston: Houghton Mifflin, 1981.

Jones, G. Brian, and Linda Phillips-Jones. *A Fight to the Better End.* Wheaton: Victor Books, 1989.

Lovenheim, Peter. *Mediate, Don't Litigate.* New York: McGraw-Hill, 1989.

Spiritual Guidance

Friesen, Garry. *Decision Making and the Will of God.* Portland: Multnomah Press, 1980.

Spiritual Warfare

Powlison, David. *Power Encounters: Reclaiming Spiritual Warfare.* Grand Rapids: Baker, 1995.

Index of Topics

abuse, physical 136–37, 259–60
anger 160
anxiety 76–77
arbitration 21, 174, 247
arbitration clause 267
Association of Christian Conciliation Services 262
attitude, changing 73–80
authority
    abusing 99
    confronting a person in 141
    respecting 99

changing 115, 119–26
character (*see* changing)
checklist 238–44
children 30, 264
Christian conciliation 249–51
Christian Conciliation Service 262
Christian Legal Society 262
church discipline 21, 175–78, 267
communication 146–65
complaining 95
conciliation clause 267
conciliators
    responsibilities 173–74
    when and how to involve 170–73
confession 109–19, 123–25
conflict
    opportunities of 26–30
    stewarding 32–34
    styles of managing 32–34
    views of 17–21, 24–31
confronting
    excuses against 138–39
    non-Christians 140–41, 174

people in authority 141
skills 146–65
when needed 132–35, 266
contract clause 266
cost of conflict 80–82
court (*see* litigation)

denial 18
devil (*see* Satan)
discipline, church 21, 175–78, 266
discussion 20

evil, overcoming 226–34

faithfulness 33–34, 98
falsehood 95
flight 18
forgiveness 183–85, 186–202, 268

gentleness 75
glorifying God 26–28, 54, 236
gospel 38, 49–50
gossip 95
growing to be Christ-like 30–31
grumbling 95
guidance
    from God 264
    from others 33, 229

heart, changing 101–3
Holy Spirit 33, 264
hypocrisy 268

"I" statements 161–62
idols 102–4, 121–22
inner peace 39–40, 264

272

insurance companies 259
interests, identifying 212–18
issues, defining 71, 212

jurisdiction 258–60

lawsuits (*see* litigation)
listening 149–56
litigation 19
    against organizations 260
    costs 248–49
    defending against 261
    when appropriate 179–80, 255
    with believers 46–49, 179–80
    with nonbelievers 255

mediation 21, 246
meekness 265
murder 19

negotiation 205–7, 245–46
non-Christians
    confronting 130
    litigation with 255

obeying God 26
opportunities of conflict 26–30
options, developing 218–24
overlooking offenses 20, 73–74, 78–79,
    142

peace
    importance of 36, 44
    with God 38
    with others 39
    within yourself 39–40
Peacemaker's Pledge, The 235–36

planning 158–61, 207–10

reckless words 94
reconciliation 183–85, 236
repentance 107
replacement principle 198–202
responsibilities, keeping 97–101
restitution 114–15, 252–54, 269
rights 82–88, 266, 269

Satan 43–44
Scripture 32–33, 122–23, 163
self-examination 91–106
serving others 28–30
Seven A's 109, 240
sin 91–94, 109–10
slander 95, 266
sovereignty of God 51–54
stewardship
    of conflict 32–34
    of possessions 86
submission 99
suffering 55, 265
suicide 19

tongue, controlling 94–97, 228
trusting God 26, 51–66
truthfulness 95, 146–65

unforgiveness, overcoming 193–98
uniformity 25, 45
unity 25, 40–43

will, God's 265
witnessing 40–43
worrying 76–77
worthless talk 96–97

Index of Persons

Adams, Jay 265, 269
Baker, Don 267
Brandon, Tom 267
Burger, Warren 47, 180, 264
Buzzard, Lynn 267
Chapman, Gary 265
Elliot, Elisabeth 60, 265
Fisher, Roger 269
Friesen, Garry 264
Gallagher, J. 269
Hansel, Tim 264
Jones, G. Brian 269
Kraybill, Ron 165, 267
Lewis, C. S. 10, 201, 268
Lincoln, Abraham 180

Mack, Wayne 265
Morison, Patrick 268
O'Flaherty, Hugh 232–33
Packer, J. I. 54–55, 264–65
Phillips-Jones, Linda 269
Piper, John 53, 265
Powlison, David 264
Scalia, Antonin 47, 179–80, 248–49, 264, 266, 269
Sproul, R. C. 99, 266
Swindoll, Charles 31, 264
Tada, Joni Eareckson 61, 265
ten Boom, Corrie 197–98, 268
Ury, William 269
Vine, W. E. 269

Index of Scripture References

Old Testament

Genesis
3:13—95
13:5–10—85
13:5–12—83
16:6–8—18
39:9—58, 92
39:11–23—58
50:15–21—192
50:19–20—74
50:19–21—58, 83, 85

Exodus
1:6–7—85
4:10–12—52
4:11–12—56, 61
21:18–23—253
21:19—253
21:22—253
21:22–24—266
21:22–35—253
21:28–29—253
22:1—253, 269
22:1–15—253
22:4—253
22:5–6—253
22:28—83

Leviticus
6:1–5—253
19:16—95
19:17—137
26:6—37

Numbers
5:5–7—252

5:5–8—254
5:5–10—253
5:6–7—92
6:24–26—37
12:3—265
14:20–23—191
25:12—37
30:2—98

Deuteronomy
22:8—253
23:23—98
24:15—99
29:29—33, 56
30:11–20—63
32:48–52—192

Joshua
9:1–19—98

Judges
5:31—37
6:23—37
6:24—29

1 Samuel
1:17—37
2:22–25—18
16:5—37
16:7—96, 176
19:9–10—18
22:6–19—214
24:1–22—214, 230
24:10—230
24:17–20—230
24:32–35—215

25:1–35—100
25:1–44—213
25:23–35—141
25:24–31—214
31:4—19

2 Samuel
12:1–13—139
12:11–14—192
12:13—192
13:1–39—192
16:5–10—192
16:5–12—83
16:21–22—192
19:1–4—192
19:18–23—192
19:19–23—83
19:22–23—85

2 Kings
5:19—37

2 Chronicles
6:37–39—108
16:9—33

Nehemiah
9:5–37—77

Esther
7:1–6—100

Job
1:6–12—53
31:13–14—99
40:1–41:34—57

42:2–3—57
42:11—53

Psalms
8:3–4—52
15:4—98
18—77
19:14—28
23:3—26
29:11—37
32:1–5—134, 196
32:3–5—93
32:5—109
32:10—51
33:10–11—54
34:1–3—21
34:14—37
36:2—93
37—231
37:1–6—236
37:4—122
37:11—265
37:31—27
37:37—37
41:4—109
46—77
51:3–4—92
62:11–12—54
68—77
71:20–22—53
73—231
73:21–22—81, 134
77—77
78—77
85:10—33
103:8–10—73
103:8–11—196
103:9–10—27
103:9–12—194
103:12—189
105—77
106—77
107—77
119:67—254
119:67–71—55
119:71—254
119:133—102
119:165—37, 39
130:3–4—189

131—57
133:1—39
135:6–7—52
136—77
139:1–18—52
139:6—52
139:23–24—93, 120
141:5—155, 266

Proverbs
2:17—98
3:5–7—26, 57
4:23—101
6:1–5—98
8:13—102
9:8—137
10:10—147
10:12—72
10:17—136, 177
10:19—147
11:12—147
11:13—95
11:27—77
12:15—33, 93
12:16—20, 72
12:18—94, 156
12:20—37
13:3—94
13:18—177
14:8—207
14:22—207
14:22b—159
14:30—134
15:1—160
15:5—155
15:18—72
15:22—33
15:23—154
15:28—150
15:31—155
16:1—52
16:2—97
16:4–5—53
16:7—37
16:9—52
16:28—95
16:33—52
17:9—72
17:10—155

17:14—20, 72
17:28—94
18:13—150
19:11—20, 72, 236
19:19—86, 192, 254
19:20—93
19:21—52
19:25—137
20:3—72
20:19—95
20:22—231
21:1—52
21:23—94
24:11–12—137
24:28—95
24:29—231
25:12—155
25:15—100, 148
26:17—72
26:20—95
27:5–6—137, 229
28:13—20, 94, 107, 119, 236
28:23—137
29:1—177
29:20—94
29:25—103

Ecclesiastes
2:26—122
5:1–7—98
8:2–5—100
9:16—215
12:13b—231

Isaiah
2:4—37
6:1–5—196
9:6—37
26:3—39, 57, 77
29:16—53
32:17—39
43:2–3—55
43:25—187, 189
45:5–7—53
46:9–10—52, 265
48:18—39
53:1–7—85
53:1–12—38
53:4–6—189

54:10—37
55:7–8—108
59:1–2—38, 134
59:2—189

Jeremiah
17:10—97
18:6—52
22:13—99
29:7—37
31:19—108
31:34b—189

Lamentations
3:37–38—53
3:40—91

Ezekiel
14:6—108, 119
18:30—119
33:11—53
34:4—177
34:8–10—177
34:25—37
36:25b–26—101
37:26—37

Daniel
1:4—221
1:4–16—192
1:6–16—100
1:8—221
1:10—221
1:11–14—141
1:11–16—221
2:14–16—100
2:20–21—52
3:1–30—27
3:9–18—100
4:27—119
4:35—52
6:1–28—27
6:6–10—100

Amos
3:6—53

Micah
4:1–4—37
6:8—34, 82, 261

Zechariah
3:1—96

Malachi
2:5—37
3:5—99

New Testament
Matthew
3:8—109
4:1—96
4:1–11—227
4:21—139
5:3—266
5:3–12—122
5:5—265
5:7—82
5:9—37, 41, 235
5:11–12—266
5:16—26
5:17—71
5:17–20—253
5:21–22—20, 41, 134
5:21–24—81, 134
5:21–48—267
5:23–24—20, 41, 133, 237
5:24—11, 183, 198, 234
5:25a—261
5:25–26—19, 81
5:33–37—98
5:38—266
5:39—138
5:48—38
6:9–10—26
6:12—186, 188, 237
6:14–15—268
6:21—121
6:24—102–3
6:25–34—77, 122
7:1—138
7:1–5—138
7:3–5—70, 236
7:5—10, 67, 138
7:9–11—122
7:12—83, 100, 206, 237
10:16—206
10:29—52
10:30–31—52
11:28–30—227

11:29—265
12:36—54
15:3–9—98, 267
15:19—101
16:18—175
17:24–27—83
17:27—85
18—169, 171, 175, 258
18:7–9—267
18:10–14—267
18:15—11, 25, 129, 137, 141
18:15–16—155
18:15–20—48, 169, 173, 178, 236, 257, 267
18:16—21, 168, 170–71, 174
18:16–20—191
18:17—21, 173, 175–77, 256
18:17–20—231, 258
18:18–20—175
18:20—180
18:21–35—83, 195, 203
18:22–27—254
18:22–33—98
18:27—188, 195
18:30—196
18:32—188
18:32–35—196
18:34—196
18:35—196, 268
19:9—98
21:12–13—135
22:37—27
22:39—39, 206
23:1–3—99, 175
23:1–4—267
23:23—34, 261, 267
23:23–32—268
24:45–51—132
25:14–21—237
25:21—16, 34
25:24–27—86
26:42—52
26:53–54—83

Mark
2:17—176

5:18–20—21
7:5–13—118
10:42–45—99
11:25—190, 236, 268
14:32–34—264

Luke
1:5–25—122
1:79—37
6:27–28—27, 41, 147,
199–200, 227, 232, 268
6:27–36—235
6:28—190
6:29–36—29
6:32–36—133
6:35–36—27–28, 227
6:36—29, 82, 119
6:36–37—268
6:43–45—101
7:42–43—188
7:50—37
8:11–15—101
8:48—37
10:30–37—83
12:4–5—103
12:13–15—71
12:16–21—102
12:27–31—102
12:27–34—103
12:29—102
12:42—32
12:42–48—132
12:47—32
15:17—107
15:19—115
15:21—113
17:3—135, 190, 267
17:3–4—194, 199
17:3–5—191
19:1–10—254
19:8—110, 115, 236
19:8–9—254, 252
22:41–44—31
22:42—53
22:43—264
23:34—27, 147, 191
23:46—52
24:36—37

John
1:3—52
3:16—38
4:1–18—176
5:30—28
6:39—52
8:29—28
8:44—95
9:1–5—55
9:22—103
11:1–4—55
12:24–26—32, 86
12:42–43—103
13:34–35—41, 237
14:15—236
14:15–17—227
14:15–31—27
14:27—37
15:4–5—120
15:8—26
17:1–19—40
17:4—26
17:20–23—40
18:11—265
21:19—27

Acts
2:23—53
2:36–41—191
2:37—266
3:19—108
4:5–17—100
4:18–19—100
4:18–20—175
4:23–31—265
4:24—59
4:27–28—53
4:27–29—59
5:1–3—103
5:3—43
5:17–42—27
5:27–32—175
5:29—100
5:40–42—265
5:41—59
6:8–15—19
6:8–7:60—27
7:54–58—19
7:59–60—147, 265, 269

7:60—190
9:15–16—85
16:16–40—80
16:22–24—83
16:25—59
16:35–39—84
16:36–38—85
19:18—110
19:35–41—85
20:26–27—165
22:22–29—85
22:25—85
22:25–29—84
23:11—85
24:1–26:32—19, 100
24:2–4—256
25:10–11—256
25:11—84–85
26:1–32—86
26:20—109

Romans
1:7—37
1:24—101
2:23–24—135, 176
3:20—38
3:21–26—53
3:23—38
3:24–30—268
5:1–2—38
5:3–4—56
5:5—63
6:23—38, 177, 189, 194
8:6–8—122
8:28—61, 265
8:28–29—30, 55, 235
8:31–32—265
9:15–16—52
11:33–36—56
12:1–2—122
12:14—147, 228
12:14–21—227, 233
12:15–16—229
12:17—229
12:17–21—236
12:18—33, 36, 39, 134,
140, 230, 237
12:19—54, 231
12:20—29

12:20–21—232
12:21—226
13:1–5—19, 231
13:1–7—99, 180, 256, 259
13:2—99
14:1—46
14:1–13—25
14:1–15:3—266
14:12—54
14:13–19—134
14:19—37, 96
15:2—96
15:5–7—45
15:7—25
15:13—37
15:14—139
15:32—52
15:33—37
16:17—176

1 Corinthians
1:10—45
2:9–15—33
2:9–16—122
4:2—33
4:3–4—122
4:5—97, 102
4:12–13—30, 147, 228
4:16—30
5:1–6—176
5:1–13—136, 177, 256
5:4–5—259
5:5—231
5:6—177
5:9–11—175, 256
5:11—96, 256, 266
5:12—256
6—171, 255–56
6:1–6—179
6:1–8—19, 21, 46–47, 50, 84, 169–70, 172–73, 175, 236, 253, 255
6:4—21
6:5—170, 255–56
6:6—255
6:7—256–57
6:9–11—120
6:10—266
7:1–40—84

7:11—198
7:15—37, 98
8:1—96
8:1–13—84, 266
9:1–18—84
9:3–15 83
9:12—85
9:24–27—124
10:6—102
10:13—33, 56
10:14—121
10:23—96
10:23–33—84
10:24—206
10:31—10, 13, 236
10:31–11:1—26, 84, 179, 236
11:1—30
12:12–31—45
13:4–7—41, 232
13:5—189, 206
13:6—157
14:26—96
15:58—233

2 Corinthians
1:3–5—55
1:3–11—56
1:6–11—55
1:9—55
2:5–11—177
2:7—201
2:7–10—188
3:18—30
4:2—95
4:7–18—59
5:12—102
5:18–20—49, 198
7:9–10—108
7:10—109
8:1—96
8:20–21—229
10:3–5—227
10:7—96
12:7–8—59
12:7–10—31, 55–56, 122
12:9–10—59, 122
12:20—95
13:11—37, 266

Galatians
1:3—37
1:10—103
2:11–14—268
5:16–21—102
5:19–22—45
5:19–26—235
5:22–23—33, 120, 227
5:22–6:2—138
6:1—132, 137, 139–40, 148, 170, 267
6:1–2—29, 75, 78, 177–78, 236
6:1–3—20
6:2—29
6:9–10—29
6:10—140
6:16—37

Ephesians
1:11–12—52
1:17–19—122
2:8–9—38, 268
2:11–18—39
2:17—37
3:16–21—33
4:1—59
4:1–2—266
4:1–3—45, 237
4:1–13—25
4:2—72
4:7–13—45
4:12—96
4:15—146–47
4:16—96
4:17—266
4:19—102
4:22–24—101, 122
4:22–32—120
4:24—123
4:26–27—43
4:29—96, 147, 163, 236
4:29–31—46
4:29–32—46, 50
4:30–31—134
4:31—96, 266
4:32—46, 73, 119, 187–88, 191, 237
5:1—27

5:1–2—119
5:5—102
5:21–24—99
5:25–33—99
6:4—99
6:9—99, 113
6:10–18—227
6:12—44
6:19–20—60

Philippians
1:9–10—26
1:9–11—120, 122
1:12–14—59
2:3–4—84, 206, 237
2:4—20, 204, 206
2:5–11—85
2:13—120
2:14—95
3:14—124
3:19—102
4:2–9—74, 236, 264
4:4–7—200
4:8—78, 200
4:9—37, 123
4:12–13—122, 265

Colossians
1:9–12—120, 122, 266
1:16–17—52
1:19–20—38
3:1–2—13, 121
3:1–4—236
3:5—266
3:5–11—120
3:5–14—236
3:8—96, 266
3:12—125
3:12–13—186, 188
3:12–15—266
3:13—20, 45, 73, 188
3:13b—187
3:15—37, 45
3:16—78, 139, 266
4:1—99
4:3—59
4:3–4—60

1 Thessalonians
2:4—103

3:10—140
4:1—120
4:10—120
5:10–11—33
5:12–13—99
5:13—37
5:13–15—45

2 Thessalonians
3:6—175
3:11—138
3:11–15—264
3:14–15—175
3:16—37

1 Timothy
1:20—231, 259
4:1–3—43
4:12—30
5:13—95, 138
5:19–20—141
6:1–2—99
6:3–6—264
6:10—102
6:11—266

2 Timothy
1:7—33
1:12—52
2:16—97
2:21—126
2:22—121, 124, 266
2:22–24—139
2:23—138
2:23–26—264
2:24–26—139, 165, 236
2:25–26—43, 107
3:2—96, 266
3:3—95
3:16–17—32
4:2–4—136
4:3—33
4:7—124

Titus
2:3—95
2:7—30
2:9–10—99
3:1–2—264

3:9—264
3:10—137

Philemon
17–18—264

Hebrews
4:12—101
5:14—125
8:10—101
10:24–25—33, 266
12:1–13—177
12:14—37, 264
13:17—99, 175
13:20—37
13:21—140

James
1:2–4—56, 236
1:13–14—53
1:19—149
2:10–11—92, 196
2:12–13—82
3:5–6—94
3:8b—94
3:14—102
3:17–18—236, 264
3:18—37
4:1–2—25
4:1–3—100, 236
4:7—44
4:8b—121
4:11–12—97
4:15—52
4:17—92
5:4—99
5:9—95, 236
5:19–20—137

1 Peter
1:6–7—55, 138
1:8—122
1:15–16—119
2:12—41, 229, 236
2:12–3:18—138
2:13–14—256, 259
2:13–25—269
2:13–3:6—99
2:15—229

2:19—237
2:19–23—100
2:20—55
2:22–25—83, 85
2:23—52, 55
2:24–25—38, 189
3:7—99
3:8–9—264
3:9—96, 147, 228
3:15–16—30, 229
3:17—53
4:8—20, 72
4:10–11—33
4:12–19—138
4:15—138
4:19—55, 237

5:1–3—99
5:8—43
5:9—44
5:10—140

2 Peter
1:4–8—119
2:10, 12—266

1 John
1:5—53
1:8—93, 236
1:9—194, 236
2:6—27, 119
2:15–17—102
3:1—96

3:4—92
3:18—201
3:21–24—39
3:23—40
4:19–21—42
5:3—27

2 John
5–6—27

Revelation
2:23—176
4:11—52
12:9—95

Attorney **Ken Sande** is president of Peacemaker® Ministries. He regularly conciliates business, family, employment, and church disputes and serves as a consultant to pastors and attorneys as they work to resolve conflicts outside the courtroom. Ken conducts seminars throughout the United States on biblical conflict resolution.